T0367458

Agricultural Markets and Prices

Agricultural Markets and Prices

~

Darren Hudson

Blackwell
Publishing

© 2007 by Darren Hudson

BLACKWELL PUBLISHING
350 Main Street, Malden, MA 02148-5020, USA
9600 Garsington Road, Oxford OX4 2DQ, UK
550 Swanston Street, Carlton, Victoria 3053, Australia

The right of Darren Hudson to be identified as the Author of this Work has been asserted in accordance with the UK Copyright, Designs, and Patents Act 1988.

First published 2007 by Blackwell Publishing Ltd

1   2007

Library of Congress Cataloging-in-Publication Data

Hudson, Darren, 1970–
   Agricultural markets and prices / Darren Hudson.
        p. cm.
   Includes bibliographical references and index.
   ISBN-13: 978-1-4051-3667-9 (hardcover : alk. paper)
   ISBN-10: 1-4051-3667-7 (hardcover : alk. paper) 1. Agricultural industries.
2. Agriculture — Economic aspects. 3. Agricultural prices. I. Title.

HD9000.5.H95 2006
381$'$.41—dc22

                                        2006025038

A catalogue record for this title is available from the British Library.

Set in 10/12pt Times by Newgen Imaging Systems (P) Ltd., Chennai, India

The publisher's policy is to use permanent paper from mills that operate a sustainable forestry policy, and which has been manufactured from pulp processed using acid-free and elementary chlorine-free practices. Furthermore, the publisher ensures that the text paper and cover board used have met acceptable environmental accreditation standards.

For further information on
Blackwell Publishing, visit our website:
www.blackwellpublishing.com

Contents

Preface

~

The study of prices in agricultural markets owes a debt of gratitude to Professors William Tomek and Kenneth Robinson for their pathbreaking text *Agricultural Product Prices*. This book also owes a debt of gratitude to these authors as well. Because of the vast popularity of their book (as well as the fact that it was from that book that I learned price analysis), I have adopted many of the conventions of their text when writing in this book. However, I have also made significant departures from their style and content in this book.

The target audience for this book is undergraduate (junior/senior) students, and beginning masters level students in marketing/price analysis. While some background in inferential statistics (with basic regression) as well as calculus is desirable and would serve to propel those students further along, I have attempted to keep the presentation at a level at which students without that background can still learn the key concepts and begin to develop empirical skills. In many places, I have added technical appendicies to augment the presentation in the chapters for more advanced students, but use of those appendicies is not necessary for understanding the content within the chapters.

I liberally employ examples and discussion questions within the text to reinforce key points. I have found that it is often the "stories" that move key points from short-term memory (which is usually flushed after the lecture is over) into long-term memory. Of course, graphs and numerical examples and exercises are also used to address different learning styles and objectives. I hope that you will also appreciate (or forgive) my obsessive need to inject a bit of humor from time to time within the text. I find that students (and instructors) need a break occasionally with some comic relief, and it is these breaks that allow our brains to "take a breath" and internalize what has been read.

The book is divided into three major parts. The first part addresses our traditional competitive market model, and is divided in much the same way as Tomek and Robinson's book. However, I attempt to have a logical progression through the first several chapters that is overt and transparent. Namely, I am attempting to construct the picture of the market from the ground up — starting with consumers and then producers. Next, competitive equilibrium is addressed, with some attention toward welfare measures. Then the simple model is augmented with stocks and international markets. Along the lines of Tomek and Robinson, I then examine the elements that affect price, such as space, time, and quality, and conclude with an introduction to futures markets.

A key element of this text is that empirical methods are integrated into each chapter directly, providing an opportunity to expose students to different empirical approaches throughout the semester/quarter rather than waiting until the end to provide them experience with empirical analysis. I believe the growing demands for graduates with quantitative skills justifies the amount of attention paid to those skills in this text. I have traditionally assigned a minimum of three major regression analysis projects during the semester and found that students do struggle with the mechanics at first, but begin to get a feel for the strengths and weaknesses over the course of the semester. But, more importantly, I believe that integrating the empirical analysis along the way gives students a better perspective for where a demand function or supply function comes from, and how to use the results of empirical research to solve problems and answer questions.

The face of agriculture has changed tremendously over the past 20 years. Global trade agreements have increased competitive pressures on production agriculture and the agricultural supply chains. All sectors of agriculture are witnessing an increasing amount of vertical integration and coordination. And there appears to be an ever-increasing level of product differentiation, even at the farm level, thus changing the overall structure and operation of agriculture. The competitive model has served agricultural economists very well over the years, but our continued devotion to this disciplinary mode of thinking is increasingly making agricultural economists irrelevant to, or at least at the fringe of, the political and economic processes unfolding before us. As such, I have devoted considerable space to the idea of imperfectly competitive markets.

The book still maintains a large discussion on our competitive models and modes of analysis, but the relative emphasis is shifted toward more understanding of imperfect competition. In particular, I have presented a lengthy chapter on vertical coordination and contracting, which I believe to be one of the richest sources of research opportunities for today's students as well as a key body of information that must be incorporated if students are to be successful in today's agriculture. I also introduce the ideas of game theory in the second part of the book, and these ideas are applied in the chapter on imperfect competition. I have attempted to keep to a level of presentation at which a junior/senior can understand the concepts, and have found that my own students do not seem to have a problem understanding the key ideas.

The final part of the book is necessarily geared toward more advanced students, typically graduate students, with the purpose of introducing more advanced techniques for analyzing behavior and decision-making. While the econometrics is certainly more complex, I would urge instructors not to underestimate the ability of good undergraduate students to grasp the concepts being presented, especially in survey design and experimental methods. Nevertheless, I felt it necessary to include this part as a primer for upper-level undergraduate and graduate students into the world of methods of analyzing individual behavior and generating primary data to analyze agricultural marketing issues.

A book of this sort is always a work in progress. I certainly welcome the comments and suggestions of those using the book so that future editions can better suit the needs of instructors (email Hudson@AgEcon.msstate.edu). My ultimate goal is to provide an experience for students that enriches their understanding of food and fiber markets and prepares them for a challenging career in agriculture by providing them basic foundations and some level of intellectual curiosity that will promote life-long learning.

D.H.
Starkville, MS
June 2006

Acknowledgments

~

As with any work of this magnitude, there are many people who have been of great assistance. I would like to thank John Lee, Don Ethridge, Steve Turner, and my parents and family for encouragement, support, and a healthy dose of caution about undertaking a project of this size. Appreciation is given to Arden Colette (my instructor in this course) for encouraging me to go to graduate school in the first place, opening up the whole world of economic research to me. I would also like to thank years of classes for enduring the fits and starts of writing this and serving as guinea pigs for the lectures, content, and exercises. Many of my students provided very useful comments and critiques on the style and content of the text.

Many of my colleagues suffered through hours of discussion, reading drafts, and providing useful comments and suggestions. In particular, I would like to thank Keith Coble and Stan Spurlock for their helpful suggestions on issues related to risk and production (and Stan for reviewing drafts of almost every chapter); Wes Wolfe and Sukant Misra for help with demand issues; Don Ethridge for assistance with product quality; Steve Turner and John Anderson for help with futures markets; and Jayson Lusk for hours of conversations about experimental economics, conjoint analysis, survey design, and economics in general.

Last, but certainly not least, I would like to thank my loving wife Lisa and my wonderful kids Nathan and Haley for their patience with long nights and weekends as I pecked away at the text. Their tugging at my shirt to do something else other than write all the time kept me sane through this process. I enjoy economics, but it is for them that I get up and go to work every day.

Introduction

~

Agricultural markets and prices are a central subject in the study of agricultural economics and agribusiness. Most of you will no doubt graduate and pursue careers in sales, marketing, or management of agribusiness firms and products. Some of you may go on to graduate school, where you will conduct research that is related to agricultural markets or marketing. Whatever your career path, the functioning of the agricultural economy, and its requisite implications on resource allocation and policy, will be central themes in your careers. Below, I will attempt to impart some perspective on the agricultural sector. Then, I will lay out the plan for this book.

0.1   The Agricultural Economy

The food and fiber marketing system continues to be an important part of the overall U.S. economy. The value of U.S. agricultural production was $213 billion in 1999, and increased to $241 billion in 2003 (a 13% increase). However, as Figure 0.1 shows, the share of agriculture in the gross domestic product (GDP) of the United States has decreased over time.

Figure 0.1 should not be interpreted as saying that the magnitude of agricultural production and processing has shrunk. Quite the contrary. Rather, the *share* of agriculture of the overall economy is shrinking. Food consumption is highly related to population growth, and the population of the U.S. is not growing as rapidly as it once was. As such, the demand for food products does not tend to grow rapidly. However, industrial and service industries are growing more rapidly than agriculture, meaning that their share of GDP is growing at the expense of agriculture.

In 2004, U.S. consumers spent $819 billion on food grown and processed in the United States, with additional expenditures on food grown and processed in foreign markets. The value of food consumption grows annually, partly due to inflation of prices and partly due to growth in population and consumer demand. However, as Figure 0.2 shows, the share of consumer expenditures spent on food has declined over time. In fact, in 1929, Americans spent about 23% of their disposable income on food, as compared to 9.5% in 2004.

This gross measure of consumer expenditures is not necessarily a "bad" phenomenon. As we have seen above, consumer expenditure continues to grow. But Figure 0.2 reveals that consumers are having to spend less of their money on food, which is a sign that

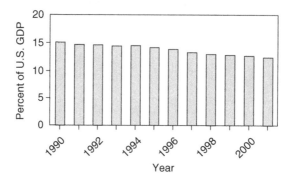

Figure 0.1 The value of agricultural production as a share of U.S. gross domestic product. *Source:* USDA, Economic Research Service.

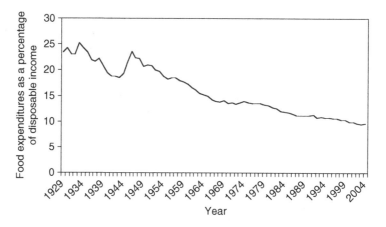

Figure 0.2 Consumer expenditures on food as a share of personal disposable income, 1929–2004. *Source:* USDA, Economic Research Service.

consumer incomes are increasing faster than food prices. So, you have more money to use on DVD players and automobiles, which has driven economic growth in this country. Sure, farmers would like to have more money but, overall, this relationship is a positive sign for the overall health of the U.S. economy. Despite this, net farm income increased from $47 billion in 1999 to $59 billion in 2003 (a 26% increase).

Food consumption has changed in a number of respects, which have implications for agricultural markets. First, the products that American consumers purchase have changed. Figure 0.3 shows changes in consumption for selected products over the 1970–2002 period. The data show a shift toward poultry, cheese, fats and oils, and fruits and vegetables, and a shift away from red meat, eggs, and milk consumption. At the same time, data show a shift toward food eaten away from home versus at-home consumption, which refects the growing importance of two-parent working households that simply do not have the time to prepare food at home. Despite this trend, about 57% of food is still purchased in stores for at-home consumption, so consumer demand for these

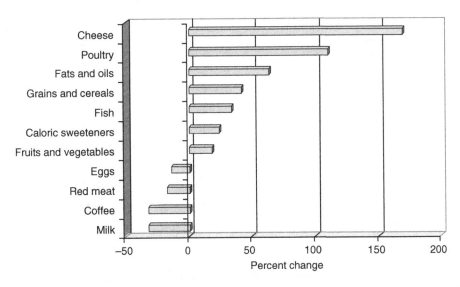

Figure 0.3 Percentage changes in food purchases by U.S. households, 1970–2002.
Source: USDA, Economic Research Service.

products is still relevant. However, even in the at-home market, a growing share of the food purchased is in highly processed, ready-to-eat forms.

The purpose of this digression into the data is to highlight several important features of the modern agricultural system. First, demand for products at the farm level is still important, but it is changes in consumer demand that drive the system. In 2004, the U.S. Department of Agriculture, Economic Research Service, estimated that the farm value of food consumption was only 19% of the final value, with the remaining 81% going to the marketing sector. As we will see in Chapter 4, this value says nothing about farm welfare, but does indicate that the farm sector is a small (and shrinking) percentage of overall food consumption. Thus, it is important to move beyond the "if we grow it, consumers will come"[1] mentality of commodity production. Rather, these data suggest that the farm sector must seriously consider its approach to food production.

Some businesses have responded by creating "branded" or differentiated products. Laura's Lean Beef and Omaha Steaks are examples of companies that have taken farm marketing to a different level by creating a differentiated product (or at least the perception of differentiation in the consumer's mind). Other companies specialize in organic foods. Farmer cooperatives such as Ocean Spray and Land O'Lakes have created products of their own and entered into vertical relationships between growers and processors. Thus, while understanding traditional, open commodity markets is still relevant today, the changing structure of agricultural supply chains has necessitated paying increased attention to imperfectly competitive markets and vertical integration and coordination. Figure 0.4, for example, shows the degree of coordination in agricultural markets.

As can be seen, products range from very low levels of vertical coordination (e.g., corn) to almost complete vertical coordination (poultry). Chapter 13 in this text addresses

---

[1] This, of course, is a take-off of the Kevin Costner movie *Field of Dreams*, where a voice in Costner's head told him "if you build it, they will come."

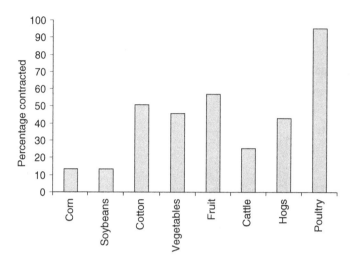

Figure 0.4   The percentage of agricultural products produced under some type of contract, 1998. *Source:* USDA, Economic Research Service.

these issues in more detail. Given the importance of imperfect competition to agriculture, an entire part of this book is devoted to the subject.

0.2   A Note on Indices

Economics often makes use of indices, or index numbers. These come in various forms, but are often key to understanding what is being presented in the data. At its most basic form, index numbers attempt to fix comparisons to some particular point, usually a point in time. Consider the example of beef prices in Table 0.1.

The table depicts beef prices in cents per pound over the 1987–2000 period. Perhaps we wish to examine relative prices of beef across time, so we select 1987 as the base period. We can calculate the index as a simple ratio of prices, with 1987 always serving as the base period:

$$Index_{88} = \frac{250.34}{238.38} = 1.05,$$

$$Index_{89} = \frac{265.66}{238.38} = 1.11, \text{ etc.}$$

We can use the resulting index to make inferences about the relative prices. For example, we can say that the 1988 price is 5% higher than the base period (1987). Likewise, we can say that the 2000 price is 29% higher than the base period. We can also use a common index, called a **deflator**, to adjust all prices to account for inflation. The most common deflator is called the **consumer price index** (or CPI). The CPI is constructed by the Bureau of Labor Statistics to reflect the price changes over time of a basket of market goods commonly purchased by consumers. The CPI is the primary measure of inflation of prices.

The prices in the table are called **nominal** prices. That is, they are the prices that are observed in the market at that period of time. To account for inflation, economists

Table 0.1 An example computation of a price index for beef prices

Year	Beef price (cents per pound)	Index (1987 = 1)
1987	238.38	1.00
1988	250.34	1.05
1989	265.66	1.11
1990	281.02	1.18
1991	288.33	1.21
1992	284.61	1.19
1993	293.44	1.23
1994	282.88	1.19
1995	284.33	1.19
1996	280.23	1.18
1997	279.53	1.17
1998	277.12	1.16
1999	287.77	1.21
2000	306.79	1.29

Table 0.2 An example computation of real beef prices using the consumer price index

Year	Beef price (cents per pound)	CPI (1999 = 1)	Real beef price (cents per pound)
1987	238.38	0.68	350.56
1988	250.34	0.71	352.59
1989	265.66	0.74	359.00
1990	281.02	0.78	360.28
1991	288.33	0.82	351.62
1992	284.61	0.84	338.82
1993	293.44	0.87	337.29
1994	282.88	0.89	317.84
1995	284.33	0.91	312.45
1996	280.23	0.94	298.12
1997	279.53	0.96	291.18
1998	277.12	0.98	282.78
1999	287.77	1.00	287.77
2000	306.79	1.03	297.85

typically convert nominal prices into **real** prices, which accounts for changes in purchasing power as a result of changes in overall price levels. Table 0.2 shows the calculation using the beef price example above.

Note, here, that the base period has changed to 1999 (the base period used by the Bureau of Labor Statistics). To calculate the real price, you simply divide the nominal price by the CPI:

$$P_{real,87} = \frac{238.38}{0.68} = 350.56.$$

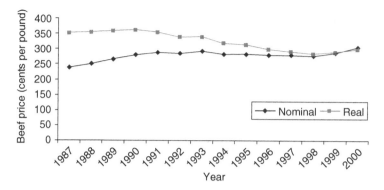

Figure 0.5   A comparison of nominal and real beef prices.

The interpretation of the CPI is relatively straightforward. In our example, 1999 is used as the base year, so all prices are measured relative to 1999. In 1987, for example, prices were only 68% of the prices in 1999.[2] By contrast, prices in 2000 were 3% higher than in 1999. This is where you will see statements in the news that the inflation rate is 3%. In this case, prices inflated by an average 3% from 1999 to 2000.

You will note that these two series generate very different prices. Figure 0.5 shows a graphical representation of these prices. While the nominal price of beef appeared to be on an upward trend over the period, real prices were on a downward trend. Why? The answer is that even though beef prices were increasing nominally, their increase was at a slower rate than the overall rate of inflation (or increase in the prices of the basket of goods). Thus, effectively, beef prices were declining in real terms.

The use of real prices is widespread in economics. We use them because we believe that economic decisions made by individuals are made in terms of real, not nominal, dollars. That is, while prices are increasing nominally, incomes are nominally increasing as well. If the price of beef in our example is increasing more slowly than overall prices, it makes beef appear less expensive *relative to* other products. As we will see in Chapter 1, this result influences our demand for beef. So, as you proceed through this text (and, indeed, through other economics courses or your career), keep in mind the definition of real prices and price indices. Most importantly, remember that when indices are used, their interpretation is *relative to* some base period or fixed point.

0.3   The Organization of the Book

The book is organized as follows. The first part relates to models and analysis of perfectly competitive markets. We note that markets are composed of producers and consumers. The first five chapters of the text are devoted to building a complete picture of a perfectly competitive market. First, we address issues of consumer demand followed by production. In Chapter 3 we combine these basic elements into a picture of market equilibrium

---

[2]Remember that the CPI is a measure of a basket of goods. So, some goods may have been more expensive in 1987 than in 1999, but the average for the basket of goods was that prices in 1987 were 68% of the level of prices in 1999.

and discuss the measurement of welfare. Next, we augment the basic model structure with a discussion of marketing margins, or vertical supply chains. Finally, in Chapter 5, we close out our discussion of the perfectly competitive model with a discussion of stocks and international markets.

Careful attention to empirical analysis is paid at each step along the way. You might wonder why this is so important. Consider the following quote by David Williams, Vice-President for International Risk Management for American Express:

> The combination of quantitative training and applied work makes agricultural economics graduates an extremely well-prepared source of employees for private industry. That's why American Express has hired over 80 agricultural economists since 1990.

In a highly competitive world, skills are what differentiate you from your competition. Those of you who understand the basic theory of markets and marketing and can combine those with quantitative skills to solve real-world problems will have a significant "leg up" on the competition for employment. In this regard, I have attempted to incorporate those skills-based exercises within the text. The moral: don't huff and puff and complain about the work. Treat every opportunity you have as your last chance to prove yourself.

Chapters 6–9 extend the basic theory of competitive markets to address issues that are central to agricultural markets: space, time, and quality. We then introduce the idea of futures markets, which are a fascinating world in themselves, but also have important uses and implications for the cash markets in which most of us will operate. These chapters comprise the treatment of the standard, perfectly competitive market.

In the second part of the book, we will turn our attention to imperfectly competitive markets. As previously discussed, imperfect competition is very important in agricultural supply chains. As such, considerable time and space are devoted to the subject. We begin with the simplest treatment—monopolies. Natural, unregulated monopolies are rare, but understanding of the monopoly structure leads to a greater understanding of something much more prevalent in agriculture—price discrimination. Here, we will examine how retailers price products in the marketplace in an attempt to maximize revenue. A brief discussion of game theory is presented in Chapter 11. Don't let the shortness of the chapter lull you into believing that game theory is not important. Rather, the mathematics of game theory can be quite complex, so Chapter 11 only introduces the concept of game theory and their logic as applied to markets. The rest of this second part (Chapters 12 and 13) is related to imperfectly competitive market models and to vertical coordination and contracting in agriculture. These are important chapters, and should not be skipped.

Finally, the third part of the book is devoted to more advanced techniques for analyzing behavior using experimental methods. This part is necessarily geared toward more advanced students, but the concepts are not difficult to grasp (although some of the econometric methods are difficult). You are all encouraged to explore this part to open your minds to new and innovative ways of addressing contemporary problems.

The entire book is geared toward upper-level undergraduate students. Prior coursework in statistics and calculus is helpful, but not necessary. I have attempted to keep the mathematics to a minimum, but some math is necessary for clarity of presentation. You will note that the math gets progressively more pervasive through the text. The hope is that as you proceed, you will become more comfortable with the notation and mathematical discussion. I hope that you find this text useful!

Part I
Models and Analysis of Perfectly Competitive Markets

~

Chapter 1

Market Demand

The demand for products and services is a central issue in the study of economics. Economists attempt to understand what drives individuals to purchase certain goods and services and to use that information to predict what impacts changes in economic conditions may have on that demand. It is important to distinguish between **demand** and **effective demand** (Kohls and Uhl, 2002). Demand represents the desire to engage in a certain activity or to purchase a given good or service. Effective demand couples that concept with the ability to pay for such goods and services. We may all want a Jaguar X-type car, but not all of us can afford to pay for it.

This chapter focuses on reviewing the fundamental concept of demand, and addresses empirical tools and techniques for analyzing market demand. You should already have had an introductory economics course before proceeding through this chapter, although considerable review material will be presented. In addition, you should already have a working knowledge of basic inferential statistics including regression analysis. While basic concepts will be presented, the objective of this chapter is not to teach you regression analysis.

1.1 Basic Demand Theory

Economists view decisions of consumers through **utility**, which is the amount of satisfaction that a particular product provides to the individual. That is, we derive some level of satisfaction from consuming our favorite food or reading our favorite book. We, as consumers, have a myriad of products and services that are available to us and, certainly, we would like to have it all. However, most of us are faced with a major constraint—income. We all have a certain level of income—some more, some less—which determines how much we can buy at an given point in time. This **budget constraint**, then, forces us to make choices about which products we are going to purchase. Naturally, we wish to use our income to purchase those goods and services that give us the most satisfaction.[1] Therefore, our study of human behavior in economic decisions is about *choices*. In the terminology of economists, we believe that consumers make choices to **maximize utility subject to a budget constraint**. That is, consumers make choices to get the most satisfaction out of a given budget.

1.1.1   Utility Maximization

Demand theory assumes that individuals seek to maximize utility. We denote the general utility function as (Deaton and Muellbauer, 1980):

$$U = u\left(q_1, q_2, \ldots, q_n\right),$$

where U is the utility and the q's are quantities of different consumption items. Further, we note that the utility function has the following properties:

1. There are only a finite number of commodities characterized numerically and there exists a measure for each commodity. That is, there are only so many commodities out there and we can measure each commodity.
2. The commodity may not be characterized by strictly negative numbers.
3. The consumer can choose different proportions from a bundle of a commodity.
4. The utility is interpreted as measuring the satisfaction derived from the consumption of alternative consumption bundles.

If these assumptions hold, utility follows several axioms of choice that are relevant to our analysis. The first is the **axiom of reflexivity**, which simply states that bundles of goods must be clearly defined. For example, suppose you were presented with the choice between bundle A and bundle B, but were given no other information. It would be hard to make a choice between these if they are not clearly defined. For utility theory to perform properly, bundles must be clearly defined if consumers are to make rational choices. Second is the **axiom of completeness**, which states that consumers must have the ability to compare bundles. For example, many times, companies with similar product bundles (say, satellite TV service) will present their products and pricing plans in such a way as to make them not comparable. It is difficult for consumers to make choices between these products because they are comparing "apples to oranges." Again, for our utility theory to make correct predictions about consumer choice, consumers must be able to compare product bundles.[2]

Third is the **axiom of transitivity**. Simply, this axiom states that if product A is preferred to product B, and product B is preferred to product C, then product A must be

---

[1] There are products and services that we must purchase, such as food, clothing, and housing. However, within these categories, we would like our income to be spent on the particular items that are most satisfying.

[2] Some students are tempted to say at this point that the obvious discrepancy between theory and reality makes the theory unreliable. However, remember that the purpose of the theory is to develop predictions about what consumers would do if these axioms held. The fact that the axiom does not hold in the example provides a means for us to understand *why* consumers may not make rational choices.

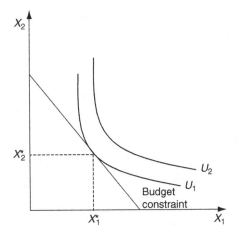

Figure 1.1 The utility-maximizing combination of X_1 and X_2 subject to a budget constraint.

preferred to product C. This axiom directly addresses the rationality of the consumer. That is, it would appear irrational to prefer C to A in this example.[3] Fourth is the **axiom of continuity**, which simply states that all choices must be in the choice set. This axiom insures that indifference curves are well defined.

These four axioms insure that a utility function exists, but do not introduce limits to choice. For this, we have the **axiom of nonsatiation**. This axiom holds that utility does not decrease for any of the elements of a person's utility function and increases for at least one element. Nonsatiation implies that the maximum utility will lie on and not inside the budget contraint because we would prefer to have more of at least one of the goods in our utility function. The **axiom of dominance** holds that if product bundle A strictly dominates product bundle B, A will always be preferred to B. Essentially, this axiom means that indifference curves with higher levels of satisfaction are always further right (on an *X–Y*, two-dimensional diagram as is Figure 1.1) and cannot intersect.[4] The properties of the utility function and the axioms of choice allow us to examine utility maximization. Figure 1.1 presents utility maximization graphically (see Appendix 1A for a mathematical treatment).

---

[3] When consumers violate this axiom, it is generally called a **preference reveral** (List, 2002). There is a great deal of scientific literature devoted to testing this axiom, with mixed results. Issues such as **bounded rationality** arise as explanations for preference reversals and other "irrational" behavior (Lusk and Hudson, 2004). While not explicitly covered here, bounded rationality basically states that people lack the mental computing capacity to evaluate all possible choices and therefore use heuristics or "rules of thumb" to make decisions. Because these heuristics often lead to sub-optimal choices, their choices appear irrational according to utility theory. The more advanced students amongst you are encouraged to explore this alternative literature.

[4] There are two more "technical" axioms as well. The **axiom of strict convexity** holds that if a consumer is indifferent between bundle A and bundle B, then a linear combination of A and B will be preferred to either A or B alone. This axiom implies that the utility function is strictly quasi-concave and indifference curves are convex and smooth. The second is the **axiom of differentiability**, which holds that strictly quasi-concave utility functions are also twice differentiable. Essentially, this axiom insures that the indifference curves are not kinked. See Deaton and Muellbauer (1980) or Varian (1992) for a more technical discussion of each of these axioms.

In this figure, U_1 and U_2 represent two of a family of indifference curves from the utility function for the consumer. An indifference curve represents the combinations of X_1 and X_2 that yield equal levels of satisfaction. The set of indifference curves represents an indifference map, which is derived from the underlying utility function. As one moves away from the origin in Figure 1.1, higher levels of utility are attained (the axiom of dominance). The budget constraint represents the maximum amount of X_1 and X_2 that can be purchased given the prices P_1 and P_2, and the slope of the budget constraint is given as $-P_2/P_1$ (and is often called the "price ratio" line). Any combination of X_1 and X_2 on or to the left of the budget constraint is a feasible purchase option, while any combination to the right would exceed the consumer's budget and, therefore, is not feasible. Thus, while the consumer would like to achieve a higher utility on U_2, it is not possible given the budget constraint.

Given the axiom of nonsatiation, we know that the optimal solution to the maximization problem will lie on the budget constraint. We also know that, in the optimum, the chosen combination must be preferred to (or at least indifferent to) any other combination for that particular budget. In Figure 1.1, this combination is given by the tangency between the indifference curve and the budget constraint, or (X_1^*, X_2^*).[5] This is the point of utility maximization, and, therefore, represents the optimal consumption bundle for the consumer.

Key Questions

1. What is the difference between demand and effective demand?
2. What are the axioms of choice?
3. Why are product bundles that lie inside of the budget contraint not utility-maximizing?
4. What does an indifference curve represent?
5. How would you verbally define the point of utility maximization?

1.1.2   Income and Substitution Effects of Price Changes

Now that we have laid out the basics, the next question becomes "What happens to utility maximization when prices change?" This question is central to understanding why consumers behave as they do when, as in the real world, prices change. Consider Figure 1.2. By decreasing the price of X_1, P_1, you have increased the quantity of X_1 that can be purchased for each level of X_2, resulting in a rotation of the budget constraint out from the origin, hinging on the y-intercept.[6] The budget constraint becomes tangent to a new indifference curve, U_2, resulting in new optimal quantities of X_1 and X_2. The optimal quantity of X_1 increases. Thus, decreasing P_1 results in an increase in the amount of X_1 that is consumed holding both income and the price of X_2 constant. In this figure, the price decrease for X_1 also results in an increase in the consumption of X_2, but this need not necessarily be so—the direction of change depends on the shape of the utility

---

[5] We note, at this point, that the slope of the budget constraint $(-P_2/P_1)$ is equal to the marginal rate of substitution (MRS) between the two goods (or the slope of the indifference curve).

[6] A good question to ask yourself at this point is "Why does the rotation hinge on the y-intercept?" Furthermore, how does one interpret the y- and x-intercepts in this figure?

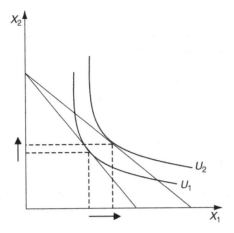

Figure 1.2 Effects on optimal quantities when decreasing the price of X_1.

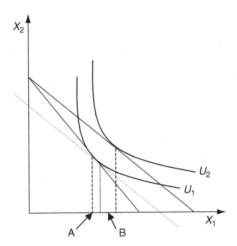

Figure 1.3 The Hicksian derivation of income and substitution effects of a price change.
Note: A in the figure represents the substitution effect and B represents the income effect.

function. In fact, this will be an issue of concern when we address whether the good is a complement or substitute.[7]

We see, then, that a decrease in P_1 has a total effect on the consumption of X_1, but that the total effect can be decomposed into two different parts (Figure 1.3) We have the total effect of the price change denoted by A + B, which is equivalent to the total change in Figure 1.2. In Figure 1.3, we "compensate" the consumer by an amount of money that will yield the same level of utility in consumption as previously realized (note that the dotted budget constraint is parallel to the new budget constraint that arose from the price decrease; this line is parallel because the compensation reduces total income, but prices

---

[7] From this figure, can you tell if X_2 is a complement or substitute?

remain the same so the slope of the budget line remains the same). The point of tangency between the dotted line and the original indifference curve bisects the total impact of the price change into its component parts—part A represents the substitution effect and part B represents the income effect. That is, part A arises because the decrease in price of X_1 induces a shift in consumption from X_2 to X_1. The income effect arises because the decrease in the price of X_1 increases real income, which allows a greater consumption of both goods.

Definition 1.1: the substitution effect *The decrease in the price of X_1 relative to X_2 results in a shift in consumption toward X_1 from X_2.*

Definition 1.2: the income effect *The decrease in the price of X_1 increases real income, which allows a greater consumption of both goods.*

The substitution effect of a price change is *always negative*. That is, as price increases, we consume less of the good and vice versa. The income effect, however, can be either positive or negative. For most goods, increases in income lead to an increase in consumption. However, for some goods, increases in income may lead to decreases in consumption. This derivation provides very useful information about how a consumer views a good—particularly the income effect (Tomek and Robinson, 1990):

Definition 1.3: normal good *A good is said to be normal when the income effect is inversely related to a price change. That is, a decrease in the price leads to an increase in the real income. As real income increases, consumption of good 1 increases as well.*

Definition 1.4: inferior good *A good is said to be inferior when the income effect is directly related to a price change. That is, a decrease in the price leads to an increase in real income. However, all of the increase in real income is spent on increasing the consumption of good 2. Thus, as income increases, consumption of good 1 decreases.*

Definition 1.5: Giffen good *The income effect of a price change is directly related to price changes as with an inferior good, but is larger than the substitution effect, making the total effect negative. That is, as the price of a good declines, consumption of that good declines as well.*

Key Questions

1. What is the income effect?
2. What is the substitution effect?
3. What are the three types of goods as defined by the income effect?

1.1.3   Deriving a Demand Function

We have now seen how consumers maximize utility and how price changes alter the utility-maximizing decisions. While understanding a person's utility-maximization decision is essential, we utimately would like to have that translated into how that individual responds—or demand. Based on these principles, we can derive an individual's demand

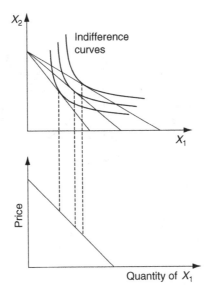

Figure 1.4　The graphical derivation of an individual's demand curve. Note that X_1 in the top panel refers to the quantity of product 1 in quantity space, and Q_1 refers to the quantity of X_1 in price–quantity space. These are the same quantities.

curve, which is a representation between price and quantity of a particular good subject to that individual's budget constraint (Figure 1.4).

By tracing out the effects of price changes for a particular product (X_1), Figure 1.4 translates the effect of price changes from utility space (X_1, X_2) into price/quantity space (X_1, P_1). In this case, the price of X_1, or P_1, is declining, generating increases in the quantity demanded of X_1, or Q_1. This is the **Marshallian demand function** for an individual consumer. In this simple case, we see that there are three main elements affecting the quantity demanded of X_1: the price of good 1 (P_1), the price of good 2 (P_2), and income (through the budget constraint). We can, therefore, represent a general Marshallian demand function as

$$Q_1 = f(P_1, P_2, I).$$

This equation states that the quantity demanded of good 1 (or Q_1) is a *function of* the prices of goods 1 and 2 as well as income.

The *market demand* is a horizontal summation of the individual demand curves, an example of which is shown in Figure 1.5. In this example, there are three consumers: #1, #2, and #3. At high prices, only consumer #2 is willing to purchase the product. As price declines, consumer #1 enters the market. Finally, as price continues to decline, consumer #3 enters the market. The resulting aggregation shows a market demand curve that changes slope as additional consumers enter the market. Thus, there are individuals who enter the market as price declines, or drop out at higher prices. This relationship means that a change in the price not only changes the quantity that each consumer will consume, but also changes the number of consumers. Because individual utility functions are generally not observable (and even if they were, there would be about 300 million of them in the U.S. alone), it is impractical to construct a demand function in this manner.

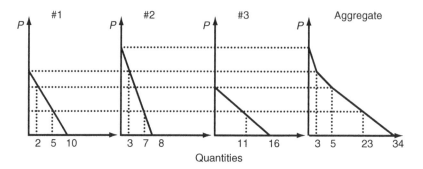

Figure 1.5   The aggregation of individual demand curves to a market demand curve.

We can construct individual demand curves from survey data, but we are most often concerned with aggregated market demand curves.[8]

Changes in Demand

An important distinction often overlooked by students (and professionals as well) is the difference between changes in demand and changes in the quantity demanded.

Definition 1.6:   changes in quantity demanded   *Movements along the demand curve resulting from changes in the price of the product under consideration.*

Definition 1.7:   changes in demand   *A shift in the demand curve resulting from a change in a factor other than the own price or quantity.*

A good rule of thumb to remember is that if the changing variable is on the axes of the graph of the demand function, the result is a change in the quantity demanded. If the variable is not on the axes, the result is a change in demand. These are further illustrated in Figure 1.6. We see that changes in demand can come in the form of increases or decreases in demand, as well as a structural change in demand. These are all driven by variables other than the own price. For example, an increase in the price of a substitute will increase the demand for the own product, while an increase in the price of a complement will decrease the demand for an own product. Structural changes can occur for a number of reasons, such as a change in government policy or a new medical finding regarding the product that changes the way in which individuals view that product in their diet (sometimes called tastes and preferences).

There are a number of factors that will change the market demand for a product. First is the size and distribution of the population. For example, we do not expect the level of demand for pork to be the same in the United States as in China. Sheer numbers of individuals mean that more is being demanded at any given price level. At the same time, the distribution of the population also plays a role. For example, there is a "Baby Boom" generation in the United States, which is larger in number than either the older or younger generations. If this group of individuals prefer something different than other

---

[8]We will examine more advanced methods of addressing individual utility and demand in a later chapter.

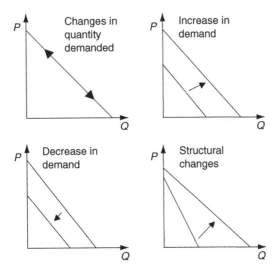

Figure 1.6 Changes in demand and quantity demanded.

generations, it will, *ceteris paribus*,[9] change demand for that product because that group of individuals is a larger portion of the population.

A second factor that affects the level of demand is income and income distribution. It should be obvious that we do not expect the level of demand for DVD players to be the same in the United States as in Africa because of the sheer difference in the level of per capita[10] income. At the same time, income distribution is important as well. If, for example, the majority of a country's wealth was concentrated in the hands of a few individuals, there would be only so many DVD players these individuals could consume. A good example of this phenomenon is the oil-rich countries of the Middle East. These countries have relatively high per capita incomes (compared to other countries of similar levels of development), but that wealth is concentrated in the hands of relatively few individuals. Thus, the market demand for goods and services in these countries remains low because of the number of individuals possessing sufficient wealth to purchase some goods and services.

A third factor is the prices and availability of substitutes and complements. More substitutes, *ceteris paribus*, lead to a decrease in demand. For example, consider the level of demand for gasoline. There are few substitutes for gasoline. What do you expect to happen to the demand for gasoline as more electric and hydrogen fuel cell automobiles are introduced? Figure 1.7 shows that an introduction of hydrogen fuel cell cars shifts the demand for gasoline to the left (decreases demand). At any given price level for gas

---

[9]Recall that *ceteris paribus* is a Latin phrase that means "all else being equal." It is a way of saying that all other variables are held constant. We, as scientists, cannot discern what is the real cause of an outcome if more than one variable is changing at a time. Later, as we examine regression techniques, we find that regression analysis is a method of imposing the *ceteris paribus* assumption on data taken from the real world.

[10]Recall that per capita is a Latin phrase meaning "per person." So, per capita income is the gross domestic product of a country divided by the population. This measure says nothing about income distribution and assumes that income is evenly divided across individuals. It is more a measure of relative wealth of a country.

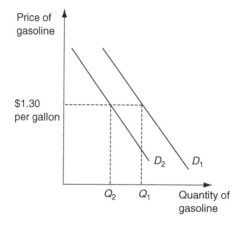

Figure 1.7   Effects of the introduction of hydrogen fuel cell cars on the demand for gasoline.

($1.30 per gallon in the figure), the demand for gasoline will be less.[11] Demand is also affected by the prices of available substitutes.

Example 1.1   *The price of Kellogg's® Frosted Flakes® is $3.00 per box. The price of the closest substitute, "Sweet Flakes," is $2.50 per box. Now, the price of "Sweet Flakes" decreases to $2.00 per box. What do you expect to happen to the demand for Frosted Flakes®?*[12]

Finally, there is the nebulous category of consumer tastes and preferences. We say that this category is nebulous because it is broad and difficult to measure. For example, consumer lifestyles alter demand for products. How do we measure consumer lifestyles? We know, for example, that an increasing portion of the population is either in single-parent households or households where both adults work. This has altered demand so that more processed foods are demanded in favor of unprocessed foods, because of the opportunity cost of time of food preparation (Kohls and Uhl, 2002). Health concerns about fat content, sugar content, and so on are increasingly driving consumption decisions as well. These phenomena are real, but difficult to capture with data in any meaningful way. These taste and preferences, however, have profound impacts on consumer demand.

Key Questions

1. How do you derive an individual demand function?
2. What are the variables in a Marshallian demand function?

---

[11]We will see later that this move also affects the elasticity of demand. In this case, the introduction of the substitute makes demand more elastic.

[12]You might be inclined to say that brand loyalty will prevent consumers from switching, and thereby prevent a decrease in demand. However, recall that market demand is a summation of individual demands. There will always be consumers who are relatively more price sensitive and will switch with a change in price. The strength of brand loyalty is exhibited through the cross-price elasticity of demand. If inelastic, a price change in "Sweet Flakes" will not alter demand for Kellogg's® Frosted Flakes® by a large amount. However, if elastic, a change in the price of "Sweet Flakes" will have a large effect on the demand for Kellogg's® Frosted Flakes®. We will return to this example when we discuss elasticities.

3. How do you derive a market demand function?
4. What is the difference between a change in demand and change in quantity demanded?
5. What are the factors that affect market demand?

1.2 Demand Elasticities

Demand elasticity is a central concept in the analysis of markets. We will briefly review the concept of an arc elasticity, and then move on to the more commonly used point elasticity of demand. An elasticity is the percentage change in one variable given a percentage change in another variable. For demand, the own-price elasticity is the percentage change in the quantity demanded given a percentage change in own price.

1.2.1 Arc Price Elasticity of Demand

The formula for the arc price elasticity of demand is given by

$$E_d = \frac{\%\Delta Q}{\%\Delta P} = \left(\frac{Q_0 - Q_1}{(Q_0 + Q_1)/2}\right) \Big/ \left(\frac{P_0 - P_1}{(P_0 + P_1)/2}\right) = \left(\frac{Q_0 - Q_1}{Q_0 + Q_1}\right)\left(\frac{P_0 + P_1}{P_0 - P_1}\right).$$

Thus, the arc elasticity is a percentage change in the quantity demanded given a percentage change in price between two points on a demand curve. We visualize the arc elasticity as in Figure 1.8. The arc elasticity of demand is useful when we have only data points, and not an estimated demand function, and wish to have some information about price responsiveness. It is a crude measure, however, because the arc elasticity is an average elasticity over a range of the demand function (the arc). Generally, the wider the range, the less accurate is the elasticity. In addition, you will note that the demand function is nonlinear in Figure 1.8. Generally, the more nonlinear the demand function, the less accurate the arc elasticity. Nevertheless, the arc elasticity is a useful device when no other data or estimated functions are available.

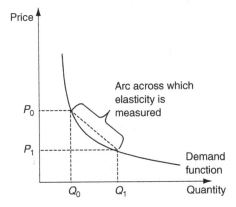

Figure 1.8 A visualization of the arc elasticity of demand.

1.2.2   Point Elasticity of Demand

A more common measure of the elasticity of demand is the point elasticity, which takes the following form:

$$E_d = \frac{\% \Delta Q}{\% \Delta P} = \frac{\partial Q}{\partial P} \frac{P}{Q},$$

where ∂ represents the partial derivative. This formulation says that the elasticity of demand is equal to the partial derivative of the demand function (Q) with respect to the price multiplied by the ratio of the price over quantity at a given point along the demand function. We usually measure the elasticity at the average price and quantity:

$$E_d = \frac{\partial Q}{\partial P} \frac{\bar{P}}{\bar{Q}},$$

but the elasticity can be measured at any given price/quantity combination. As above, we can visualize the point elasticity as in Figure 1.9. Recall that a derivative of a function is the slope of a line tangent to that function at a given point (the dashed line in Figure 1.9). The points, in this case, are $\bar{P}$ and $\bar{Q}$. Thus, this point elasticity is called the *elasticity of demand at the means*, referring to the point of reference being the average price and quantity. Consider the following example:

Example 1.2   *The following is an estimated global demand function for cotton:* $Q_c = 100.6125 - 0.393 P_c$. *Assume that the average consumption of cotton over the 1965–1999 period was 61.33 million bales and the average price (deflated by the U.S. consumer price index) was 74.54 cents per pound. The point elasticity of demand at the means is then given by*

$$E_d = \frac{\partial Q_c}{\partial P_c} \frac{\bar{P}_c}{\bar{Q}_c} = -0.393 \left(\frac{74.54}{61.33} \right) = -0.48.$$

Thus, the own-price elasticity of demand for cotton at the means was -0.48.

1.2.3   Cross-Price and Income Elasticities

We are also concerned with cross-price and income effects. Assume that you have the following demand function:

$$Q_1 = f(P_1, P_2, I),$$

where P_2 is the price of a substitute or complement and I is income. The cross-price elasticity of demand for good 1 with respect to changes in the price of good 2 is

$$E_{12} = \frac{\partial Q_1}{\partial P_2} \frac{P_2}{Q_1}.$$

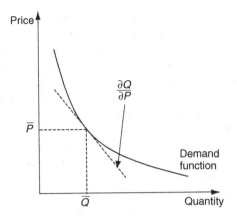

Figure 1.9 A visualization of the point elasticity of demand.

Again, we typically evaluate this expression at the mean values of all variables, but it can be evaluated at any price/quantity combination. The sign of this elasticity determines whether the goods are substitutes or complements. For substitutes, as the price of the competing good increases, this makes the first good relatively less expensive, so demand for the first good will increase (giving the elasticity a positive sign). For example, if the price of pork increases, this makes beef relatively less expensive, therefore increasing the demand for beef. Conversely, if the price of a complement good increases, it makes the joint consumption of goods more expensive, thereby decreasing the demand for the first good. For example, if the price of shortcake increases, the demand for strawberries will decrease (giving the elasticity a negative sign).

You should note that the substitute/complement relationship can be inferred directly from the signs on the coefficients of the demand function. For example, consider the following hypothetical demand equation for beef:

$$Q_{beef} = 155 - 0.05P_{beef} + 0.25P_{pork} - 0.12P_{potatoes} + 0.07I.$$

The positive sign on the coefficient for pork implies that as the price of pork increases, the demand for beef will increase, thus indicating a substitute relationship between beef and pork. Conversely, the negative sign on the coefficient for the price of potatoes indicates that potatoes and steak are complements.

The strength of the complement/substitute relationship is reflected in the cross-price relationship. Returning to our Kellogg's® Frosted Flakes® example, if the "Sweet Flakes" are a strong substitute for Kellogg's® Frosted Flakes®, we expect to see a larger cross-price elasticity than if they were not strong substitutes. The same is generally true for complements (in absolute value). Thus, understanding cross-price elasticities can be a useful tool for understanding marketing implications for products in consumer markets.

We can similarly derive the income elasticity from the demand function:

$$E_{1I} = \frac{\partial Q_1}{\partial I} \frac{I}{Q_1}.$$

The income elasticity carries special importantance because it can be used to classify the good as either normal or inferior. A **normal good** is identified by a positive sign on the income elasticity—an increase in income leads to increases in demand for that good. Most goods are normal. For example, if your income increases, do you consume more beef? An **inferior good** is identified by a negative sign on the income elasticity—an increase in income leads to decreases in demand for that good. When you finish college and get a job, are you actually going to increase your consumption of SPAM®?

In reality, some income elasticities are very close to zero. Consider toilet paper. Does your level of income really influence the amount of toilet paper you use? (Let's hope not!) Rather, as income increases, consumers often reallocate consumption within a product group toward higher-quality items. For example, when you graduate and get that high-paying job, you may not actually increase your beef consumption. Rather, you will likely switch from ground beef (Hamburger Helper) toward ribeye steaks. Thus, we may not observe a strong income effect for broad classes of goods (such as beef), but observe strong income effects for specific products within that class (ground beef versus ribeye steaks).

1.2.4   Interpretation of Elasticities

There are three possible interpretations of the elasticity of demand (or any calculated elasticity):

$|E_d| > 1 \Longrightarrow$ The demand for the product is **elastic**. The percentage change in the quantity demanded is greater than the percentage change in price.

$|E_d| = 1 \Longrightarrow$ The demand for the product is **unitary**. The percentage change in the quantity demanded is equal to the percentage change in price.

$|E_d| < 1 \Longrightarrow$ The demand for the product is **inelastic**. The percentage change in the quantity demanded is less than the percentage change in price.

Returning to the previous cotton demand example, we see that the elasticity of demand is equal to -0.48, which, when the absolute value is taken, is less than 1. Therefore, we would conclude that the own-price elasticity of demand is inelastic. As we will see in a moment, the value of the elasticity is important, but knowledge of whether the elasticity of demand is elastic, inelastic, or unitary has important implications in marketing.

1.2.5   Units of Measure on Elasticity

What are the units of measure on elasticity? Consider the following equation:

$$E_d = \frac{\partial Q(\text{lbs})}{\partial P(\$)} \frac{P(\$)}{Q(\text{lbs})},$$

where the units of measure of the underlying variables are in parentheses. By cross-multiplication, the units of measure drop out, leaving no units of measure for the elasticity. Thus, elasticity is a *unitless measure* of responsiveness of demand to price changes. This

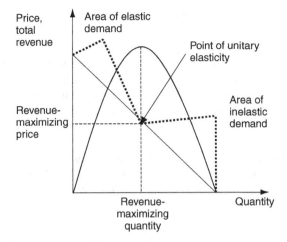

Figure 1.10 The relationship between total revenue and own-price elasticity of demand.

is an important finding because it means that we can compare elasticities across commodities. It is important to remember that while the measure is unitless, the interpretation is not. We interpret the elasticity as a percentage change in one variable with respect to a percentage change in another variable.

Example 1.3 *Assume that the own-price elasticity of demand for beef is −0.35, while the own-price elasticity of demand for pork is −0.53. Because elasticities are unitless, we can directly compare these elasticities. From this, we conclude that demand for beef is more price inelastic than pork. Therefore, changes in the price of beef will have less of an impact on the quantity demanded of beef than changes in the price of pork on the quantity demanded of pork.*

1.2.6 Elasticity and Total Revenue

There is an important and useful relationship between the own-price elasticity of demand and the total revenue for an industry, which is shown in Figure 1.10. This figure depicts the total revenue function (the curved line) and the demand function. Note that the demand function intersects the total revenue function at the *x*-axis. In practical terms, this means that when the price is zero, total revenue is zero. We can bisect the demand curve by noting that maximum revenue is achieved at the point of unitary elasticity. The area to the left of this point on the demand curve is the elastic portion, while the area to the right is the inelastic portion.

This figure provides a powerful tool for understanding economic behavior in markets. Below are some key points to be noted:

1. If demand is in the elastic portion of the demand curve, total revenue can be increased by decreasing the price of the product (or, conversely, increasing the quantity).
2. If demand is in the inelastic portion of the demand curve, total revenue can be increased by raising the price (or, conversely, decreasing the quantity).

This construct offers some immediate applications:

Example 1.4   *Assume, as is often appropriate, that the own-price elasticity of demand for farm products is inelastic (or that demand is in the inelastic portion of the demand curve). If your objective was to increase farm income, what action would you take? (Note: The farm sector is a price taker. You, therefore, cannot set price.) Does this justify the use of acreage control programs that were in place in the United States in the 1980s and 1990s?*

Example 1.5   *Assume that you are a retailer of blue jeans.*[13] *You note that the own-price elasticity of demand for blue jeans is elastic at the retail level. If your objective is to increase total revenue, what action would you take? (Note: You are at the retail level, so you have pricing power.)*

There are many complexities surrounding these examples that are not captured in the figure. However, you can see that this simple construct can be used to understand the underlying fundamentals of economic decisions that are made in the real world every day.

Key Questions

1. What is the difference in calculation between arc and point elasticities?
2. What is the sign (positive or negative) on the cross-price elasticities of demand for a substitute and for a complement?
3. What is the relationship between own-price elasticity of demand and total revenue?
4. How do we classify goods based on the income elasticity of demand?

1.3   Derived Demand

The subject of **derived demand** is of particular interest to agricultural markets. Up to this point, we have been talking about the consumer and their demand for products. Demand at the retail level for final goods and services is called **primary demand**. Most agricultural products, however, serve as inputs into processes used to make these final goods. We say that demand for agricultural products is "derived" from the consumer's demand for the final goods. Thus, we think of demand for agricultural products as a derived demand. The relationship between primary and derived demand is shown in Figure 1.11. Primary demand represents the consumer's demand for final products (say, steak), while the derived demand represents processor demand for the input into that production process (say, steers). The difference in price between the two market levels represents the **marketing margin**, which we will address in detail in Chapter 4. It is important to remember that there are multiple levels of these derived demands.

Example 1.6   *The demand for steaks at the retail level represents the primary demand. The demand for wholesale cuts of meat is derived from this primary demand. The demand*

---

[13]We are making a conceptual leap here, as there are many brands, brand loyalty, and so on. However, this example provides an illustration of the rationale for retailer behavior.

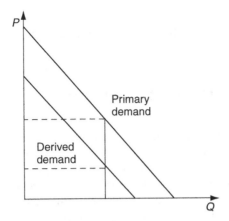

Figure 1.11   The relationship between primary and derived demand.

for beef carcasses is derived from the wholesale demand for meat cuts. Demand for live cattle is derived from the demand for carcasses, and so on, all the way back to the cow-calf operation.

You should also note that derived demands go into other markets:

Example 1.7   *The demand for steaks at the retail level represents the primary demand. This generates a derived demand for labor to process and transport wholesale cuts of meat. The processor demand for live cattle not only generates a demand for feeder cattle, but also generates a derived demand for corn, hay, and other feed inputs.*

Thus, the simple act of you going to the grocery store to purchase a steak sets off a chain reaction of derived demands in multiple markets. Agricultural economists spend considerable time trying to understand the implications of changes in consumer demand on these derived demands. Empirically, derived demand is treated somewhat differently than primary demand. Factors such as consumer income, population, tastes and preferences, and so on are still important, but we must also be mindful of the demand factors in the higher market levels if we are to best understand derived demand.

Example 1.8   *Assume that you are attempting to analyze demand for corn. Of course the price of corn is relevant. What are the complements? What are the substitutes? What other factors might be important? Cattle on feed? The price of sugar?*

In many ways, analyzing derived demand is sometimes more difficult than analyzing primary demand. The diversity of uses of agricultural products as inputs into different products means that there are many factors that may affect derived demand. In the previous example, corn is used both as a sweetener (high-fructose corn syrup) as well as a feed input for livestock production. If the price of sugar increases, the demand for corn sweetener will increase as well (that is, corn sweetener and sugar are substitute sweeteners in food products). If, at the same time, consumer demand for beef decreases because of health concerns, the demand for corn will decrease as well. Because these factors in different markets are all changing simultaneously, understanding the impacts on corn markets can be quite difficult. We will address this topic in more detail in Chapter 4.

1.4 Estimating Demand Functions

Empirical estimation of demand functions can be an important part of an applied economist's job. In this section, we explore the basic techniques of demand function estimation. I proceed under the assumption that you have taken a basic course in regression analysis. Although not completely necessary, this experience will enable you to concentrate on the economic aspects of demand estimation without getting bogged down in econometric intricacies. Further, this section is not intended to be a substitute for a course in econometrics, but is focused on imparting the basic tools of demand estimation.

1.4.1 Empirical Demand Functions and Functional Form

We begin by recalling that the the general demand function is denoted by

$$Q_1 = f(P_1, P_2, \ldots P_n, I),$$

where P_1 is the own price, $P_{-2}, \ldots, P_{-n}$ are the prices of complements and substitutes, and I is income.[14] This general function, however, says nothing about the form the equation will take for estimation purposes. We must decide on the **functional form** that our estimated equation will take. The most common functional form chosen is the linear-additive function form, which is expressed as follows:[15]

$$Q_1 = \alpha + \beta_1 P_1 + \beta_2 P_2 + \cdots + \beta_n P_n + \beta_X I,$$

where α is the intercept term and the β's are the demand coefficients to be estimated.[16] The function is linear because the parameters form a straight line (recall the equation of a line is $Y = a + bX$, so that changes in X result in a line). The equation is additive because, in theory,[17] the value of each parameter is independent of the other

---

[14]Identification of the demand function is essential to estimation. Appendix 1B at the end of this chapter discusses the issue of identification in more detail. Those not familiar with the concept of identification should read Appendix 1B before proceeding.

[15]Note that this is an equation *to be* estimated. An estimated equation must have an additional term, ε, which represents the random error in the estimated equation. Recall that in ordinary least squares regression, we assume $\varepsilon \sim N(0, \sigma^2)$, or that the error term is normally distributed with a mean value of zero and a constant variance σ^2. Tests of this assumption can be made (Greene, 2000), but we assume this characteristic of the error terms holds here for simplicity.

[16]You should note that the β's in the estimated linear equation can be interpreted as the impact multipliers. See Ferris (1998) for a more complete discussion on the interpretation of impact multipliers.

[17]We say "in theory" because in practice, there are correlations between parameters, called multicollinearity. If the demand function is properly specified, multicollinearity should not be a problem, and therefore, the function is linear and additive.

and the derivative of the function with respect to any variable is equal only to its parameter. The own-price elasticity of demand arising from this functional form is given by

$$E_d = \frac{\partial Q_1}{\partial P_1} \frac{P_1}{Q_1} = \beta_1 \frac{P_1}{Q_1}.$$

As you can see, β_1 is a constant, so the own-price elasticity of demand changes with changes in P and Q. This yields the familiar figures from above of a linear demand function whereby the slope, β_1, is constant, but the elasticity changes as one moves up or down the demand function.

A popular alternative to the linear model is the double-log model of demand, denoted by

$$Q_1 = A P_1^{\beta_1} P_2^{\beta_2} \ldots P_n^{\beta_n} I^{\beta_I}$$

or

$$\ln Q_1 = \ln A + \beta_1 \ln P_1 + \beta_2 \ln P_2 + \ldots + \beta_n \ln P_n + \beta_I \ln I,$$

where ln is the natural logarithm of the associated variable. The second equation represents a linearized version of the first for estimation purposes. The double-log model has the advantage of allowing for a nonlinear demand function. It also has the special property that the elasticity, and not the slope, is constant:

$$E_d = \frac{\partial Q_1}{\partial P_1} \frac{P}{Q} = \beta_1 A P_1^{\beta_1 - 1} P_2^{\beta_2} \ldots P_n^{\beta_n} I^{\beta_I} \left(\frac{P_1}{A P_1^{\beta_1} P_2^{\beta_2} \ldots P_n^{\beta_n} I^{\beta_I}} \right) = \beta_1.$$

Note also that the estimated coefficient, β_1, is the elasticity. This formulation appears daunting at first. However, in practice, it simply involves taking the natural logarithm of all of the data prior to estimation. Then, the estimated coefficients are the elasticities with respect to their corresponding variables. Other commonly used functional forms and their respective derivatives are found in Tomek and Robinson (1990) or Ferris (1998).

Given the wide variety of functional forms, the question becomes "How does one select the appropriate functional form?" Tomek and Robinson (1990) provide three criteria that are useful for consideration. First are economic considerations. That is, does a functional form provide reasonable estimates across the range of data used for analysis?[18] Consider the situation in Figure 1.12. Assume that the true demand function is represented by the nonlinear function in the figure. However, assume that data range from only P_1 to P_2 and from Q_1 to Q_2. In this case, a linear approximation to the true demand function would likely result in elasticity estimates that

---

[18] I prefer to think of this as the range of experience. That is, we may have only observed prices for corn between $1.80 and $3.00 per bushel. But this does not, however, mean that prices cannot fall outside of that range. Nevertheless, we must be concerned with the appropriateness of the elasticity estimates across the range of experience that we possess.

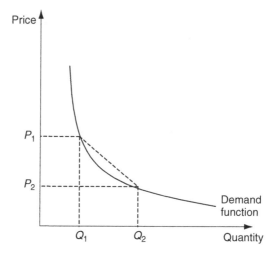

Figure 1.12 The choice of experimental functional form based on range of data issues.

are very reasonable. However, if our range of experience is wider than that depicted in the figure, our linear function might not give a good approximation to the true demand function. In that case, a nonlinear form such as the double-log model would be more appropriate. In practice, we do not know the shape of the true demand function. However, for fairly narrow ranges of experience, a linear function may perform well, but for wider ranges of experience, the more flexible nonlinear forms should be chosen.

The second criterion is purely statistical. That is, we should choose, all else being equal, the functional form that exhibits the best statistical properties. These include measures of goodness of fit such as R^2. While these measures are useful, they **cannot and should not**, in themselves, determine the appropriate functional form. Models with alternative functional forms can, in fact, have very similar measures of goodness of fit.[19] Furthermore, decisions made purely on statistical grounds can lead to incorrect conclusions about the appropriate functional form to choose (Theil, 1971). Nevertheless, statistical guidelines can be useful in assisting in the decision on choice of functional form, but theoretical considerations should be implemented first and foremost.

Finally, the choice of functional form should consider the principle of Occam's Razor. That is, all else being equal, the simplest explanation of a problem is usually the correct one. In this case, simple models are preferred to complex ones, and a smaller set of explanatory variables should be preferred to a larger set.[20]

---

[19]There are statistical techniques for comparing between alternative functional forms. The more advanced readers amongst you should consult Greene (2000) for a discussion of these measures.

[20]Note that this consideration is under the assumption of all else being equal. One should not be parsimonious in variable use for parsimony's sake. That is, you should include the minimum number of variables needed to correctly specify your equation, no more or no less. Easy to say . . . difficult to do.

1.4.2   Price-Dependent Demand (Inverse Demand)

An alternative to the quantity-dependent demand presented above is the price-dependent (or inverse) demand function. The general form for this type of model is

$$P_1 = f(Q_1, Q_2, \ldots, Q_n, I),$$

so that the price of the own product is a function of the quantity of the own and complement/substitute products and income. We typically use the inverse demand function for products where quantity is relatively fixed or predetermined and demand for that product is essentially whatever is produced. Examples are perishable products such as fruits and vegetables. The "elasticity" in this case is calculated as

$$F = \frac{\partial P}{\partial Q} \frac{Q}{P},$$

which is called the **price flexibility**. This measure indicates the percentage change in price with a percentage change in quantity demanded. Estimation procedures and issues as well as data issues are similar to quantity-dependent demand functions as described above.

1.4.3   Data and Aggregation

A second topic of importance in empirical demand estimation is the data source and level of aggregation (in time, space, and form). There are two basic types of data—primary and secondary. **Primary data** are data derived from direct observation. For example, these data can take the form of individual transactions data as used by Brown et al. (1995) or survey data used by Hite, Hudson, and Intarapapong (2002).[21]

The most common form of data used in empirical demand estimation is **secondary data**, which are data derived from a published source. These data have been collected by other parties and have typically been aggregated in some manner. The **level of aggregation** refers to how individual data are combined. It would be very expensive (if not impossible), for example, to publish every individual's beef consumption. However, we can *spatially* aggregate consumption to a national, regional, state, or even city level. For example, for *any given period of time*, we could report the national beef consumption (one data point), beef consumption in the Northeast, Southeast, Midwest, Southwest, and Northwest (five data points), beef consumption by state (50 data points), or beef consumption by city (many data points).

Note that at each subsequent level of aggregation, we are "losing" information. That is, when we move from a city to state level of aggregation, we are losing the information gained by the variation in beef consumption between cities. Statisticians are acutely interested in variation because it is the variation that identifies the differences between individuals and allows us to explain the factors that influence demand. If we proceed

---

[21] In a later chapter, we will address more advanced issues of individual utility and demand estimation, and the creation of primary data from surveys and experimental economics techniques.

up the level of aggregation, we arrive at the national level, which only provides us information about the total demand at any given point in time. There is a trade-off to be made here. On the one hand, lower levels of aggregation allow greater variation, which allows for richer explanations about differences in demand. However, it is much more expensive to collect data at lower levels of aggregation.

Related to this is the level of *time* aggregation. That is, data can be collected for a single point in time, resulting in a **cross-sectional** data set. That is, a cross-sectional data set provides a "snapshot" of the level of demand for a given point in time. For cross-sectional data, we should be acutely aware of the level of spatial aggregation. In this case, we would like to have the lowest level of aggregation possible (even individual consumer data) so as to capture the maximum amount of variation across the cross-section.

Most typically, however, we will utilize **time series** data, which are observations on a particular variable, say national per capita beef consumption, across time. There are a variety of levels of time aggregation in time series data—daily, weekly, monthly, annually. The choice of the level of time aggregation depends on two factors: (1) the problem you are attempting to address and (2) the availability of secondary data. Some problems will require data with a daily frequency. For example, Lusk and Schroeder (2002) attempted to examine the impacts of meat recalls on the price of beef. Because meat recalls occur on a particular day and the price impacts of that meat recall are likely to be felt immediately, they needed daily price information for beef. However, other problems may require less frequent data. For example, Hudson and Hanson (1999) examined seasonality effects in catfish prices (and marketing margins). Daily data were not required, but monthly data were desirable in this case. Other problems, such as problems of structural changes in demand, occur over longer periods of time and, thus, only require annual observations.

Data availability is often a constraining factor in choosing the level of time aggregation. For example, in the Hudson and Hanson (1999) analysis, if daily observations were needed, it would not be possible to get them from secondary sources. There are no published data on the daily consumption of catfish in the United States. Thus, data availability would have constrained the analysis to monthly observations at best.

It is important to remember that research of this type is an iterative process. That is, we first develop a conceptual model of the demand function we wish to estimate. We use this conceptual model to guide the empirical estimation process. Your problem may dictate that you need monthly data, but after searching for data sources, you find that monthly data do not exist. This will force you to reconsider your problem and research objectives. It may be that you can obtain the needed data from primary sources, or you may have to find an alternative way to define your problem to fit the data that you do have. In either case, it is most important to properly define your conceptual model of demand before proceeding to empirical estimation. If you fail to do so, you will likely either make a mistake in the empirical estimation, or create an empirical model that has no relevance to the problem you were attempting to address.

Exercises

Problem 1.1   *Assume that a story has been broadcast on Dateline NBC that announces that too much consumption of red meat increases the risk of heart disease. What impact do you expect this report to have on beef demand? Explain your answer graphically.*

Problem 1.2　*Based on the following data for corn:*

Amount of corn sold (billions of bushels)	Price per bushel ($)
3.0	4.00
3.4	3.75
3.8	3.50
5.0	3.00
5.7	2.75
6.4	2.50
7.2	2.25

suppose that the price of corn decreases from $3.00 to $2.75 per bushel. What is the own-price elasticity of demand? (Note: At those prices, the quantity demanded of corn goes from 5.0 to 5.7 billion bushels.) Interpret your result.

Problem 1.3　*Based on the following demand equation for cotton:*

$$Q_c = 88.83 - 0.34P_c,$$

suppose that the average quantity consumed, $\bar{Q}_c$, is 63.2 million bales and the average price paid, $\bar{P}_c$, is 74.5 cents per pound. What is the own-price elasticity of demand at the means? Interpret your result.

Problem 1.4　*Assuming the demand for agricultural products is inelastic, what would be the impact on total farm revenue if the supply of agricultural products were restricted by the government (say, an acreage control program)? Why?*

Problem 1.5　*Assume that the demand for beef can be expressed as $Q_{beef} = 127 - 0.23P_{beef} + 0.15P_{pork} + 0.27P_{chicken} + 1.07I$. Also assume that the average per capita beef consumption is 75.73 pounds, the average price of beef is 190.88 cents per pound, the average price of pork is 145.52 cents per pound, the average price of chicken is 68.48 cents per pound, and the average disposable income is $7,715.49. (1) Interpret this equation for substitutes and complements, as well as whether beef is a normal or inferior good; (2) calculate the own-, cross-, and income-elasticities of demand, and interpret your results.*

Problem 1.6　*If the own-price elasticity of demand at the means is −0.09, the coefficient on the own price in the demand function is −3.3457, and the average quantity is 95.26, what is the average price?*

Problem 1.7　*Recall that the total effect of a price change is equal to the substitution effect plus the income effect and the income effect is always negative. If the total effect is negative, is this a normal, inferior, or Giffen good?*

References

Brown, J., D. Ethridge, D. Hudson, and C. Engels. "An Automated Econometric Approach for Estimating and Reporting Daily Cotton Market Prices." *Journal of Agricultural and Applied Economics*, 27(1995): 409–422.

Chiang, A. *Fundamental Methods of Mathematical Economics*, third edition. McGraw-Hill, New York, 1984.

Deaton, A. and J. Muellbauer. *Economics and Consumer Behavior*. Cambridge University Press, New York, 1980.

Ferris, J. *Agricultural Prices and Commodity Market Analysis*. WCB–McGraw-Hill, New York, 1998.

Greene, W. *Econometric Analysis*, fourth edition. Prentice Hall, Upper Saddle River, NJ, 2000.

Hite, D., D. Hudson, and W. Intarapapong. "Taxpayer Willingness to Pay for Water Quality: The Case of Precision Application Technology." *Journal of Agricultural and Resource Economics*, 27(2002): 433–449.

Hudson, D. and T. Hanson. "An Examination of Farm/Processor Price Spreads in Catfish Markets." *Aquaculture Economics and Management*, 3(1999): 222–227.

Kohls, R. and J. Uhl. *Marketing of Agricultural Products*, ninth edition. Prentice Hall, Upper Saddle River, NJ, 2002.

List, J. "Preference Reversals of a Different Kind: The 'More is Less' Phenomenon." *American Economic Review*, 92(2002): 1,636–1,643.

Lusk, J. and D. Hudson. "Effect of Monitor–Subject Cheap Talk on Ultimatum Game Offers." *Journal of Economic Behavior and Organization*, 54(2004): 439–443.

Lusk, J. and T. Schroeder. "Effects of Meat Recalls on Futures Market Prices." *Agricultural and Resource Economics Review*, 31(2002): 47–58.

Theil, H. *Principles of Econometrics*. John Wiley, New York, 1971.

Tomek, W. and K. Robinson. *Agricultural Product Prices*, third edition. Cornell University Press, Ithaca, NY, 1990.

Varian, H. *Microeconomic Analysis*, third edition. W.W. Norton and Company, New York, 1992.

Appendix 1A: Mathematical Treatment of Utility Maximization and Demand Derivation

Using these techniques and the axioms from this chapter, we can derive a simple Marshallian (uncompensated) demand function from a utility function. Consider the following utility function:

$$U = x^2 y^2.$$

Note that the utility function is nonlinear. The utility this consumer derives from consuming products 1 (x) and 2 (y) is *multiplicative* (that is, multiplied by each other). If we plot the utility function, we get Figure 1.13. As you can see, increases in x, holding y constant, slightly increase utility. The same is true for increases in y, holding x constant. However, when both x and y increase, utility increases rapidly. In fact, without a budget constraint, this consumer would prefer to consume an infinite amount of both x and y.

We now introduce the budget constraint:

$$I = p_1 x + p_2 y,$$

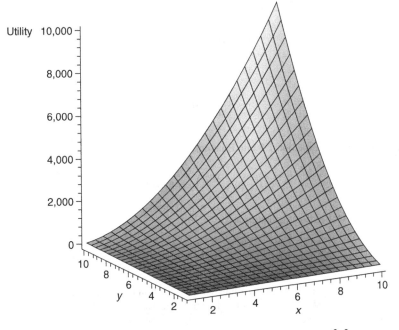

Utility

Figure 1.13 A graphical representation of the given utility function: $U = x^2 y^2$.

where the P's are prices and I is income. This constraint says that our total expenditures on x and y cannot exceed our total income. From these, we get the following Lagrangian function[22] to be maximized:

$$\max L = x^2 y^2 + \lambda \left(I - p_1 x - p_2 y \right).$$

To solve this maximization problem, we must find the first-order conditions[23] of maximization by differentiating the above with respect to x, y, and λ, yielding

$$\frac{\partial L}{\partial x} = 2xy^2 - \lambda p_1 = 0, \tag{1.1}$$

$$\frac{\partial L}{\partial y} = 2yx^2 - \lambda p_2 = 0, \tag{1.2}$$

$$\frac{\partial L}{\partial \lambda} = I - p_1 x - p_2 y = 0. \tag{1.3}$$

---

[22] The Lagrangian function is a function used in mathematical economics that introduces the budget constraint into the utility function. Essentially, maximizing the Lagrangian function is equivalent to saying "maximizing the utility function subject to a budget constraint." You are referred to Chiang (1984) for a complete treatment of the Lagrangian function.

[23] We are skipping the second-order conditions for maximization here to preserve clarity of the argument. However, you should be mindful to examine the second-order conditions for maximization in practice. Do the second-order conditions hold here?

We can rewrite Equations 1.1 and 1.2 and set them equal to one another:

$$\frac{2xy^2}{p_1} = \frac{2yx^2}{p_2},\qquad(1.4)$$

which solves to

$$x = \frac{yp_2}{p_1}.\qquad(1.5)$$

We can then substitute Equation 1.5 into Equation 1.3:

$$I - p_1\left(\frac{yp_2}{p_1}\right) - p_2 y = 0,$$

which yields the Marshallian demand for y:

$$y = \frac{I}{2p_2}.$$

You should also solve for the Marshallian demand function for q_1. The important item to note here is that in this simple form for a utility function, the Marshallian demand function contains two primary arguments: the own price and the income or total expenditure, I. In more complicated utility functions, we will also begin to see cross-price arguments. Thus, this leads us to a general form for a Marshallian demand function:

$$q_1 = f(p_1, p_2, \ldots p_n, I),$$

where I represents income.

Appendix 1B: Identification

Identification of the demand (or supply) function is not as easy as it might seem. Consider the situation in which you are analyzing soybean demand using annual data. For each year, you have two pieces of information—average price for the year and quantity sold. Assuming that you have data over time, an X–Y scatter plot of the data might look like Figure 1.14.

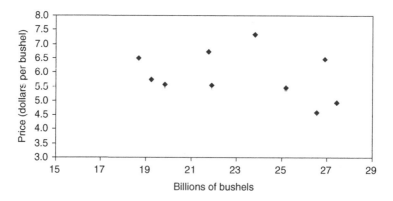

Figure 1.14   A scatter plot of annual observations on soybean quantity and price.

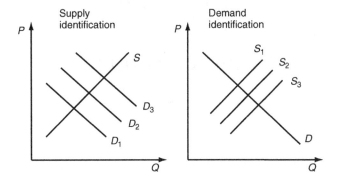

Figure 1.15 Supply and demand function identification.

If supply were completely stable (that is, the supply function did not change over time), then annual changes could be used to trace out a supply function. Conversely, if demand were completely stable, then annual changes could be used to trace out a demand function (see Figure 1.15). However, both supply and demand are generally changing through time, thus complicating the process of identifying either a supply or demand function. We include demand shifters in our estimation (or supply shifters if we are estimating supply) to help us identify the demand function. While not perfect, this greatly improves our ability to identify these functions.

Chapter 2

Market Supply

The supply of products into the marketplace is a crucial aspect of economics, but one that receives relatively little attention as compared to demand. This is due in part to the complexity of supply relationships. This chapter outlines production relationships and relates them to market supply. The chapter is not intended as a substitute for a good course in production economics. Rather, the purpose is to highlight production and supply relationships so that a clear and complete picture of the market emerges. First, we will address the decisions of the individual producer, then aggregate the individuals to the market level. Then, we will address factors that shift or alter supply. Finally, we will end with some discussion of supply estimation.

2.1   The Producer

There is a technical relationship between the inputs in a production process and the output, known as the **production function**. For example, there is a relationship between the amount of fertilizer applied and the ouput of the resulting crop. This relationship is traditionally shown as in Figure 2.1.[1] The total amount of production for each level of input is called the **total physical product** (*TPP*). The production function shows a level of nitrogen input at which marginal increases in nitrogen applications lead to greater than proportional responses in yield. That is, there is an increasing marginal effect.[2] There comes a point at which yield is still increasing, but increasing at a decreasing rate. So, adding more fertilizer will increase yield, but each additional unit of fertilizer increases yield by a successively smaller amount. Finally, the relationship will reach a

---

[1]The figure depicts a transcendental production function, which is only one of many methods to represent a production relationship. The transcendental form is convenient because it generates the classical three stages of production.

[2]Said another way, yield is increasing at an increasing rate.

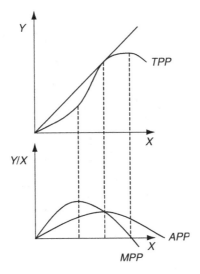

Figure 2.1   The production function (total physical product, or *TPP*) and the associated marginal physical product (*MPP*) and average physical products (*APP*).

point at which an additional unit of fertilizer actually decreases output. This is the point of maximum production. Note that the **marginal physical product** (*MPP*) relationship is equal to zero at that point, suggesting that increases in fertilizer will decrease total output.

The importance of this technical relationship cannot be overlooked. While there is no "economic" (that is, prices) content in the production function, these technical relationships play a major role in economic decisions. For example, assume you have two types of fertilizer. Fertilizer A generates twice as much yield for each unit of fertilizer as fertilizer B. By this, how much more would you be willing to pay for fertilizer A relative to B? You would probably pay as much as twice as much for A relative to B. We will now relate the technical relationship to costs. The production function is then related to cost and supply through the cost functions (Figure 2.2).[3]

The total cost for the firm is given by:[4]

$$TC = VC + FC, \tag{2.1}$$

where *VC* is the variable cost and *FC* is the fixed cost. Variable cost is a function of output, *Y*, and input prices, r_n:

$$VC = f(Y, r_1, r_2, \ldots, r_n). \tag{2.2}$$

---

[3] The cost relationships are linked to the technical production function through isoquants and isocost curves. These issues are skipped here to conserve space and preserve clarity. However, readers should investigate these relationships to gain a more complete picture of the relationship between costs and production. See Beattie and Taylor (1993) as an example.

[4] The more advanced readers amongst you are encouraged to examine the Appendix 2A derivation of conditional input demand functions and average and marginal cost functions.

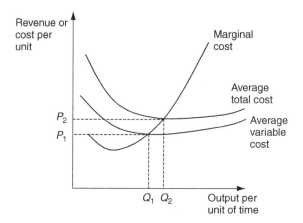

Figure 2.2 Cost relationships for the individual producer.

In Figure 2.2, the average total cost is

$$ATC = \frac{TC}{Y} \tag{2.3}$$

and average variable cost is

$$AVC = \frac{VC}{Y}. \tag{2.4}$$

The marginal cost for the firm is

$$MC = \frac{\partial TC}{\partial Y}. \tag{2.5}$$

In a static analysis, the producer will produce at the point at which marginal cost is equal to marginal revenue (see Appendix 2B for a mathematical treatment of a simple profit maximization problem). Note that average variable cost and average total cost get closer together as output is increased in Figure 2.2. This is because the difference between total cost and variable cost is fixed cost. Given that fixed cost is constant across all levels of output, the average fixed cost declines across output. Marginal cost represents the addition to cost from an additional unit of output. Recall from Figure 2.1 that as output increases, you reach a point at which output is increasing at a decreasing rate. Thus, cost is increasing at an increasing rate beyond that point. It is a mathematical property of cost functions that marginal cost will always equal both average variable cost and average total cost at their respective minimums.

As a price taker, the marginal revenue for the individual producer is the price. Now, let's examine the impact of changes in marginal revenue (price) on optimal levels of output. At some low level of price, say P_1, the marginal revenue is equal to the marginal cost at the point at which marginal cost is equal to average variable cost. This point is known as the **short-run shutdown point**. For any price below P_1, the marginal revenue will not be sufficient to cover variable operating expenses. In the short run, the producer can afford to operate by covering variable expenses, but at P_1, the producer is not paying any fixed expenses (including management).

Now examine the relationship when the marginal revenue is equal to P_2, which corresponds to the point at which marginal revenue is equal to marginal cost when marginal cost is equal to average total cost. This point is known as the **long-run shutdown point**. Here, the producer is just covering all costs (including management), and is, therefore, not earning an economic profit. It should be apparent from Figure 2.2 that the optimal output when the producer is facing P_2 is higher than when facing P_1. Thus, there is a direct relationship between the price of the product and the optimal output. How responsive the producer is to changes in price (that is, how much optimal output goes up or down with a price increase or decrease) depends on the slope of the marginal cost function.

This leads us to an important conclusion regarding individual behavior. Namely, the marginal cost function *above the minimum of average variable cost* is the *short-run supply function* for the individual producer. Why is it only above the minimum of average variable cost? Recall that the minimum of average variable cost is the shutdown point in the short run. At any price less than P_1, the producer could not afford to pay variable expenses. Do you think the banker would be willing to loan you money if he or she did not think you would be able to pay back the loan? Of course not. By the same regard, the producer will not produce.

Key Questions

1. What describes the technical relationship between inputs and output?
2. What is the unique relationship between marginal cost and average or variable cost?
3. What is the point of profit maximization?
4. What is the difference between the shutdown point in the short and long run?
5. What is the short-run supply function?
6. If, in perfect competition, we have a zero profit condition in equilibrium, does this mean that all producers are earning zero profit?

2.2 Market Supply

We have established the basic relationships for the individual producer, and we now turnover attention to market supply. Put simply, the market supply function is the horizontal summation of all individual supply functions. That is, we add all producers together to get the market, in much the same way that we add all individual consumers to get the market demand function. This construction is convenient in that we can rely on the logic of decisions made by the individual to infer market behavior. Thus, as we discuss the issue of market supply, we will move back and forth between the individual and the market as needed to trace out the logic.

2.2.1 Length of Run

The length of time allowed for adjustment, or the **length of run**, plays an important role in how we interpret supply relationships. Most importantly, the length of run affects the "fixity" of the inputs in the production process. For example, in the *very short run* (say, after harvest), all production inputs are fixed and the producer cannot respond to changes

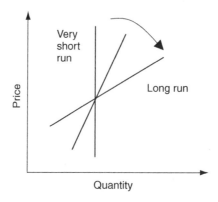

Figure 2.3   The impacts of length of run on the supply function.

in price.[5] In the *short run* (say, during the growing season), most inputs are fixed (land, labor, seed, etc.), but the producer may alter timing and amounts of irrigation, fertilizers, or pesticides, depending on the price of the product. Thus, some, but not significant, supply reponse to price is available.

In the *medium run* (say 1–2 years), many of the inputs become variable. The producer can change equipment and cropping patterns in response to the prices available in the market. Higher cost and less liquid[6] inputs, such as land, remain relatively fixed. In this case, a greater degree of price response is exhibited by the producer. Finally, in the *long run*, all factors of production become variable. The producer can move out of production totally if wished and/or can alter locations, crop mixes, equipment, and all other inputs. The impacts of length of run on the supply function are shown in Figure 2.3. In the very short run, supply is perfectly inelastic. The producer cannot alter the level of production, no matter what the price. As the length of run gets longer, the supply function becomes flatter (or more elastic), suggesting that price changes have larger impacts on the quantity supplied. This result highlights a very commonsense relationship.

Example 2.1   *Suppose that you were to be assigned a paper where the grade was based on the number of pages you produced. In the very short run (say 15 minutes), you could only produce one page, no matter what the grade. However, if you were given a week, the number of pages you could produce would depend greatly on the grade you received for each additional page.*

Thus, clearly, one must consider the length of time that is covered when thinking about supply, because it affects our interpretation of the supply relationship. Generally speaking, the longer the length of time considered in the analysis, the more elastic would be the expected supply elasticity.[7]

---

[5] We are abstracting here from the possibility of storage. We will return to the issue of storage in a later chapter.

[6] Liquid, in this case, means easily disposable. For example, it may be feasible to sell and buy equipment over this time horizon, but buying and selling different plots of land is more difficult.

[7] Recall from Chapter 1 the elasticity calculation. For supply, we are simply calculating the supply elasticity from the supply function, not the demand function. Because the supply function is upward sloping, the supply elasticity is positive.

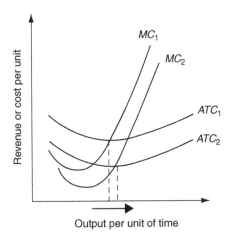

Figure 2.4   The impacts on cost of production and optimal output of a decrease in herbicide price.

2.2.2   Changes in Supply

As with a demand function, it is useful to distinguish between changes in supply and changes in the quantity supplied. Changes in the quantity supplied are movements along the market supply curve. There are a number of factors that change supply (or shift the supply function), which are summarized below.

Factor Prices

As discussed in the first section of this chapter, the physical relationship between inputs and output is important. Changes in the prices of inputs used in the production process are obvious sources of changes in supply. Analysis by example will help to understand the logic of the changes.

Example 2.2   *Roundup*® *has been a popular herbicide for many years. Assume that the patent on this herbicide has now expired so that lower-cost "generic" brands with the same effectiveness are available on the market. What impact will this have on the production of the individual producer? What will be the impact on market supply?*

The individual producer is attempting to maximize profit (see Appendix 2B). As such, the producer will continue to use inputs until the last unit of additional input pays for itself. That is, the **marginal value product** (MVP) must equal the **marginal factor cost** (MFC) (Beattie and Taylor, 1993). Assuming that the producer is following this maximization pattern, we can simplify the analysis by examining the impacts of the herbicide price change on costs and optimal output (Figure 2.4). Starting with the original marginal cost relationship, MC_1, under the original herbicide price, the producer will produce some optimal level of output in equilibrium.[8] Now, a reduction in the cost of the herbicide

---

[8]Recall that in equilibrium, the producer produces where marginal cost equals average cost. "Average cost" is used here to simplify the graphical presentation. For the short run, this would be average variable cost, but would be average total cost for the long run. The logic is the same.

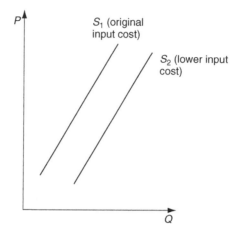

Figure 2.5   The impact of a lower herbicide price on market supply.

would shift both the marginal cost to the right and average total cost downward (reflecting a lower per unit cost for the herbicide). Clearly, then, the optimal level of production would increase.

But what happens to market supply? Given that market supply is simply a summation of individual supplies, the result of the lower herbicide price is a rightward shift in the market supply function (Figure 2.5). Thus, at any given price level, the producer (and the market) is willing to supply more output. Obviously, the opposite would be true if the price of the herbicide were to increase.

Competing Products

The profitability of products that compete for the same set of resources is also important in determining the level of supply of a given product. Corn and soybeans in the Midwest provide a classic example. Assume that you are attempting to analyze the supply of corn in the United States (and the Midwest is the primary producer). Soybeans represent a primary competitor for the land resource used to produce corn. If the profitability of soybeans were to increase relative to corn, we would expect to see the supply function for corn to shift to the left, and vice versa. This relationship is transparent and easy to visualize. But it is important to note that other resources are also important to consider.

For example, in the Delta area of Mississippi, it may be the case that a producer is choosing between soybeans and cotton. There are obvious cases where soil types are more suited to either cotton or soybean production, and so either crop will be planted on its most appropriate soil type. However, these two crops compete in terms of time for the manager and cultivation equipment. As the profitability of cotton increases relative to soybeans, the producer may not necessarily devote more land to cotton, but will devote more management and equipment time to that crop. This example illustrates a marginal change in the supply of cotton, but a change nonetheless.[9]

---

[9]Hudson and Ethridge (2000) provide an example of competition between cotton and sugarcane in Pakistan. In this case, the trade-off was not necessarily for land (although that was important as well), but for irrigation water. This provides another example of the impact of the profitability of competing crops.

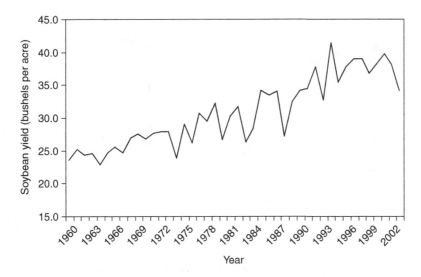

Figure 2.6 The average soybean yield in the United States, 1960–2003.
Source: U.S. Department of Agriculture, Economic Research Service, *Oilseeds Yearbook,* 2004.

As can be seen, competing product relationships can be complex and may depend heavily on the technology being used or the production environment. For example, in areas where double-cropping is possible, competition for the land resource may be less important. So, to fully understand supply relationships, an understanding of competing products is important.

Technology

The technology used by producers is also important, although changes in technology tend to be a longer-run issue. Compare, for example, the output of a given acre of land in the 1920s, when there were little or no mechanical tractors or harvesters, with the situation today. The difference in productivity[10] is enormous. Even over shorter periods, technology can have important impacts. Figure 2.6 shows soybean yields in the United States from 1960 to 2002. As can be seen, even over this period, there have been substantial increases in average yield.

What is the likely marginal impact of technological change between this year and last? Generally, technological progress is slower, and viewed more over the long term. However, technology can make "leaps" as well. An example is spatial technology. Spatial technology (also known as site-specific farming) is a combination of global positioning systems, yield monitoring, soil testing, and technology that allows producers to alter the application rates of fertilizers and pesticides moving across the field (Hudson and Hite, 2003; Isik et al., 2003; Hudson et al., 2004). This technology holds the potential to revolutionize farming practices by allowing producers to optimize inputs on subunits of a field. That is, rather than applying a single rate of nitrogen fertilizer, for example,

[10]Productivity is defined as output per unit of input. In this case, we are referring to the yield per acre.

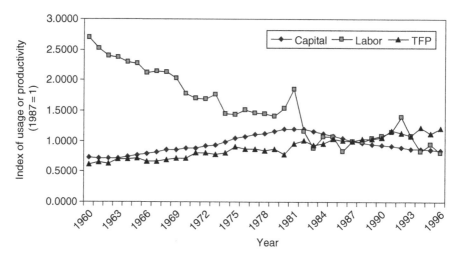

Figure 2.7 Indices of input use and total factor productivity (*TFP*) in U.S. agriculture, 1960–1996.
Source: U.S. Department of Agriculture, Economic Research Service, *Agricultural Productivity in the U.S.,* 1998.

to the entire field, the producer can now apply the optimal amounts at specific points in the field. While the impacts of spatial technology on farm profitability are still uncertain (Swinton and Lowenberg-DeBoer, 1998), the technology may prove to be a major shift in technology in agriculture. Another example is genetic engineering and biotechnology.

Figure 2.7 shows indices representing labor and capital usage in U.S. agriculture as well as total factor productivity (TFP). As can be seen, there has been a steady decline of labor usage over time. At the same time, there has been a relative increase in the usage of capital. This figure represents the relative substitution of capital for labor in agriculture, which is a function of technology. An important point to note here is that TFP is increasing over time, suggesting that input usage is becoming more efficient, leading to greater output. So, the *combination* of inputs is generating greater productivity, even though the mix of inputs is changing. We will discuss the issue of technology adoption in more detail in a moment.

Joint Products

Sometimes, a product that is produced has a joint product as well. For example, the production of wool is joint with the production of mutton. The production of soybean oil is joint with the production of soybean meal. Because these products are jointly produced, the price of one product will impact the supply curve of the joint product.

Example 2.3 *Assume that the price of soybean oil has increased. What will be the impact on the supply of soybean meal?*

An increase in the price of soybean oil will increase the quantity supplied of soybean oil (by increasing the crush of soybeans). But meal is a by-product of the crush, so this change will shift the supply function for soybean meal to the right. This decreases the price of soybean meal, *ceteris paribus*. Thus, it is important to consider the impact of joint products. Failure to do so will lead to erroneous conclusions about the product under question.

Risk[11]

Risk (both price and yield) plays an important role in the decisions of farmers. In the traditional profit maximization model of producer decisions, producers are assumed to be **risk neutral** (that is, indifferent to the level of risk). However, if producers are to be assumed **risk averse** (that is, willing to forgo some level of income to avoid risk), riskiness becomes a major issue. Sandmo (1971) illustrates an important concept: all things being equal, price risk reduces the optimal level of output. That is, when producers faces price risk, the response is to reduce the level of applied inputs, and therefore, reduce output.[12] Yield risk also plays an important role.

As Helmberger and Chavas (1996) demonstrate, production decisions are based off *expectations* of future prices. That is, a farmer is not looking at last year's price alone in making cropping decisions. Rather, the producer is forming an expectation about what the likely price *will be* at harvest time. If prices are risky (that is, highly variable), it is difficult for the producer to form expectations and, thus, difficult to make cropping decisions.

If risk reduces output, risk-shifting will increase output. For example, if price risk induces a producer to reduce the optimal level of output, the existence of a forward or futures market or a government program that guarantees price will allow the producer to shift risk and increase output. In addition, new technologies that reduce risk will have a similar effect.

Empirical studies examining the impact of risk on supply have found a couple of important results (Traill, 1978; Hurt and Garcia, 1982). First, as predicted by the theory, risk has an inverse relationship with supply. That is, as the level of risk is increased, supply is reduced. Second, and perhaps more importantly, inclusion of risk in models of supply suggests that the impact of price becomes more important. That is, models with the inclusion of risk predict *more* price responsiveness than models without risk (Tomek and Robinson, 1990). This result is important because it suggests that when accounting for risk, supply is more responsive to price. In terms of predictions, this result means that models without risk will *underpredict* the impact of price on supply.

Institutional Factors

Institutional factors such as government programs and market structure will also impact supply. Obviously, acreage allotments affect supply because they represent direct supply control. However, factors such as mandatory marketing orders are implicit supply control because they limit the level of product that can be marketed at any given point in time. Past farm programs have had a substantial impact on production (see Gardner, 1995). Acreage

---

[11]Risk is an important concept in all economic relationships, not just production. This section only highlights the impacts of risk. For a more complete discussion of production under risk, see Helmberger and Chavas (1996) or Beattie and Taylor (1993). We will return to risk issues later in the book.

[12]More specifically, risk-increasing inputs are decreased while risk-reducing inputs are increased. For example, irrigation is a risk-reducing input. So, more risk would lead to a greater use of irrigation.

allotments, set asides, and other supply control mechanisms have been important, but changes in farm programs recently have likely decreased the importance of these program effects. Of greater importance of late have been environmental programs and regulations. Programs such as the Conservation Reserve Program (CRP) and the Wetland Reserve Program (WRP) are intended to take land out of production for conservation purposes. Regulations on pesticide and herbicide use, restrictions on nonpoint-source pollution, and other environmental regulations are becoming increasingly important. All these factors affect land availability, cropping patterns, and costs and, therefore, ultimately affect market supply.

Another important factor is the structure of the market. We have been trained to think about price in an open market and the responsiveness of individual producers to changes in price. However, what if the market is completely vertically integrated?[13] For example, in poultry, individual producers are often not paid per pound for chickens produced. Rather, they are paid a flat fee plus bonuses for efficiency. Clearly, the poultry producer is not responding to a price in the traditional sense. Rather, the level of production is determined by the needs of the poultry processors. A contract, in this case, has replaced the market and the producer is no longer responding directly to price. It is, therefore, difficult to visualize a supply function in the traditional sense.

Key Questions

1. What impact does length of run have on market supply?
2. What are the factors that affect supply?
3. What impact will lower production costs have on the producer and on market supply?
4. What impact might vertical integration have on supply responsiveness?
5. What impact does risk have on supply?

2.3   Technology Adoption and Supply Adjustment

A critical issue in agriculture is the role of technology adoption and the adjustment of supply. Figure 2.4 shows the cost effects of a reduction in pesticide cost. A similar analysis can help understand the implications of new technology:

Example 2.4   *Assume that the Roundup Ready® seed technology has just been introduced in the soybean market. This technology allows the producer to apply Roundup herbicide to soybeans directly without damage to the crop. Presumably this technology lowers cost of production by decreasing weed control costs (Couvillion et al., 2000). What impacts will this have on the market?*

We can examine the impact of technology on the individual producer as in Figure 2.8. The adoption of the Roundup Ready seed lowers the average cost from AC_1 to AC_2, shifting the marginal cost from MC_1 to MC_2. Producers who adopt the technology upon introduction could likely expect to receive P_1 even after adopting because their marginal

---

[13] Vertical integration and contracting are important topics in agriculture today. We only touch on the issue here, but a later chapter is devoted to the subject.

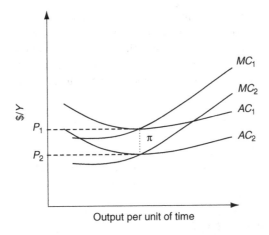

Figure 2.8 The impacts of technology adoption on firm cost and profits in the short run.

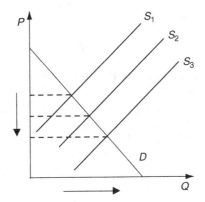

Figure 2.9 The impacts of technology adoption and the technology treadmill in the market.

contribution to market supply would not alter the market price. Thus, they would receive an economic profit of π.

However, this result can only be a short-run outcome. Other producers will observe the profit, π, that is available from technology adoption and will adopt the technology as well. As more producers adopt the technology, the market supply begins to shift outward, thus lowering price. Finally, producers that do not adopt will exhibit an average cost that is higher than the market price and *must* adopt the technology or exit production.

The issue of technology adoption and the above relationship leads to an important concept called the **treadmill theory**, or the technology treadmill. As we have just seen, technology adoption offers up short-term economic profits that encourage adoption. As the profits are dissipated when supply adjusts, producer seek newer technologies to "lower costs." The effect of this technology treadmill can be seen in Figure 2.9. The market supply increases with successive levels of technology development and adoption, resulting in higher levels of output. Assuming that demand remains unchanged, prices decline as well. What is more likely the case, demand will be changing as well, so the price effect will depend on both demand and supply changes (an issue discussed in Chapter 3).

The important feature of the treadmill theory is that cost-reducing technology has important implications for supply. In the short run, some producers earn economic profits, enticing other producers to adopt. This cycle generates a supply function constantly shifting outward (other things being equal). As we discussed above, this process of supply adjustment may ultimately lead some producers to exit production even though supply is increasing.[14]

Key Questions

1. What is the treadmill theory?
2. What impact does technology have on farm profits of adopters in the short run, and in the long run?

2.4   Measuring Supply

Keeping in mind the data considerations discussed in the previous chapter, we can visualize a supply function as being composed of the following:[15]

$$S = f(P, PC, JP, T, R, IF),$$

where P is the price of the product, PC is the profitability of competing crops, JP are the prices of joint products (if any), T is technology, R is risk, and IF are institutional factors. Operationalizing (or specifying with specific variables) these concepts is straightforward for some and difficult for others. The price of the product under question is clear,[16] as is the price of joint products. However, what about the profitability of competing crops?

A primary difficulty with competing crops is that costs of production of corn, for example, are much different in the Southeast than the Midwest. Further, costs are different across farms. A common method of specifying competing crops in the supply model is simply to use the price of competing crops. This necessarily introduces measurement error. That is, price is a *proxy*, but not a perfect representation for profitability of competing crops. However, numerous empirical studies have shown this to be an effective approach to competing crops.

Another important issue is how to measure technology. Technological change is difficult to measure. (How do you measure the impacts of incremental changes in the horsepower of tractors?) Some analysts resort to the use of simple time trends to capture the trend of technological change.[17] If discrete changes in technology (e.g., the

---

[14]This result can occur if the technology makes some producers relatively more productive than others. The relatively higher-cost producers would be forced out of production because the market price would be below average total cost.

[15]At this point, it is important to note that we are ignoring stocks and imports as sources of supply. In the strictest sense, what follows is a discussion of estimating domestic production. We will explore the issue of stocks and imports/exports in a later chapter.

[16]The issue becomes significantly more complex when using "expected" prices. The formulation of expectations is quite complex. See Helmberger and Chavas (1996) for a discussion of supply models with expectations.

[17]An interesting side note is that a simple time trend implies that the rate of technological change is increasing at a decreasing rate. For example, a time trend is typically specified as $t = 1, 2, 3, ..., n$. What is the percentage

introduction of the tractor) can be identified, dummy variables can be used. Additionally, accounting for the level of adoption of a technology may be possible. For example, Khanna, Epohue, and Hornbaker (1999) and Hudson and Hite (2003) provide recent examples of measuring the level of adoption of precision agriculture technology. If precision agriculture technology is production increasing, then increases in the percentage of producers adopting this technology would be expected to increase supply.

Institutional factors are likely to be modeled with dummy variables. For example, peanuts previously were produced under quota. However, in 2002, the quota system was abandoned. In supply models for peanuts, a dummy variable would be needed to identify the potential structural shift in supply that occurred with the elimination of the peanut quota. Other factors such as minimum support prices may also need to be considered.

Recognizing that: $S = Yield * Acreage$, it may be useful for some applications to separate yield and acreage into two separate equations.

$$Yield = f(P, W, T, R),$$
$$Acreage = g(P, PC, IF, R),$$

where W is weather and the other variables are as previously defined. This approach explicitly accounts for how factors affect both yield and acreage, which, when taken together, determine supply. Pragmatically, it is sometimes more difficult to accurately estimate yield equations, forcing some to assume that yield is given and estimate acreage response equations (Hudson and Ethridge, 2000).

Whatever the chosen method of analysis, it is important to recognize that supply estimation is one of the most difficult tasks an economist faces. Supply decisions are dynamic (Chavas and Johnson, 1982), are subject to considerable random variation due to weather, are dependent on farmer expectations, and subject to considerable interference by the government. Thus, while supply is a very important variable in market analysis, it remains an area of great challenge to applied economists wishing to estimate supply relationships.

Exercises

Problem 2.1 *Describe the technical relationship between an input and output.*

Problem 2.2 *Assume that the total cost function (TC) is given by the following equation: $TC = 100 + 2.5y + 0.05y^2$, where y is output.*

1. *What is the fixed cost?*
2. *What is the average total cost (ATC)?*
3. *What is the average variable cost (AVC)?*
4. *What is the marginal cost (MC)?*

---

change between time = 1 and time = 2? What is the percentage change of time = 2 and time = 3? Progressively, the percentage change between time periods gets smaller. Thus, the implied growth rate in technology is increasing at a decreasing rate. An alternative to a simple time trend is to enter it as the natural logarithm of time, ln t.

Problem 2.3   *Assume that the government has placed a regulation on the emissions from farm diesel that will increase the cost of diesel. Graphically and verbally describe the impacts of this regulation on the individual producer as well as market supply.*

Problem 2.4   *Assume you have estimated the following supply equation for corn:*

$$Q_{corn} = 150 + 1.2P_{corn} - 0.8P_{soy} + 0.05Time.$$

Also assume that the average price of corn is $2.20 per bushel, the average output is 0.36 billion bushels, the average price of soybeans is $3.20 per bushel, and Time is a linear trend from 0 to 20.

1. *How do you interpret the coefficient on Time?*
2. *What is the own-price elasticity of supply? Interpret your answer.*
3. *What is the cross-price elasticity of supply with respect to soybean price? Interpret your answer.*

References

Beattie, B. and C. Taylor. *The Economics of Production.* Krieger Publishing, Malabar, FL, 1993.

Chavas, J. and S. Johnson. "Supply Dynamics: The Case of U.S. Broilers and Turkeys." *American Journal of Agricultural Economics*, 64(1982): 558–564.

Couvillion, W., F. Kari, D. Hudson, and A. Allen. "A Preliminary Economic Assessment of Roundup Ready Soybeans in Mississippi." Department of Agricultural Economics, Mississippi State University, Research Report 2000-005, May 2000.

Gardner, B. *Plowing Ground in Washington: The Political Economy of U.S. Agriculture.* Pacific Research Institute for Public Policy, San Francisco, CA, 1995.

Helmberger, P. and J. Chavas. *The Economics of Agricultural Prices.* Prentice Hall, Upper Saddle River, NJ, 1996.

Hudson, D. and D. Ethridge. "Income Distributional Impacts of Trade Policies: A Case in Pakistan." *Journal of Agricultural and Applied Economics*, 32(2000): 49–61.

Hudson, D. and D. Hite. "Producer Willingness to Pay for Precision Application Technology: Implications for Government and the Technology Industry." *Canadian Journal of Agricultural Economics*, 53(2003): 39–53.

Hudson, D., L. House, B. Barnett, and M. Isik. "GPS, Inc.: A Case of Investment under Uncertainty." *Review of Agricultural Economics*, 26(2004): 303–312.

Hurt, C. and P. Garcia. "The Impact of Price Risk on Sow Farrowings, 1967–1978." *American Journal of Agricultural Economics,* 64(1982): 565–568.

Isik, M., K. Coble, D. Hudson, and L. House. "A Model of Entry–Exit Decisions and Capacity Choice under Demand Uncertainty." *Agricultural Economics*, 28(2003): 215–224.

Khanna, M., O. Epohue, and R. Hornbaker. "Site-Specific Crop Management: Adoption Patterns and Incentives." *Review of Agricultural Economics*, 21(1999): 455–472.

Sandmo, A. "On the Theory of the Competitive Firm under Price Uncertainty." *American Economic Review*, 61(1971): 65–73.

Swinton, S. and J. Lowenberg-DeBoer. "Evaluating the Profitability of Site-Specific Farming." *Journal of Production Agriculture*, 11(1998): 439–446.

Tomek, W. and K. Robinson. *Agricultural Product Prices*, third edition. Cornell University Press, Ithaca, NY, 1990.

Traill, B. "Risk Variables in Econometric Supply Response Models." *Journal of Agricultural Economics*, 29(1978): 53–61.

Appendix 2A: Cost Function

In order to appreciate the complexity underlying the cost functions presented in this chapter, it is useful to derive these functions for a specific case. Assume that the production is described by a Cobb–Douglas production function and we have perfect competition in both input and output markets:

$$Y = AX_1^{b_1} X_2^{b_2}, \tag{2.6}$$

where Y is the output, X_1 and X_2 are inputs, A is a constant, and b_1 and b_2 are the technical coefficients relating levels of X_1 and X_2 to levels of output. Using this, we can minimize the cost of production for a given level of output, Y^0, as

$$\min C = r_1 X_1 + r_2 X_2 + FC + \lambda \left(Y^0 - AX_1^{b_1} X_2^{b_2} \right), \tag{2.7}$$

where the r's are input prices, FC is the fixed cost, and λ is the Lagrangian multiplier. The first-order conditions for cost minimization are as follows:[18]

$$\frac{\partial C}{\partial X_1} = r_1 - \lambda A b_1 X_1^{b_1 - 1} X_2^{b_2} = 0, \tag{2.8}$$

$$\frac{\partial C}{\partial X_2} = r_2 - \lambda A b_2 X_1^{b_1} X_2^{b_2 - 1} = 0, \tag{2.9}$$

$$\frac{\partial C}{\partial \lambda} = Y^0 - AX_1^{b_1} X_2^{b_2} = 0. \tag{2.10}$$

Solving Equations 2.8 and 2.9, respectively, for λ yields

$$\lambda = \frac{r_1}{A b_1 X_1^{b_1 - 1} X_2^{b_2}}, \tag{2.11}$$

$$\lambda = \frac{r_2}{A b_2 X_1^{b_1} X_2^{b_2 - 1}}. \tag{2.12}$$

Equating Equations 2.11 and 2.12 yields

$$\frac{r_1}{A b_1 X_1^{b_1 - 1} X_2^{b_2}} = \frac{r_2}{A b_2 X_1^{b_1} X_2^{b_2 - 1}}$$

and rearranging yields

$$\frac{r_1}{r_2} = \frac{b_1 X_2}{b_2 X_1}$$

or solving for X_2 yields[19]

$$X_2 = \frac{b_2 r_1}{b_1 r_2} X_1. \tag{2.13}$$

---

[18] As with the previous chapter, we are ignoring the second-order conditions to preserve clarity of presentation. However, you should evaluate second-order conditions.

[19] Note that this equation is the expansion path for the firm with a Cobb–Douglas production function with constant factor prices (Beattie and Taylor, 1943).

Equation 2.13 can be substituted into the production function (Equation 2.6) to derive the **conditional input demand** function for X_1:

$$X_1^c = \left(\frac{Y}{A}\right)^{1/(b_1+b_2)} \left(\frac{b_1 r_2}{b_2 r_1}\right)^{b_2/(b_1+b_2)}. \tag{2.14}$$

Equation 2.14 is "conditional" because it depends on the level of output. That is, we have been minimizing cost *given* a level of output, Y^0. We can rearrange Equation 2.13 to solve for X_1 and then derive the conditional input demand function for X_2, which is

$$X_2^c = \left(\frac{Y}{A}\right)^{1/(b_1+b_2)} \left(\frac{b_2 r_1}{b_1 r_2}\right)^{b_1/(b_1+b_2)}. \tag{2.15}$$

Recall that the variable cost function is

$$VC = r_1 X_1 + r_2 X_2. \tag{2.16}$$

We substitute the conditional demand functions (Equations 2.14 and 2.15) into the variable cost function (Equation 2.16) as follows:

$$VC = r_1 \left[\left(\frac{Y}{A}\right)^{1/(b_1+b_2)} \left(\frac{b_1 r_2}{b_2 r_1}\right)^{b_2/(b_1+b_2)}\right] + r_2 \left[\left(\frac{Y}{A}\right)^{1/(b_1+b_2)} \left(\frac{b_2 r_1}{b_1 r_2}\right)^{b_1/(b_1+b_2)}\right]$$

$$= \left[YA^{-1} r_1^{b_1} r_2^{b_2}\right]^{1/(b_1+b_2)} \left[\left(\frac{b_1}{b_2}\right)^{b_2/(b_1+b_2)} + \left(\frac{b_2}{b_1}\right)^{b_1/(b_1+b_2)}\right]. \tag{2.17}$$

Using Equation 2.17, we can derive the marginal cost function as

$$\frac{\partial VC}{\partial Y} = \frac{\left[YA^{-1} r_1^{b_1} r_2^{b_2}\right]^{1/(b_1+b_2)} \left[(b_1/b_2)^{b_2/(b_1+b_2)} + (b_2/b_1)^{b_1/(b_1+b_2)}\right]}{(b_1 + b_2)Y}. \tag{2.18}$$

Thus, as Equation 2.18 indicates, the cost relationships can be quite complex (that is, ugly). However, it reinforces the general formula presented in Equation 2.2 that variable, and thus marginal, cost is a function of output and the prices of inputs. Different functional forms for the production function will, of course, alter the formulation of the marginal cost function.

Appendix 2B: Profit Maximization

We begin a simple analysis by assuming that the producer wishes to maximize profits. The producer is in perfect competition in both the input and output markets so that he or she has no influence on either output or input prices. We further assume that there is only one variable input and that the maximization problem is unconstrained for simplicity.[20] To add context to the problem, we

---

[20] A constrained optimization problem allows for the introduction of technical constraints. For example, if you could only apply so many pounds of nitrogen for regulatory reasons, we could add a constraint setting a maximum nitrogen application. These problems are significantly more complex, but add realism to situations and are, therefore, useful tools.

will assume that the producer is a corn producer and only the amount of applied nitrogen affects output.[21] We begin by denoting the production function:

$$y = f(x),$$

where y is the output of corn and x is the amount of nitrogen applied. The profit function for the producer is defined as

$$\pi = py - rx,$$

where p is the price of corn and r is the price of nitrogen fertilizer.[22] To find the maximum profit point, we must find the point at which the slope of the profit function is equal to zero.[23] This calculation is accomplished by taking the partial derivative of the profit function with respect to the nitrogen application and setting that equal to zero:

$$\frac{\partial \pi}{\partial x} = p\frac{\partial y}{\partial x} - r = 0.$$

We note that $\partial y/\partial x$ is simply the change in corn output with respect to a change in nitrogen application, which is the *MPP* relationship defined at the beginning of this chapter. Thus, we can redefine this equation as

$$\frac{\partial \pi}{\partial x} = pMPP - r = 0.$$

The price of nitrogen, r, is constant, so each additional unit of nitrogen costs r. We define this as the **marginal factor cost (MFC)**, or the addition to cost with each additional unit of input. The price of corn to the producer is also constant at p. Multiplied by the *MPP*, this generate the **marginal value product (MVP)**. We can rearrange this equation as

$$pMPP = r,$$

or

$$MVP = MFC.$$

Thus, at the point of profit maximization, the *MVP* will equal the *MFC*. In addition to this condition, we must also meet the condition that total revenue must exceed variable cost (the short-run shutdown point). More generally, we note that the point of profit maximization is denoted by the point at which marginal revenue is equal to marginal cost ($MR = MC$), where total revenue exceeds total cost.

---

[21] Of course, this is an oversimplification of the problem. We assume only one variable input for simplicity. The concepts presented are applicable when more than one input is used, but the mathematics gets more complex.

[22] Note that there are no fixed costs in this equation. Fixed costs do not enter the calculation at the margin and so are omitted. You could simply add the fixed cost to the end of the equation, but it drops out in the subsequent analysis.

[23] As with Chapter 1, we are not checking second-order conditions here for brevity. You are advised to check second-order conditions to insure that they have identified a maximum point.

Chapter 3

The Market

So far, we have laid the foundations for consumer choices and demand as well as producer decisions and supply. While we have alluded to the market, we have yet to explicitly define market equilibrium. In many ways, "equilibrium" is a process of movement toward a stable balance between supply and demand. In static terms, it is the point at which supply and demand are equal. Equilibrium arises through market competition. Producers attempt to sell products in the market in competition with other producers, so the incentive is to produce the product at the lowest possible price. Consumers are purchasing products subject to a budget constraint, and so are attempting to purchase products at the lowest possible price. Consumers "compete" by attempting to purchase products from a finite, limited supply of goods and must balance making purchases before the available supply is gone with their budget constraint. This interaction leads the market to a point at which products are offered at a price that induces just the "right"[1] amount of production and a price at which the "right" amount of consumers are willing to pay, or equilibrium.

We live in a world of incomplete information. Buyers and sellers attempt to learn more about how much is being produced and consumed, constantly updating prices in a process of movement toward an equilibrium. Unfortunately, supply and demand are constantly changing, thus complicating this process. For the time being, we will ignore the adjustment process, or how prices move from one equilibrium to another as conditions change. Rather, we will initially focus on the static states of equilibrium and changes in equilibrium. We will then focus on the distribution of benefits between consumers and producers in equilibrium and the impacts of changing market conditions on that distribution. It is important to note that we are abstracting from several important

---

[1] "Right" is in quotation marks because the word carries with it a value judgment about what is "fair" or equitable. However, in this context, we are not making a value judgment about equity, but are simply stating that equilibrium is a condition that satisifes both consumers and producers given market conditions (that is, factor prices, consumer preferences, budget constraints, etc.). You are cautioned not to "over-interpret" the meaning of equilibrium. An equilibrium may arise that has all of the products going to just a few individuals or all of the profits going to just a few producers. Equilibrium, therefore, is a result of efficiency, not equity. We will address the relative distribution of benefits later in this chapter.

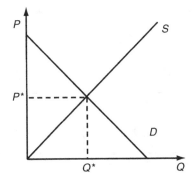

Figure 3.1 Market equilibrium.

elements in the market—stocks and international trade. We will return to these issues in later chapters. However, the equilibrium concept will translate directly to those situations as well.

3.1 Competitive Equilibrium

3.1.1 The Equilibrium Concept

Market equilibrium is defined graphically as the intersection between the market supply function and the demand function (Figure 3.1). Given both supply and demand conditions, market equilibrium is given by (Q^*, P^*). It is important to note that the equilibrium concept is based on the **marginalist principle** (Nicholson, 2002). The marginalist approach was introduced in the 1850s as a potential solution to the water–diamond paradox. Before that time, economists assumed that a product derived value, and therefore, price, from its overall usefulness to the consumer. However, water is extremely useful but has a low price, where as diamonds are not particularly useful[2] but have a high price. The marginalist principle supposes that it is the usefulness of the *last unit* consumed that matters. Because water is relatively plentiful, consumption of another pint is likely not particularly valuable, resulting in a low price. By contrast, diamonds are relatively scarce, so consumption of an additional diamond is more valuable.[3]

Viewing Figure 3.1 from this perspective, we note that the demand function is downward sloping because each additional unit of consumption is progressively less valuable to consumers. By contrast, the supply function is upward sloping because each additional unit of output employs progressively less productive resources (marginal cost is increasing). At the equilibrium point, the last unit of consumption is worth the same as the last

---

[2] Remember that this analysis was being conducted in the 1850s, so industrial uses for diamonds were essentially nonexistent. Today, diamonds have many industrial uses.

[3] Historically, this was the paradox. However, note that water prices, especially in the Western U.S., are increasing rapidly. Perhaps one day, water will be more valuable than diamonds!

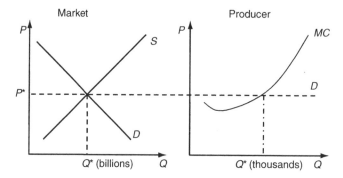

Figure 3.2   The relationship between market equilibrium and equilibrium at the producer level.

unit of production. It is also important to note that this process happens **simultaneously**.[4] Which blade on a pair of scissors cuts the paper? It is likewise difficult to say that either supply or demand cause price. It is the interaction between the two that generates price.

For the individual producer, the demand function is simply a horizontal line at the market price (marginal revenue is constant) as shown in Figure 3.2. Because the output of the individual producer has no impact on the market price, the demand function the producer faces has no slope. Imagine walking into your local elevator, and the sign posted on the wall saying "If you bring 1,000 bushels, your price is X. If you bring 2,000 bushels your price is Y, etc." Rather, the price offered may change over time, but no matter how many bushels you bring in, you get one price (assuming a homogeneous quality; we will discuss the impact of quality on price in Chapter 8). The optimal ouput for the producer is given by the intersection of the horizontal demand curve with the marginal cost curve for that producer (again, assuming that the market price is equal to or exceeds the average variable cost in the short run).

3.1.2   An Example Equilibrium Derivation

To illustrate the derivation of market equilibrium, consider the following example. Assume that you are examining the market for chicken sandwiches in your local market. You determine that the daily demand for chicken sandwiches in this market is given by

$$Q_d = 10,000 - 5,000P,$$

where Q_d is the quantity demanded of chicken sandwiches and P is the price of the chicken sandwich. Further, we note that the daily supply function of chicken sandwiches is

$$Q_s = 5,000P.$$

---

[4]This is a general statement. There are alternative models that incorporate lags and expectations (Helmberger and Chavas, 1996; Ferris, 1998). We address these issues empirically in later chapters.

To solve for the equilibrium (or "market clearing") price of chicken sandwiches, we set the quantity demanded equal to the quantity supplied:

$$Q_d = 10,000 - 5,000P = Q_s = 5,000P.$$

We use this equation to solve for the equilibrium price:

$$10,000 - 5,000P = 5,000P,$$
$$10,000 = 10,000P;$$

so the equilibrium price is

$$P^* = 1.$$

We can use the equilibrium price to determine the equilibrium quantity, as follows:

$$Q_d^* = 10,000 - 5,000P^* = 10,000 - 5,000(1) = 5,000.$$

Note that if we insert the equilibrium price into the supply equation, we get the same result:

$$Q_s^* = 5,000P^* = 5,000(1) = 5,000.$$

Thus, at the equilibrium price, supply and demand are equal, or they are in balance.

Key Questions

1. How is equilibrium defined?
2. What is the marginalist principle?
3. Mathematically, how does one calculate equilibrium?

3.2 Impacts of Changes

3.2.1 Graphical Analysis

Turning our attention to the impacts of changes in supply or demand on market prices and quantity, we note that impacts of supply or demand changes on price and quantity depend on the elasticities of supply or demand. Consider Figure 3.3. When supply is relatively inelastic, an increase in demand leads to larger increases in price than when supply is relatively elastic. The reason for this outcome can be explained through the price responsiveness of the supply function. When supply is inelastic, the quantity supplied to the market is relatively fixed, so that increases in price have little effect on the quantity supplied. Therefore, as demand increases, the quantity supplied cannot increase substantially, leading to a large increase in price. In recent times, the price of oil has increased

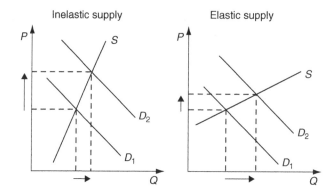

Figure 3.3 Impacts of changes in demand with inelastic and elastic supply.

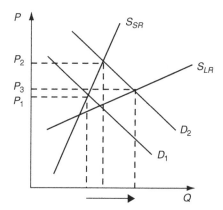

Figure 3.4 The relationship between length of run in supply and the impacts of demand changes.

substantially. Given that the supply of oil is relatively inelastic,[5] and also given that more nations are demanding more oil, as China, India, and other heavily populated nations become more affluent and developed, it is easy to see why the price of oil has increased so rapidly.

Conversely, when supply is relatively elastic, the quantity supplied can be increased substantially with only small changes in price. This situation can be typically found in newer products. In newer products (for example, new technologies), expansion of production can occur with only slight increases in marginal cost. Thus, for these industries, increases in demand lead to relatively smaller increases in price. We should recall from Chapter 2 that the elasticity of supply is dependent on the length of run. So, we can examine what happens to equilibrium over time (Figure 3.4). Assume that in the short run, demand increases from D_1 to D_2, resulting in an increase in price from P_1 to P_2. As supply adjusts over the long run, supply shifts (or rotates) from S_{SR} to S_{LR}, leading to a decrease in price to P_3.

[5] There is, according to the experts, a finite supply of oil. But even in the intermediate term, exploration for and extraction of additional oil supplies is quite expensive. Thus, short-run supply is relatively inelastic.

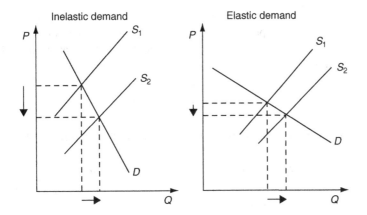

Figure 3.5 The impacts of changes in supply with inelastic and elastic demand.

Similarly, we can analyze the impacts of changes in supply when demand is elastic or inelastic (Figure 3.5). When demand is inelastic, an increase in supply leads to larger decreases in price relative to elastic demand. We assume that demand for farm products is relatively inelastic. By Figure 3.5, then, we would predict that increases in supply of farm products would lead to a relatively large decrease in price (as compared to the situation when demand was elastic). Conversely, at the retail level, demand for individual food products tends to be more elastic, so increases in supply would have a relatively smaller impact on the retail price. We will return to the farm-level/retail-level discussion in the next chapter.

3.2.2 A Mathematical Examination of Changes

Returning to our chicken sandwich example, now suppose that the cost of production of chicken sandwiches increases (say, the minimum wage has increased), so that the new supply function is given by

$$Q_s = 4{,}000P.$$

Again, solving for the equilibrium condition, we get

$$Q_d = 10{,}000 - 5{,}000P = Q_s = 4{,}000P,$$
$$10{,}000 = 9{,}000P,$$
$$P^* = 1.11.$$

Note that with an increase in the wage rate, supply has shifted to the left, holding demand constant. This results in an increase in price of $0.11 per sandwich. The equilibrium quantity is given by

$$Q_d^* = Q_s^* = 10{,}000 - 5{,}000P^* = 10{,}000 - 5{,}000(1.11) = 4{,}444.$$

Thus, the increase in price is accompanied by a decrease in the equilibrium quantity. Suppose now that a news report has come out saying the chicken sandwiches are particularly healthy, resulting in an increase in demand for chicken sandwiches. The new demand function is

$$Q_d = 12,000 - 5,000P.$$

Using the original supply function, our equilibrium condition is given by

$$Q_d = 12,000 - 5,000P = Q_s = 5,000P.$$

Solving for P as above yields

$$12,000 - 5,000P = 5,000P,$$
$$12,000 = 10,000P,$$
$$P^* = 1.20,$$
$$Q^* = 6,000.$$

So, an increase in demand (holding supply constant) increases the equilibrium price and quantity of chicken sandwiches. The important item to note in this example is that there is a mathematical relationship between demand and supply in determining the equilibrium price and quantity.

Key Questions

1. What is the impact of elasticities on changes in equilibrium price and quantity?
2. How does the length of run in supply affect equilibrium price and quantity?
3. Mathematically, how do supply and demand changes alter equilibrium price and quantity?

3.3 Producer and Consumer Surplus

We have alluded to the impacts of market changes. It is useful to have some measure of the economic impact of these changes on the economic agents involved. For this, we will use a measure called **surplus**.

3.3.1 The Surplus Concept

We begin by examining the consumer side of the market (Figure 3.6). We note that consumer 1 was willing to pay P_1 to consume Q_1. But the market price is P^*. Thus, consumer 1 earns a "surplus" of $(P_1 - P^*)$ by being able to consume Q_1 at the price P^*, which is lower than his or her willingness to pay. Consumer X, by contrast, is the last

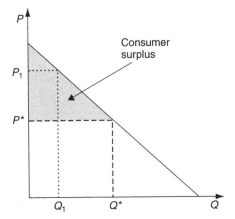

Figure 3.6 Consumer surplus.

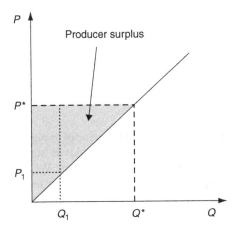

Figure 3.7 Producer surplus.

consumer in the market, consuming that last unit of the good. He or she is willing to pay P^* for that unit and, thus, earns no surplus.[6]

We can make an analogous argument on the supply side of the market (Figure 3.7). Producer 1 is a low-cost producer and would be willing to supply Q_1 for P_1. But the market price is P^*, so producer 1 earns a "profit" or surplus equal to $(P^* - P_1)$ on his or her output Q_1. By contrast, producer X is a higher-cost producer and is willing to supply his or her production at P^*, and, therefore, earns no surplus on production.

We can combine these two concepts to get a generalized picture of economic welfare in markets (Figure 3.8). We visualize **consumer surplus** as the area above the equilibrium price and below the demand curve. **Producer surplus**, by contrast, is the area below the equilibrium price and above the supply curve. It should be obvious that, as

---

[6]This is what we mean by "at the margin." At the margin, here, consumers earn no surplus on the last unit of consumption.

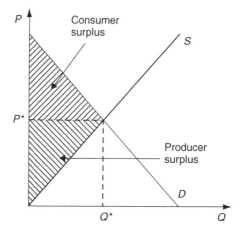

P

Consumer
surplus

S

P*

Producer
surplus

D

Q*

Q

Figure 3.8 Producer and consumer surplus.

discussed previously in this chapter, the elasticities of supply and demand affect the
relative distribution of benefits within the market.

3.3.2 Measuring Surplus

We can now turn our attention to calculating the value of producer and consumer surplus.
With linear demand functions, calculation of surplus is simple geometry[7] (and you
thought you would never use that geometry you learned). We note that in Figure 3.8 the
consumer surplus is a triangle. Recall that the formula for the area of a triangle is half
the base of the triangle times the height of the triangle. Thus, if the y-intercept for the
demand function is labeled P_d in Figure 3.8, we denote the consumer surplus as

$$CS = \frac{1}{2} \left(P_d - P^* \right) \left(Q^* - 0 \right).$$

Likewise, we can calculate the producer surplus as

$$PS = \frac{1}{2} \left(P^* - 0 \right) \left(Q^* - 0 \right).$$

---

[7]For nonlinear functions, the calculation is more complex. Assuming our demand function is $D(P)$, the
consumer surplus is

$$CS = \int D(P) \mathrm{d}P,$$

which is the integral of the demand function across the prices under question. We focus on the linear case
because it is computationally less difficult, but the concept of measurement is the same.

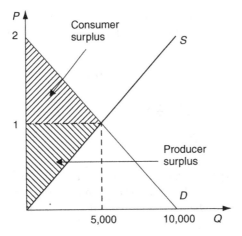

Figure 3.9 Producer and consumer surplus and equilibrium price and quantity for chicken sandwiches.

A brief example will illustrate the calculation. Recall that our chicken sandwich example has the following supply and demand functions:

$$Q_d = 10,000 - 5,000P,$$
$$Q_s = 5,000P.$$

We note that the x-intercept for the demand function (that is, the quantity demanded when $P = 0$) is 10,000. Further, the y-intercept (that is, the price when the quantity demanded is equal to zero) is

$$Q_d = 10,000 - 5,000P,$$
$$0 = 10,000 - 5,000P,$$
$$5,000P = 10,000,$$
$$P = 2.$$

Likewise, when price is equal to zero, no chicken sandwiches will be supplied. Using this information, we can graph the supply and demand functions for chicken sandwiches as well as the equilibrium price and quantity (Figure 3.9).

To calculate consumer surplus:

$$CS = \frac{1}{2}(2 - 1)(5,000 - 0),$$
$$CS = \frac{1}{2}(5,000),$$
$$CS = \$2,500.$$

Thus, at equilibrium, the total consumer surplus from the chicken sandwich market is $2,500 per unit of time (in this case, per day). For producer surplus:

$$PS = \frac{1}{2}(1 - 0)(5,000 - 0),$$

$$PS = \frac{1}{2}(5,000),$$

$$PS = \$2,500.$$

So, the total benefit to producers is $2,500 per day as well. The total to the economy is $PS + CS$, or $5,000 per day. In this case, the economic benefit is evenly divided, but this does not necessarily have to be the case. As stated above, relative elasticities of supply and demand will affect the distribution of benefits.

Now consider the case in our example where demand has shifted. Again, solving for the endpoints of the demand function yields an x-intercept of 12,000 and a y-intercept of $2.40. Recall that the equilibrium price was $1.20 and an equilibrium quantity of 6,000 chicken sandwiches. The resulting calculation for the consumer surplus is

$$CS = \frac{1}{2}(2.4 - 1.2)(6,000 - 0) = \$3,600,$$

and the producer surplus is given by

$$PS = \frac{1}{2}(1.2 - 0)(6,000 - 0) = \$3,600.$$

Therefore, we can define the change in consumer surplus as a result of the demand shift as the difference between our new consumer surplus and the original consumer surplus:

$$\Delta CS = \$3,600 - \$2,500 = \$1,100.$$

The change in producer surplus is calculated similarly. The result, then, is that a change in demand results in an increase in total welfare.[8]

Key Questions

1. What is "surplus"?
2. How do you define consumer surplus, and producer surplus?
3. How is surplus measured?
4. How do changes in supply or demand change surplus?

---

[8] The changes in surplus can be measured directly through geometry as well. But, in this case, a trapezoid is formed, which is the difference between the new triangle and the old triangle. The computations are slightly more complex, but not terribly so.

3.4   Summary

The idea of equilibrium should not be new to you at this point in your academic career. But it is important to recall and retain the idea of competitive equilibrium as we proceed through the remainder of this part of the book. Clearly, equilibrium arises from the interaction of supply and demand, so that one cannot consider demand without supply or vice versa if one is to fully understand market phenomena. Also important in this chapter was the introduction of the idea of surplus as a measure of economic welfare. The policy-making process is often interested in understanding who gains and who loses as a result of economic or policy changes. The welfare concept gives us one method of being able to understand and predict these effects directly from demand and supply functions. Thus, the surplus concept is something important to carry out of this discussion. Finally, it is important to realize that those nasty supply and demand elasticities that I am sure you would like to forget rear their ugly heads again (and will continue to do so). This just reinforces the importance of supply and demand elasticities in applied analysis.

Exercises

Problem 3.1   *The Atkins diet craze has led to an increase in demand for beef products. Discuss (graphically and verbally) short-run and long-run impacts of this change on equilibrium price and quantity for beef.*

Problem 3.2   *Assume that the demand function for yellowfin tuna sushi (in dollars per pound per day) is $Q_d = 200 - 15P$, and the supply function is $Q_s = 20P$. Derive the equilibrium price and quantity.*

Problem 3.3   *In Problem 3.2, calculate the consumer and producer surplus at equilibrium.*

Problem 3.4   *Graph the supply and demand functions in Problem 3.2. Assume that the demand function shifts as a result of an advertising campaign to $Q_d = 280 - 15P$. Graph the new demand function on the same graph, showing the new equilibrium price and quantity.*

Problem 3.5   *In Problem 3.4, calculate the change in consumer and producer surplus.*

References

Ferris, J. *Agricultural Prices and Commodity Market Analysis*. WCB–McGraw-Hill, New York, 1998.

Helmberger, P. and J. Chavas. *The Economics of Agricultural Prices*. Prentice Hall, Upper Saddle River, NJ, 1996.

Nicholson, W. *Microeconomic Theory: Basic Principles and Extensions*, eighth edition. South-Western, 2002.

Chapter 4

Marketing Margins

~

We have now established the principles of demand, supply, and the determination of price. In an abstract sense, prices are a result of the interaction of economic agents within a market. However, these interactions occur at all different levels of a market. That is, consumers rarely interact directly with producers to purchase agricultural commodities. Rather, producers interact with buyers who represent processors. Those processors then interact with wholesalers and distributors, and these interact with retailers, who then interact with consumers. This process can be viewed as a **supply chain**.

We will now turn our attention to how changes in supply and demand interact within these various market levels to determine prices and resource allocation. To accomplish this, we will be primarily concerned with the issue of **marketing margins**, which are the differences between the prices paid by a consumer and the prices received by a producer. Obviously, both producers and consumers are concerned about marketing margins. What is the size of the marketing margin and what influences the size? How do changes in supply and demand affect consumers and producers? The questions surrounding marketing margins go beyond the welfare implications of these changes on producers and consumers. They affect business planning in response to these changes. The goal of this chapter is to provide you with the tools necessary to understand the impacts of changes on the different market levels.

4.1 Defining Marketing Margins

There are two basic ways in which to view marketing margins (Tomek and Robinson, 1990). First, we may view marketing margins simply as the difference in price paid by consumers and the price received by producers. Second, we may view the marketing margin as the price of a collection of services that are performed in getting the product from the producer to the consumer. As we shall see, these are not mutually exclusive views, but provide a different perspective on the problem at hand—marketing margins. In the following, we will discuss the different perspectives.

4.1.1   Price Differences

We are perhaps most accustomed to viewing a marketing margin as a difference between the price paid by consumers for a product and the price received by the original producers of that product. This relationship is depicted in Figure 4.1. The retail price is a result of the intersection of the derived supply and primary demand. Primary demand is a reflection of the preferences of the final consumers. Empirically, the primary demand function is described by retail price and quantity data. The farm-level price is a result of the intersection of the primary supply and derived demand functions. Empirically, the derived demand function is described by farm-level price and quantity data.

It is important to note that the primary demand for the product is really a joint demand. First, consumers are demanding the underlying product, say cereal. At the same time, they are demanding the processing/marketing components of the product, or the conversion of wheat into the cereal, the packaging, the transportation to the grocery store, the shelf space, and so on. These services are often referred to as the utilities of time, space, and form (Kohls and Uhl, 1998). Thus, we can conceptually divide primary demand into the demand for the farm product and the demand for the processing/marketing services.

We typically assume that final products are produced from fixed proportions of the farm product and other inputs. For example, each box of cereal is assumed to be made of one-tenth of a bushel of wheat, one minute of labor, and two units of capital. The fixed-proportions assumption is akin to assuming that the elasticity of substitution between farm and marketing inputs is equal to zero, or that you cannot substitute labor for grain in the production of cereal. This certainly seems to be a realistic assumption for many cases. However, if farm product prices increase enough, this may induce firms to use labor to reduce wastage, thereby meaning that the elasticity of substitution is not zero. Gardner (1975) provides a general analysis when the elasticity is not zero, but that is beyond the scope of this text. Second, we assume that the supply function for marketing services is static.

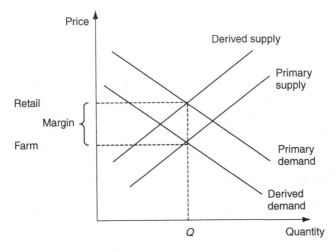

Figure 4.1   Basic market margins—primary and derived demand and supply functions.

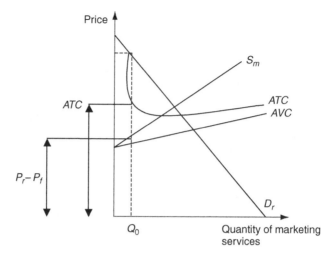

Figure 4.2   The cost functions of a marketing firm and determination of the marketing margin.

Given these assumptions, we can surmise that the farm-level price for a product is simply the retail price of the product less the per unit cost of the marketing services provided. A simple example follows:

Example 4.1   *The price of beef at the retail level is $2.80 per pound. The price of slaughtering, packaging, transportation, advertising, and firm profits is $2.00 per pound. From this, we can surmise that the price of beef at the farm level is $0.80 per pound.*

Thus, the derived demand for farm products represents the demand for the farm component in the final product. In empirical analysis, we often need to adjust prices so that we are pricing consistent components. For example, a ribeye steak only makes up a small proportion of the overall beef carcass. It would not be appropriate to simply compare the price of ribeye steaks to the farm-level price for beef, because not all the final components of the beef carcass are included in the ribeye price.

4.1.2   Marketing Costs

A second way to view the marketing margin is the cost of a collection of services that move and transform the farm product into a product for the final consumer. Helmberger and Chavas (1996) provide an analysis of marketing margins from this perspective. Let us first assume a short-run situation so that the supply of farm product is fixed at at given level, Q_0. We will also assume that the marketing firm is passive; that is, it does not attempt to influence price and simply serves as a pass-through agent, moving and transforming the product. This situation is depicted in Figure 4.2. The demand function for the final product by the consumer is given by D_r. The average total cost of processing the farm product is given by ATC.[1] The marginal cost of marketing is given by S_m, which

---

[1] Note that the total cost of processing does not include the cost of the farm product. This is simply the cost associated with the marketing services.

is also the supply function for marketing services. The average variable cost of marketing is given by *AVC*.

Now, given a level of farm product, Q_0, we can determine the size of the marketing margin by the intersection of this quantity with the supply function for marketing services.[2] The size of the marketing margin is given by $P_r - P_f$, which is the difference between the retail and farm-level prices. At this level of output, we would expect to see a retail price of P_r and the average total cost given in the figure. Because this is a short-run analysis, we see that it is possible for the marketing firm to operate at a margin less than the average total cost of production. Under the assumption of perfect competition, what would we expect to be the size of the marketing margin?

Key Questions

1. What is a supply chain?
2. What is a marketing margin?
3. What are the two views of marketing margins? How are they different? How are they similar?

4.2 Marketing Costs and Size of Margins

There are three general assumptions that we might make about how marketing costs respond to changing volumes of product moving through the system, each having a different impact on the size of the marketing margin. We will discuss each of these in turn. For the following, we will assume for simplicity that farm supply is perfectly inelastic (short run) and that 100% of farm output is transformed into retail output. We make this assumption so that we have only one supply relation with which to concern ourselves.

- **Assumption 1** The supply of marketing services is perfectly elastic; that is, there is no price response in marketing services as the demand for those services increases.

In this case, it does not matter how much product is moved through the marketing system; the price for marketing services does not increase. This yields the classic view of marketing margins that is found in Figure 4.1. From a pragmatic perspective, this amounts to assuming that increases in the amount of product moving through the system do not bid up the price of labor, capital, electricity, and so on. This assumption is not likely to hold over the long run, but is a useful analytical device for understanding the determination of the marketing margin.

- **Assumption 2** The supply of marketing services is upward sloping; that is, increases in the demand for marketing services increases the price of those services.

---

[2]This result is under the assumption that there is no wastage in the production process. Helmberger and Chavas (1996) provide a more general model that includes wastage. You are encouraged to explore this model as well.

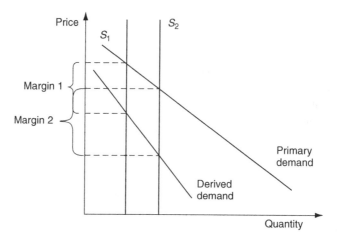

Figure 4.3   The size of the marketing margin with an upward-sloping supply function for marketing services.

This is similar to the situation depicted in Figure 4.2. Increases in the supply of the farm product will lead to increases in the size of the marketing margin, as shown in Figure 4.3. At low levels of farm supply, S_1, there is a relatively smaller marketing margin, Margin 1. As farm supply increases to S_2, the demand for marketing services increases. With an upward-sloping supply function for marketing services, the price of marketing increases, leading to a larger marketing margin, Margin 2.

- **Assumption 3**   There are economies of scale in marketing, leading to a downward-sloping supply function for marketing services; that is, as the farm supply increases, there should be a decline in the marketing margin.

At a relatively low level of farm output, S_1, marketing firms are under-utilizing plant, equipment, and/or labor (Figure 4.4). As farm output increases, firms gain efficiencies, leading to a decline in the marketing margin. There is some appeal to this assumption because we believe that there are economies of scale in processing. However, this assumption is likely to hold only in some region of the supply curve for marketing services.

To summarize, then, changes in the marketing margin are dependent on what we assume about the effects of changes in volume on marketing costs. It is likely that all three assumptions are valid in different situations. For example, over some range of farm output, we may expect to see declining costs because the marketing sector was under-utilizing its capacity. Over other ranges, we may expect to see relatively constant marketing costs, and over some higher range of output, we may expect to see increasing costs. This demonstrates the importance of understanding conditions of the market under study. Diligent observation will improve the reasonableness of assumptions, and therefore improve the accuracy of predictions about behavior.

Key Questions

1. What are the different assumptions we can make about marketing costs?
2. What are the implications of these assumptions on our predictions about changes in marketing margins?

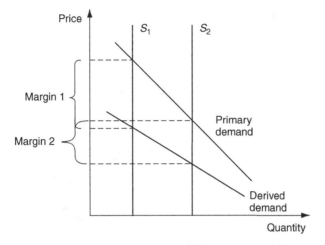

Figure 4.4 The size of the marketing margin with a downward-sloping supply function for marketing services.

4.3 The Impacts of Marketing Margin Changes on Producers and Consumers

A central concept is the impact of changes in supply and demand conditions on consumers and producers. The preceding discussion should highlight the fact that these impacts will be different depending on the underlying cost structure of the marketing firm or industry. At the same time, changes in retail demand or farm-level supply will also have an impact on the distribution of economic welfare between producers and consumers. Finally, the structure of the market will play a role in determining the distribution of welfare as a result of changes in the market. We will discuss each of these questions in the following sections.

4.3.1 The Effects of Cost Structure

Building upon the previous discussion about the assumptions on costs of marketing, we can begin to gain some understanding about the effects of changes in market forces. Assume that markets are competitive. Now assume that the cost of a marketing input (say, labor) has increased. What will be the impact on producers and consumers? To answer this, one must remember that the distance between the curves in the preceeding graphs (the marketing margin) is a function of marketing costs. Thus, any increase in marketing costs will increase the marketing margin.

From the marketing firm's perspective, an increase in labor costs will decrease the demand for labor. Less labor means less product can be moved through the marketing firm, thus shifting the derived demand for farm products to the left. At the same time, there is less product available at the retail level so that the derived supply shifts to the left. So, in Figure 4.5, the result of the shift in derived supply and derived demand (the

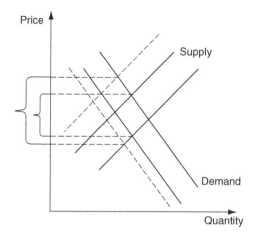

Figure 4.5   The impact of an increase in marketing costs on the marketing margin.

dashed lines in the figure) is an increase in the marketing margin. It is important to note that the relative magnitude of the shifts depends on many factors.

Example 4.2   *The question of product labeling has become more important with the advent of growth hormones, genetic modification, and nutritional concerns. Assume that some milk producers use bovine somatotropin (bST), which is a growth hormone that stimulates milk production. Assume also that the Food and Drug Administration (FDA) has mandated that all milk carry a label at the retail level signifying bST or non-bST-treated milk. This label will add 1 cent per gallon of milk cost. What do you think will be the magnitude of the shifts in derived demand and/or derived supply?*

Example 4.3   *Suppose that the government plans to increase the minimum wage rate from $5.50 per hour to $6.50 per hour. Assume that meat processing is fairly labor intensive, with per unit labor costs being the largest overall marketing cost component. What do you think will be the magnitude of the shifts in derived demand and/or derived supply?*

These two examples highlight two key features of the impacts of a change in cost: the actual cost increase and the share of that cost component in the overall marketing cost. Other things being equal, any marketing cost increase will increase the marketing margin, but the magnitude of that change in the marketing margin can vary greatly depending on how the cost increase fits into the overall marketing margin. Given that marketing margins are also functions of items such as waste, spoilage, and productivity, technology can also play an important role in the size of the marketing margin. Some technologies reduce the per unit cost of production on all units, leading to parallel shifts in the demand and supply curves. However, some technologies favor larger production (that is, cost savings increase as output increases). This change results in nonparallel shifts in curves and result in marketing margins that decline with volume (such as that seen in Figure 4.4). Finally, risk may also impact the cost structure of the firm (Brorsen et al., 1985). That is, when a marketing firm faces significant price or other risks, the firm must take action to mitigate that risk. Those actions carry costs and, therefore, affect the optimal level of production.

4.3.2 Added Services

A slightly different, but related, problem is that of adding new services. Consider the following example:

Example 4.4 *In the 1950s, bologna was typically purchased in a "tube" and either sliced at home or sliced by the meat market. Over time, companies began to recognize the value of having bologna pre-sliced for the consumer's convenience. Now, it is difficult to find bologna that is not pre-sliced in resealable packages. What is the impact of adding the pre-sliced service?*

Obviously, the added service was of value and demanded by customers, but it adds cost (try to compare the per pound cost of pre-sliced bologna to that of bologna purchased unsliced). The added cost means that the marketing margin is greater for pre-sliced bologna than for unsliced. A new combination of inputs (labor and capital) has been used and the final product has been transformed. So what happens to demand and supply? The quick answer is that it depends. If, for example, the addition of the new service entices new consumers to adopt the product, then demand has increased. If, however, the added cost of the service leads some consumers to drop the product, then a decrease in demand has occurred. To the extent that the added service changes the demand for the underlying product (bologna), changes in derived demand for the components of bologna will change as well.[3]

4.3.3 The Incidence of Margin Changes

Incidence, or the impacts of changes on various groups, is an important question that economists must answer. This question can be effectively subdivided into two parts: the introduction of a new service versus changes to the factors related to an existing service. With the addition of the new service, as above, the analysis is relatively simple. That is, the cost of the additional service is typically reflected in a higher retail price. In general, then, the incidence of the margin change lies primarily at the retail level and derived demand remains unchanged. However, in some cases, the additional service may increase overall demand, thereby increasing derived demand and farm-level prices as well.

The more common problem relates to changes in the cost of providing an existing service. In this case, the effect is generally to change both farm- and retail-level prices. The magnitude of the change on both market levels depends on the relative demand and supply elasticities (or the relative slopes [in absolute value] of linear demand and supply functions). Generally speaking, if the slope of the demand curve is steeper than the supply curve (that is, demand is more inelastic than supply), changes in cost will have

---

[3] You are challenged to actually identify what is in bologna.

a greater impact on the retail level than the farm level, and vice versa. As Tomek and Robinson (1990) note, supply at the farm level is generally thought to be more inelastic than demand. According to theory, then, cost changes will have a larger impact at the farm level.[4]

Key Questions

1. What factors influence the impact of cost changes on marketing margins?
2. How does adding services affect marketing margins?
3. What is incidence?
4. Why do cost changes typically fall more heavily on the farm sector?

4.4   The Farmer's Share of the Retail Dollar

As agricultural economists, we have traditionally been concerned with the distribution of benefits to producers and consumers. Policy-makers often ask what will be the impact of a particular policy or economic change. The **farmer's share of the retail dollar** is an often quoted and often misused statistic in the popular media regarding farmer welfare, which deserves some special attention. Generally, the farmer's share of the retail dollar is simply the ratio of the farm-level price over the retail-level price:[5]

$$\frac{P_{farm}}{P_{retail}}.$$

Obviously, a higher number for this ratio indicates that the farmer is receiving a higher proportion of the final retail value. As layers of marketing are added (e.g., processing, storage, transportation, advertising, etc.), this ratio declines. The final value (price) of the product is distributed through the marketing channel. Consider Table 4.1, from Bondurant and Ethridge (1998).

As can be seen in Table 4.1, the farmer's share of the retail dollar for cotton jeans is 4.14%, while the retail share is 55.67%. Is that situation "fair?" It is difficult to make a qualitative judgment about the equity of the distribution of the retail dollar from the data. Clearly, blue jeans are a heavily processed product (for an extensive discussion of what affects this ratio, see Kohls and Uhl, 1998). Compare this with the distribution for eggs, where the farmer's share of the retail dollar is upward of 90%. Is the egg farmer any better off than the cotton farmer?[6] Using the same assumptions as in Table 4.1,

---

[4]Note that if supply were perfectly inelastic, the entire incidence of a margin change would fall at the farm level. This result challenges the "conspiracy theory" notion that retailers are unfairly treating producers. That is, this theoretical model shows that the result of having changes in cost disproportionately fall upon the farmer is an artifact of the demand and supply relations, not a conspiracy. However, we will return to the issue of market structure impacts later, which alters the interpretation a bit.

[5]Often, people just take the ratio of these prices without consideration of transformation. For example, some people would take the ratio of the price of a ribeye steak to the price of live cattle. This obviously inflates the retail price relative to the farm price because of transformation losses. That is, the entire steer is not a ribeye steak! To get an accurate comparison, one must adjust for the product transformation. An example is provided below.

[6]Try asking an egg farmer!

Table 4.1 The distribution of retail price—cotton jeans

Market segment	Per pound of cotton ($)	Per pair of jeans ($)	Proportion of retail value (%)
Farm	0.632	1.327	4.14
Ginning	0.088	0.185	0.58
Accumulated value after ginning	**0.720**	**1.512**	**4.72**
Warehousing	0.049	0.103	0.32
Shipping	0.239	0.502	1.57
Accumulated value at mill door	**1.008**	**2.117**	**6.61**
Mill processing	1.315	2.762	8.62
Accumulated value after textile mill	**2.323**	**4.879**	**15.23**
Manufacturing	4.439	9.321	29.10
Accumulated value after manufacturing	**6.762**	**14.200**	**44.33**
Retailing	8.505	17.830	55.67
Total retail value	**15.267**	**32.030**	**100.00**

Bondurant and Ethridge (1998) also calculated the farmer's share of the retail dollar for other products.

As can clearly be seen in Table 4.2, the farmer's share of the retail dollar is different for different products. However, the *price* received by the farmer is the same in each of these cases. So, is the farmer better off with jeans or men's dress shirts? The answer is that the farmer is equally well off in both cases.[7] The question of equity is important. Consider the following example:

Example 4.5 *Return to the example of bologna. Assuming that Oscar Meyer® has decided to pre-slice bologna and place it in resealable packages, we have seen that this will increase the retail price of bologna (and the marketing margin). Does the pork or beef producer deserve any of that increase in price? Why or why not? Note that the farmer's share of the retail dollar has declined.*

This result highlights the difficulty in making judgments about farmer welfare using the farmer's share of the retail dollar as the measurement device. The farmer's share of the retail dollar is a useful means for comparing the relative marketing costs of different products. For example, it should be obvious from Table 4.2 that the marketing costs for dress shirts are much higher than for blue jeans. At the same time, tracking the farmer's share of the retail dollar can be useful in making judgments about changes in marketing costs through time.

Key Questions

1. What is the farmer's share of the retail dollar?
2. What factors affect this ratio?
3. Can the ratio be used to make judgments about farmer welfare?

---

[7] We are abstracting from the demand issue here and assuming that an equal quantity of cotton is consumed in both cases.

Table 4.2 Farmer's share of retail dollar—cotton products

Product	Proportion at farm level (%)
Men's blue jeans	4.14
Terry towels	3.26
Woven bed sheets	2.37
Men's knit briefs	2.01
Women's sweat pants	1.45
Men's dress shirts	0.75

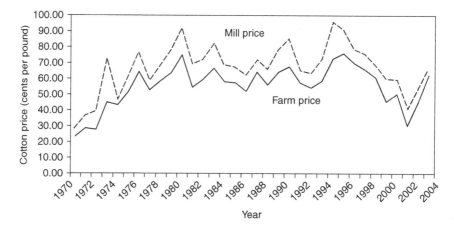

Figure 4.6 The price spread between farm- and mill-level cotton prices.
Source: U.S. Department of Agriculture, Economic Research Service, *Cotton and Wool Situation and Outlook Yearbook,* various issues.

4.5 Measuring Marketing Margins

A general means of measuring the marketing margin between market levels is the price spread. As can be seen in Figure 4.6, there is a relationship between the prices at different market levels (in this case, the textile mill and the farm). However, the price spread (or the difference between these two prices) changes.

Gardner (1975) clearly shows that, from a theoretical perspective, the volume of product moving through the market channel as well as the relative demand and supply elasticities determine the size of the marketing margin. There are a number of methods for specifying marketing margins. These are presented below.

4.5.1 Mark-Up Models

A general specification for a marketing margin is a **mark-up pricing** relationship:

$$M = c + aP_r,$$

where M is the difference between retail- and farm-level prices, $c \geq 0$ is the constant portion of the margin, and $0 \leq a \leq 1$ is the fixed percentage mark-up. This specification conveniently yields a relationship between the retail- and farm-level elasticities of demand:

$$E_f = E_r \left[1 - \frac{c}{(1-a)P_r} \right],$$

where E_f is the farm-level own-price elasticity of demand and E_r is the retail own-price elasticity of demand. Clearly, if there is no constant mark-up (that is, $c = 0$), the farm-level own-price elasticity will equal the retail own-price elasticity. While somewhat popular empirically, simple mark-up pricing models are often criticized because, from a theoretical perspective, simple mark-up relationships should not exist in competitive markets (Gardner, 1975).

An alternative to the simple mark-up model is the **dynamic mark-up model** (Heien, 1980). A simple form of the model is:

$$P_r = \alpha + \beta_1 P_{r,t-1} + \beta_2 P_f + \beta_k C_k,$$

where P_r is the retail price, P_f is the farm price, and C_k are marketing costs. This model can be further extended by including a variable representing the volume of product moving through the marketing system. The lagged retail price, $P_{r,t-1}$, is used to capture price dynamics resulting from lagged adjustments in the market channel. Products are not instantaneously transformed from the farm product to the retail product, suggesting that price changes (and margin changes) may take time to adjust. The dynamic model allows for this price adjustment by including the lagged price as an explanatory variable. The advantage of the dynamic model from a theoretical perspective is that it bridges the gap between Gardner's theoretical contruct of competitive marketing margins and the empirical observation that mark-up relationships exist in the food industry. That is, Heien's analysis demonstrates that mark-up relationships can exist in competitive markets when one considers the lagged adjustments from one equilibrium point to another.

4.5.2 Margin Models

An alternative to the mark-up class of models are those that explicitly model the margin directly. Wohlgenant and Mullen (1987), for example, provide two general types of margin models:

$$M = b_1 P_r + b_2 P_r Q + b_3 C,$$

$$M = c_0 + c_1 Q + c_2 C,$$

where Q is the quantity of product moving through the marketing channel. The first of these equations is the **relative price spread equation** and the second is the **real price spread equation**. Note that the relative price spread equation has no intercept term, indicating that the hypothesis is that there is no fixed relationship between farm and retail prices. The real price spread specification views the price spread as a price of a bundle of marketing activities.

The real difference between these models and those of the mark-up pricing class is that the Wohlgenant and Mullen approach explicitly accounts for farm supply and retail demand changes. This is advantageous from the point of view that we are often faced with situations in which fundamental changes in the underlying characteristics of supply and demand (changes in demographics or technology, for example) are occurring, and we must ascertain what impacts these changes will have on margins.

As with supply and demand models, data aggregation is an issue with marketing margin models. For example, Lyon and Thompson (1993) have found that the selection of the appropriate model is more complicated as both spatial and temporal aggregation increase. That is, selecting the most appropriate model using annual data is more difficult than using monthly data. Or, selecting the most appropriate model using national data is more difficult than using regional data. The literature is replete with examples from all levels of aggregation, so model selection is possible, but researchers should be aware of the difficulties of data aggregation.

Key Questions

1. What is a mark-up pricing relationship and what are its weaknesses?
2. What is a dynamic mark-up relationship and how is it different than a mark-up relationship?
3. What is the difference between a relative and real price spread equation?

4.6 Summary

This chapter has outlined the basic concepts of marketing margins, or vertical price relationships. The costs of transforming farm products into final consumer goods represents the marketing margin, but the relationship between the margin and quantity depends on how marketing costs respond to changes in output. In some cases, we may see marketing costs (and the margin) decline as output increases due to economies of scale. In other cases, the margin may be relatively constant. Or, margins may increase as output increases due to constraints on capacity.

The farmer's share of the retail dollar is affected by marketing costs. As the degree of processing of a farm product increases, the farmer's share of the retail dollar will decline. But, as we have seen, this relationship says nothing about farm welfare. In fact, farm welfare can increase even as their share of the retail dollar declines if marketing costs are increasing faster than farm prices.

In short, vertical price relationships are quite important to agriculture. It is through these vertical relationships that final consumer demand for food and fiber products is transmitted to the farm level, thus determining resource allocation. There are a number of empirical techniques for analyzing vertical price relationships as discussed, and having a firm understanding of the empirical relationships between market levels aids decision-makers within the market to plan for future changes in these markets.

Exercises

Problem 4.1 *What are the three assumptions about the relationship between marketing costs and the marketing margin? In what situations would you expect each of these assumptions to hold?*

Problem 4.2 *Assume that you have estimated a mark-up pricing relationship as $M = 0.76 + 0.45P_r$. If the retail-level price elasticity of demand is -0.57 and the retail level price is 2.62, what is the farm-level price elasticity of demand?*

Problem 4.3 *Suppose that the Food and Drug Administration has mandated that all food processing facilities close down for one full shift for cleaning of equipment and inspection. What impact do you think this will have on the marketing costs, on producers, and on consumers? Graphically demonstrate your answers and clearly state your assumptions.*

References

Bondurant, J. and D. Ethridge. "Proportions of the Retail Dollar Received by Cotton Industry Segments: Selected Consumer Goods." *Proceedings of the Beltwide Cotton Conferences*, 1998, 1: 306–311.

Brorsen, B., J. Chavas, W. Grant, and L. Schnake. "Marketing Margins and Price Uncertainty: The Case of the U.S. Wheat Market." *American Journal of Agricultural Economics*, 67(1985): 521–528.

Gardner, B. "The Farm-Retail Price Spread in a Competitive Food Industry." *American Journal of Agricultural Economics*, 57(1975): 399–409.

Heien, D. "Markup Pricing in a Dynamic Model of the Food Industry." *American Journal of Agricultural Economics*, 62(1980): 10–18.

Helmberger, P. and J. Chavas. *The Economics of Agricultural Prices*. Prentice Hall, Upper Saddle River, NJ, 1996.

Kohls, R. and J. Uhl. *Marketing of Agricultural Products*, eighth edition. Prentice Hall, Upper Saddle River, NJ, 1998.

Lyon, C. and G. Thompson. "Temporal and Spatial Aggregation: Alternative Marketing Margin Models." *American Journal of Agricultural Economics*, 75(1993): 523–536.

Tomek, W. and K. Robinson. *Agricultural Product Prices*, third edition. Cornell University Press, Ithaca, NY, 1990.

Wohlgenant, M. and J. Mullen. "Modeling the Farm-Retail Price Spread for Beef." *Western Journal of Agricultural Economics*, 12(1987): 119–125.

Chapter 5

Stocks and International Markets

~

To complete the picture of a market, we must turn our attention to stocks and international markets. Many agricultural products such as fresh fruits and vegetables or milk are not storable in their raw form because they are perishable. However, many other products such as grains and oilseeds are storable. In this chapter, we will investigate the impacts of stocks on our market model. Next, we will turn our attention to international markets. The concept of international trade is similar to that of spatial equilibrium, which will be discussed in Chapter 6. However, there are key features of international markets such as exchange rates that need special attention. Finally, we will revisit the idea of equilibrium to include the effects of stocks and international trade.

5.1 Storable versus Nonstorable Products

5.1.1 Price Determination without Stocks

For nonstorable commodities, the supply of the good at harvest represents the total supply for that year (if there are no imports). Because supply is fixed, the short-run supply function is vertical (perfectly inelastic) as in Figure 5.1. Given demand, if the supply of the product is small, say S_1, the price will be "high." If, however, harvest is good yielding a supply of S_2, the market price will be lower. From this, you should deduce that the price is determined by the quantity supplied to the market, given a level of demand. Thus, empirically, we will often specify the short-run demand for a nonstorable good as inverse demand, or $P = f(Q)$, as discussed in Chapter 1. Of course, in the longer run, the supply of even nonstorable commodities will adjust to prices, giving a supply function with some positive slope. But, in the short run, all production decisions have been made so that the supply is fixed at the quantity harvested.

   The result of nonstorability is that prices can change substantially from year to year, depending on the level of output (assuming no changes in demand). Even assuming no changes in demand, it is logical to assume that weather conditions and other supply

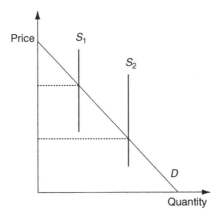

Figure 5.1 Short-run price determination without stocks.

shifting variables will change from year to year. Without stocks available to augment supplies, rapid changes in price are possible.

Example 5.1 *During 1999, the U.S. government initiated a pilot program to provide insurance to watermelon growers. Because the program shifts risk for growers, output expanded by 11%. That year, price decreased by 16%.*

The example here illustrates the substantial impact that a change in supply can have on a nonstorable commodity. The simple addition of a program to provide crop insurance altered output (along with weather and other factors), resulting in a large change in farm-level price. Thus, for nonstorable commodities, careful attention to expected output is a primary indicator of potential price impacts.

5.1.2 The Impacts of Stocks on Price

For storable commodities, the short-run situation looks a bit different. Assume that there are stocks of wheat in elevators across the country prior to this year's harvest. Figure 5.2 shows the post-harvest situation in the wheat market. The quantity Q_T represents the total available quantity, which includes both current production, Q_1, and available stocks. As price increases from low levels toward P_T, individual stockholders are induced to augment current production by moving wheat out of elevators onto the market, giving an upward-sloping supply function, S'. At some point, however, stocks will be exhausted (at Q_T), and no more product can be supplied to the market, making the supply function perfectly inelastic.

The existence of stocks has an important impact on price. If the amount harvested this year were Q_1 and there were no stocks, the resulting short-run price would be P_1. However, with stocks available, the resulting short-run price is P^*.[1] Thus, stocks generally

---

[1] Note that at this price level, total available supply is not exhausted, meaning there will be stocks available for the next growing season.

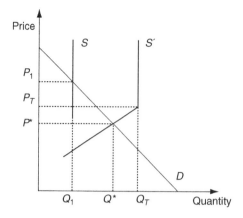

Figure 5.2   Short-run price determination with stocks.

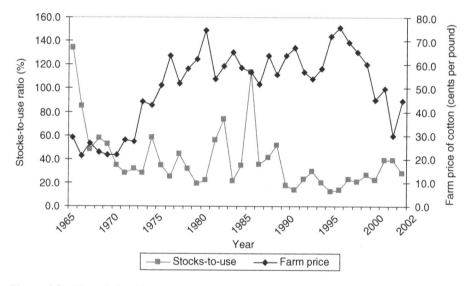

Figure 5.3   The relationship between stocks-to-use and farm price for U.S. upland cotton, 1965–2002.
Source: U.S. Department of Agriculture, Economic Research Service, *Cotton and Wool Situation and Outlook Yearbook,* 2003.

put downward pressure on price.[2] This relationship is often viewed through something called the **stocks-to-use ratio**, which is simply the ending stocks of a commodity relative to the amount used of that commodity.[3] Figure 5.3 shows the relationship between the stock-to-use ratio for cotton and U.S. farm price for cotton. The figure shows that in early

---

[2] In the next section, we will discuss the demand for stocks, and will find that when harvests are large, the demand for stocks can actually increase price.

[3] Use can mean a lot of things, but most typically, use in this context means domestic consumption plus exports.

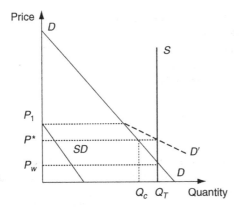

Figure 5.4   The effects of the demand for stocks on price.

periods (1965) when stocks-to-use was at its highest, price was low. As the stock-to-use has trended downward, the price has increased. The strength of the stocks-to-use ratio analysis shown in the figure is its simplicity. However, because of its simplicity, it does tend to leave a considerable amount of the variation in farm prices unexplained, and thus, is only a gross predictor of price behavior. Nevertheless, the relationship shown in the figure does demonstrate that increasing stock levels does put downward pressure on price, and vice versa.

5.1.3   Demand for Stocks

If there are stockholders, it makes sense that there would be a demand to hold stocks. Demand for stocks takes two general forms. First, **speculative demand** for stocks arises from traders who believe that the price of the commodity will increase over time, yielding profitable opportunities for purchasing the product today, holding it in storage, and then selling it at some point in the future. Second, there are **operational stocks**, which arise because processors must hold inventory to keep plants operating throughout the year.

Example 5.2   *Kellogg's® produces cereal throughout the year. However, there is not sufficient capacity to process all of their required corn for the year when it is harvested. Therefore, they hold operational stocks of corn to process as needed through the year.*

Helmberger and Chavas (1996) provide a general model of demand for stocks as shown in Figure 5.4. The demand for the commodity for current consumption is given by the demand curve DD, and stock demand is given by the demand curve SD. At prices below P_1, traders are willing to purchase the commodity and place it in storage, so the effective demand curve for the market becomes DD'.[4] Without stock demand, the intersection

---

[4]Note that the stock demand curve is downward sloping as well, implying that as the market price decreases, the quantity demanded for stocks increases. The "kink" in the market demand curve at P_1 arises because we are adding (horizontal summation) the stock demand to the consumption demand. This is a similar construction to that found in Chapter 1, where we horizontally summed individual demand to form market demand.

of the supply curve and consumption demand curve *DD* yields a market price of P_w. However, with stock demand, the relevant intersection is between the supply curve and total demand *DD'*, resulting in a higher equilibrium price of P^*. Thus, the result is that the total supply of Q_T is exhausted, but is now divided between current consumption, Q_c, and the amount demanded for stocks, $(Q_T - Q_c)$.

5.1.4   Summary

The impacts of stocks on price are twofold. First, when current production is relatively tight, the existence of stocks can augment current production, resulting in a price that will be lower than would be the case with no stocks. Second, when current production is relatively abundant, the demand for stocks can augment demand for current consumption, yielding a price that is higher than without stock demand. Thus, the net effect of stocks is to "smooth" available supply and reduce overall price volatility as compared with a situation without stocks. This *does not mean* that stocks eliminate price volatility, nor does it mean that products with stocks are necessarily less volatile in price than products without stocks. It does mean that stocks act as a price buffer against more adverse effects of short or bumper crops. As such, accounting for the effects of stocks is necessary to properly understand price dynamics in storable commodities across time.

A second item to remember about stocks is that the existence of stocks links current and future prices. That is, what you anticipate price to be in the futures affects your decision to store or not store today. In this regard, stocks act as a link between present and future supply/demand situations. But, it is also important to remember that these decisions are based on *expectations* about the future, which means that it is based on the best available information from today. As information changes, expectations change, and product is moved in and out of storage in response to those changes in expectations.

Key Questions

1. What are the types of demand for stocks?
2. What impact do stocks have on market price?
3. What is speculative demand for stocks? What is operational demand?
4. What is the stocks-to-use ratio?

5.2   Exports and Imports

Another important component of markets is international trade. In 2003, the U.S. exported $59.5 billion in agricultural products. At the same time, the U.S. imported $47.4 billion. One may be tempted to think of trade as a modern phenomenon, but trade is probably as old as human civilization. The ancient Phoenician society, for example, was centered around trade (Irwin, 1996). It was not until the late 1990s that the volume of global trade exceeded the trade volumes seen in the early 1900s prior to the two world wars. It is also important to remember that trade is global. Figure 5.5 shows the distribution of agricultural exports from the United States in 2002. While the majority of agricultural exports from the U.S. are sent to countries of the Western Hemisphere

Figure 5.5   The distribution of U.S. agricultural exports, 2002.
Source: U.S. Department of Agriculture, Foreign Agricultural Service.

($15.9 billion), substantial exports are sent to Asia, Australia, Europe, Africa, and the Middle East. Thus, international trade remains important and will continue to increase in importance over time and a firm understanding of the impacts of trade are important. This section, however, is not intended as a substitute for a good course in international trade.[5]

5.2.1   Export and Import Demand

Before delving into the specifics of trade, it is useful to gain some perspective on the types of products that are traded. Table 5.1 shows the value of both exports and imports for some selected product categories.

First, it should be obvious that there are several important export products for the U.S.—animals, grains, vegetables, oilseeds, and cotton. At the same time, however, you probably notice that for many of these products, imports are large as well. The explanation for this is twofold. First, in many cases, data are reported as in Table 5.1 in broad product categories. As such, there are some specific products within that category that are almost completely exported, where other specific products are almost completely imported. Combining the data in this fashion gives the impression that imports are as large

---

[5]Those interested in trade topics are directed to Koo and Kennedy (2005) as an example text on international trade. We focus here on the primary economic variables relevant to trade and their impact on prices and distribution of goods and services. However, there is a world of issues related to trade policy, exchange rates, and the macroeconomy that are important as well.

Table 5.1   The value of exports and imports for selected categories, 2003

Exports ($billion)	Category	Imports ($billion)
9.4	Animals and animal products	8.9
16.2	Grains and feeds	3.9
2.9	Fruits and fruit preparations	4.7
2.0	Nuts and nut preparations	0.8
4.8	Vegetables and vegetable preparations	6.4
1.7	Sugar and sugar-related products	2.1
0.0	Rubber	1.0
0.7	Beverages (excluding fruit juices)	6.6
9.1	Oilseeds	2.1
1.5	Vegetable oils and waxes	1.6
3.9	Cotton (excluding linters)	0.0
0.9	Seed–home and field	0.5
0.0	Cut flowers and bulbs	0.6

Source: USDA, Foreign Agricultural Service.

as exports, but the combination masks the underlying differences in specific products. Second, for some products such as fresh fruits and vegetables, production is seasonal. So, when those products are in season in the U.S., domestic consumers purchase them and some are exported. When those products are not in season, domestic consumption is satisfied by imports. Thus, for these specific products, we may observe both exports and imports, but they are generally occurring at different points during the year.

There are many economic variables that influence trade, with comparative advantage being the driving economic force (Nicholson, 2002; Koo and Kennedy, 2005). Comparative advantage gives rise to gains from trade, which are the benefits accruing from specialization of production. Here, we focus on the specific factors that influence and the impacts of export/import demand. From the perspective of an individual country, **import demand** or **excess demand** represents the demand for goods and services that are not satisfied by domestic production. This can be visualized in Figure 5.6.

In the figure, the world price of the product is P_w. At this price, domestic consumers would like to consume Q_d. However, at this price, domestic producers are only willing to supply Q_s. The difference, $Q_d - Q_s$, is excess demand. To satisfy this excess demand, the county would turn to international markets to supply imports. There are two basic views of the impacts of imports on world market price, as illustrated in Figure 5.7. Under the **small-country assumption**, the excess demand of the importing country is assumed to be small enough relative to the overall market that these imports have no effect on world price (Houck, 1992). Thus, the excess demand function for trade (*ED*) is horizontal; that is, no matter the amount imported (which, again, is assumed to be a small amount), there is no impact on the price. Thus, the intersection of the excess supply function (*ES*) and *ED* yields an amount imported by the domestic country of X, which will equal the amount ($Q_d - Q_s$) in Figure 5.6.

Conversely, under the **large-country assumption**, the amount of imports by the domestic country are assumed to be large enough to have an impact on price, resulting

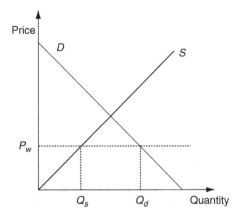

Figure 5.6   An illustration of excess demand for a domestic market.

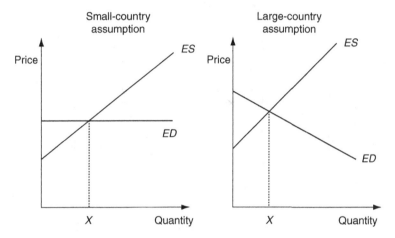

Figure 5.7   Large- and small-country assumptions about the impacts of import demand.

in a downward-sloping excess demand function. Again, the intersection of *ES* and *ED* yields the amount traded. However, in the large-country case, any changes to the excess demand function (or the excess supply function) will alter the world market price.

Turning our attention to exports, Figure 5.8 shows a similar relationship to that for imports in Figure 5.6. In this case, at the world price of P_w, domestic consumers are willing to purchase Q_d, but domestic producers are willing to supply Q_s. The resulting difference is called **excess supply**. To dispose of this excess, the country would turn to international markets to export the excess supply.[6] As with imports, exports are subject to the same large/small-country distinction. In the case of the small country, the amount made available for exports is small relative to the overall market and those exports have no

---

[6] The demand curve in the figure represents total demand, including domestic consumption and the demand for stocks; thus, the excess supply is net of the amount that is placed in domestic stocks.

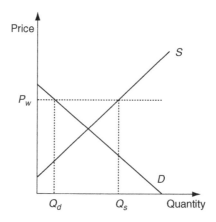

Figure 5.8   An illustration of excess supply for a domestic market.

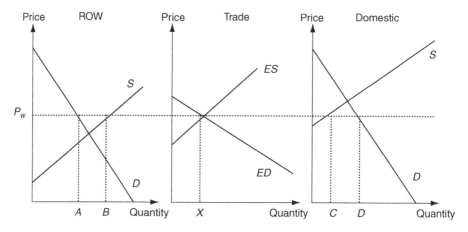

Figure 5.9   The market equilibrium with international markets under the large-country assumption.

impact on price, resulting in a horizontal excess supply function. For the large country, exports are large relative to the overall market, leading to an upward-sloping excess supply function.

We can combine these to get a more complete picture of market equilibrium with international markets in Figure 5.9.[7] Here, we are assuming that the domestic country is a net importer of the product and that it is a large country. At any price above the "equilibrium" price in the rest of the world (ROW), the ROW would be willing to supply product to international markets. Thus, the horizontal difference between the supply and demand functions in the ROW generates the excess supply function *ES*. At the same time, at prices below the domestic equilibrium price in the domestic market, domestic consumers would like to import the product so that the horizontal difference between the

---

[7] At this point, we are ignoring transfer (or transportation) costs. We will revisit the impacts of transfer costs on spatial markets in the next chapter.

supply and demand function below the domestic equilibrium price generates the excess demand function *ED*. The intersection of the *ED* and *ES* functions estabishes the world market price, P_w. At the world price, consumers in the ROW are willing to consume A, and producers are willing to supply B. The difference, $(B - A)$, is exported (which is equal to X in the center panel). At the same time, domestic producers are willing to produce C, while domestic consumers are willing to purchase D, with the difference, $(D - C)$, being imported (which is also equal to X in the center panel.

Two important features should be obvious about the effects of international trade. First, for exporting countries, the existence of international markets actually increases the price of the exported product above what would be observed without international markets. This, of course, benefits producers of that product, but consumers must now pay increased prices. At the same time, trade decreases the price of the product as compared to the situation with no trade for the importing country. This lowers the price producers would have received in the absence of trade, but benefits consumers by lowering the price paid for that product. To analyze the net effect of trade, we would employ the consumer/producer surplus measure discussed in Chapter 3. But, it is clear that international trade will have an impact on market price.

5.2.2 Exchange Rates

Analysis of export/import demand is very similar to that of consumer demand, with the same general economic variables having an influence. When one wishes to examine the demand for imports, it is important to note that it is the characteristics of the importing country that are most relevant. For example, import demand (*ED*) may be viewed by the following general functional relationship:

$$ED = f(P_o, P_{s/c}, I, P),$$

where P_o is the price of the product under question, $P_{s/c}$ are the prices of substitutes and complements, I is the income in the importing country, and P is the population in the importing country. Conversely, if one wishes to examine the demand for exports from a country (or excess supply), it is the characteristics of the importing countries that are relevant. That is, it is the prices of substitutes and complements, income, and population of the countries that are demanding the exports that are relevant (Hudson and Ethridge, 2000).

An important variable (not shown in the equation above) that is relevant to both export and import demand is the **exchange rate**. The exchange rate represents the amount of one currency it takes to purchase one unit of another currency (Koo and Kennedy, 2005). For example, one U.S. dollar may purchase 103 Japanese yen. Thus, the dollar/yen exchange rate would be 1 for 103. Changes in exchange rate have important impacts on trade. When the dollar increases in value relative to other currencies, or the dollar has **appreciated**, it takes fewer dollars to purchase foreign goods (and makes U.S. goods more expensive to foreign buyers). Thus, currency appreciation typically leads to increased imports and decreased exports, *ceteris paribus*. Conversely, if the dollar declines in value relative to other currencies, or the dollar has **depreciated**, it takes more dollars to purchase foreign goods (and makes U.S. goods less expensive to foreign buyers). Thus, currency depreciation typically leads to fewer imports and more exports.

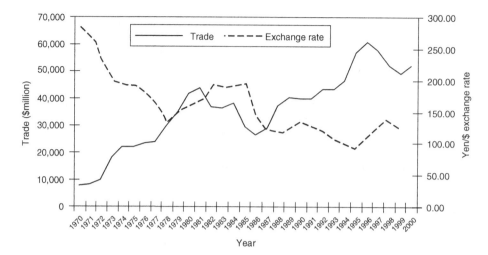

Figure 5.10   The relationship between exchange rates and U.S. agricultural exports.
Source: U.S. Department of Agriculture, Foreign Agricultural Service and Economic Research
Service.

Example 5.3   *During 2004, the U.S. dollar depreciated by up to 40% relative to other
currencies. What do you think was the impact on exports and imports in the U.S.?*

The relationship between exchange rates and U.S. exports can be illustrated in
Figure 5.10. In the early 1980s the dollar/yen exchange rate was approaching 1 to 300.
Since that time, the dollar has been on a downward trend, implying that the dollar has
been depreciating versus the Japanese yen. At the same time, U.S. agricultural exports
have been on an upward trend. Thus, the conclusion is that exports and currency value are
negatively correlated as implied by the discussion above.[8] Thus, to more fully capture
the factors influencing export/import demand, exchange rates must be considered.[9]

Key Questions

1. What is excess demand? What is excess supply?
2. What impact does trade have on prices in the exporting country, and on those in the
   importing country?
3. What is currency appreciation? What is currency depreciation?
4. What impact do changes in exchange rates have on imports and exports?

---

[8] In fact, the correlation over the time period presented in the figure is −0.81. Thus, while the exchange rate is a
key variable in explaining the variation in exports, it is not the only variable as noted in the previous equation.

[9] You should be aware that you will find two primary types of exchange rates reported in the data—nominal
and purchasing power parity (PPP). The nominal exchange rate is the common exchange rate found in the
newspapers, which is derived from either currency markets or stated government exchange rates, where they
are controlled by the government. The PPP exchange rate takes nominal exchange rates and attempts to make
adjustments for costs of living. There is some debate in the economics literature as to the proper exchange rate
to use. But the most common form used in empirical analysis (and the easiest to find) are nominal exchange
rates. An example of a PPP exchange rate called the "Big Mac Index," is published by *The Economist* magazine.
Here, exchange rates are adjusted by the price of a McDonalds Big Mac, which is used as a proxy for the
cost-of-living differentials across countries.

5.3 Equilibrium Revisited

We have now completed our journey through the basic structure of a perfectly competitive market. By now, it should be obvious that there is quite a bit of information contained within the catch phrase "it's supply and demand." Hopefully, you have expanded your understanding to see that the demand for a product is a function of the characteristics and preferences of domestic consumers, but price is ultimately linked to the expectations of stockholders and the characteristics and preferences of foreign consumers as well. Likewise, domestic production is tied to the technology and management of domestic producers as well as other supply shifting variables, and, at the same time, linked to these same variables around the globe.

Example 5.4 *Closely examine the market equilibrium illustrated in Figure 5.9. Think about all of the variables underlying each of the curves found in the figure. Now, think about the standard quip "What does that have to do with the price of tea in China?"*

It is important to note that what is found in Figure 5.9 is something called **partial equilibrium**. That is, the figure only represents one sector, not the economy as a whole. We know that changes in any of the underlying variables will shift curves in our diagram, leading to changes in prices, quantities, and so on. But, our figure only gives us a partial picture, because it does not tell us what the impact of the changes are on the rest of the economy. For that, we would need a **general equilibrium** model (Nicholson, 2002). General equilibrium is beyond the scope of this book, but you should be aware that while the partial equilibrium model is extremely useful in analysis, it is not the final picture. Nevertheless, our partial equilibrium model is the most typical level of analysis and serves as a useful device for understanding the impacts of changes in economic variables on prices and quantities of interest.

5.4 Summary

This chapter has outlined two key components of agricultural markets—stocks and international markets. The ability to hold stocks obviously adds flexibility for market participants to adjust stocks to expected futures prices, and also provides the market with a buffer against short and large harvests. Although our models appear simple, analyzing stock behavior can be quite complex because of the myriad of reasons that people will hold stocks—speculative and operational. Nevertheless, stocks play a significant role in the price determination of storable commodities.

International markets have always been, and are becoming increasingly, important to agricultural markets. A large share of U.S. agricultural production is exported. Trade agreements such as the North American Free Trade Agreement (NAFTA) and the World Trade Organization (WTO) are altering tariffs and quotas (taxes and quantity constraints) on exports and imports, which is changing the dynamics of international trade. In addition, factors such as transport costs play a significant role in trade as well. Because U.S. agriculture is dependent on international trade, understanding the forces underlying trade is important as well. As we have seen, ultimately, it is international markets that tie the consumers of one nation together with the producers of another. So, policies, natural disasters, and tastes and preferences around the globe interact together to determine international prices.

Exercises

Problem 5.1 *Assume that there has been a hurricane in Florida that has destroyed a large portion of the tomato crop. What do you expect to happen to prices of tomatoes in the short run? Analyze this situation graphically and verbally.*

Problem 5.2 *The current level of stocks for corn is 14 million bushels. The current use (consumption + exports) of corn is 10 million bushels. What is the stocks-to-use ratio?*

Problem 5.3 *The stocks-to-use ratio for wheat has declined from 120% to 80%. What do you expect will happen to wheat price? Why?*

Problem 5.4 *Assume that the United States is a large country exporter of corn. Congress is expected to pass a law requiring that corn-based ethanol be used as a blending agent for gasoline. What impact will this have on exports and world price of corn? Analyze this problem graphically and verbally (Hint: What impact will passage of the law have on domestic demand for corn?).*

Problem 5.5 *If the exchange rate has gone from 103 yen to the dollar to 140 yen to the dollar, is this currency appreciation or depreciation? What impact will the change have on exports from the U.S.? Why?*

References

Helmberger, P. and J. Chavas. *The Economics of Agricultural Prices.* Prentice Hall, Upper Saddle River, NJ, 1996.

Houck, J. *Elements of Agricultural Trade Policy.* Waveland Press, Prospect Heights, IL, 1992.

Hudson, D. and D. Ethridge. "Income Distributional Impacts of Trade Policies: A Case in Pakistan." *Journal of Agricultural and Applied Economics*, 32(2000): 49–61.

Irwin, D. *Against the Tide: An Intellectual History of Free Trade.* Princeton University Press, Princeton, NJ, 1996.

Koo, W. and L. Kennedy. *International Trade and Agriculture.* Blackwell, Oxford, 2005.

Nicholson, W. *Microeconomic Theory: Basic Principles and Extensions*, eighth edition. South-Western, 2002.

Chapter 6

Price Variation Across Space

~

To this point (with the exception of Chapter 5), we have not explicitly considered the role of space in prices. That is, we have essentially treated production and consumption as occurring in the same place at one price. However, production clearly occurs nationwide, as does consumption. Clearly, then, there are a multiplicity of observed prices in different areas at the same point in time. Casual observation would show that the price for Choice steers is different in Amarillo, TX, and Omaha, NE. What causes these differences? Is there any relationship between prices in different areas? In this chapter, we will explore what generates differences in price across space and what ties prices across space together.

6.1 The Law of One Price

6.1.1 Arbitrage

Agricultural markets are generally believed to follow a principle called the **law of one price**, which holds that prices in different markets do not differ by more than transfer costs. More generally (Tomek and Robinson, 1990):

1. Prices between any two markets or regions that trade a product cannot exceed transfer costs.
2. Price differences between any two markets or regions that do not trade will be less than or equal to transfer costs.

An important concept in economics, called **arbitrage**, drives this relationship.

Example 6.1 *Assume that corn is selling for $2.80 per bushel in Greenville, MS, and selling for $3.20 per bushel in Cairo, IL. Assume also that the transfer cost between these two points is $0.20 per bushel. What would you do?*

The answer to the above should be obvious. If you can buy corn in Greenville for $2.80 and ship it to Cairo for $0.20, your total cost would be $3.00 per bushel. You could then sell it for $3.20 and make $0.20 per bushel profit. Assuming others have access to the same information, this price difference would entice shippers to ship grain from Greenville to Cairo until the price came down in Cairo, up in Greenville, or both, until the point at which the difference in prices just equaled the transfer cost of $0.20. This is an example of arbitrage in action.

Arbitrage is a central feature of well functioning markets. As Carter (2003) points out, arbitrage is essential in futures markets. As we can see above, arbitrage is essential in determining the proper allocation of product across space and equilibrating prices. The profit motive of individuals in the economy is a strong force insuring that the incentive to arbitrage markets is present.

There are limits to arbitrage, however. As mentioned above, traders must have access to the information that reveals price differences between regions. If not all traders have access to this information, arbitrage will be slow or completely ineffective, leading to long-term or permanent violation of the law of one price. In addition, access to transportation services may inhibit the normal working of arbitrage. For example, if there were an insufficient number of barges available on the Mississippi River, it would be more difficult or costly to ship corn from Greenville to Cairo. These difficulties tend to be more short term in nature. Finally, consumer preferences may create a situation in which price differences exceed transfer costs. That is, consumers may prefer onions from Georgia to those from Texas, in which case price differences can persist above transfer costs for long periods of time (or permanently).

In addition to these limitations, there are market structure considerations as well. That is, arbitrage is generally believed to hold in competitive markets subject to the limitations just discussed. However, in imperfectly competitive markets, there may be other explanations for linkages in prices between spatially dispersed markets that have little to do with arbitrage (Faminow and Benson, 1990). At the very least, market structure has an impact on the effectiveness of arbitrage in equilibrating prices (Brorsen, Chavas, and Grant, 1991; Kawaguchi, Suzuki, and Kaiser, 1997). Thus, while arbitrage is important, it is important to note that this is a phenomenon that may be limited to competitive market structures.

6.1.2   Transfer Costs and Market Boundaries

The preceding section made reference to the term **transfer cost**, which is the single most important variable in determining spatial price relationships (Tomek and Robinson, 1990; Fuller, Fellin, and Erikson, 2000). One might be tempted to use the average transportation cost between two points as the transfer cost, but this could lead to erroneous conclusions. Typically, transfer cost includes a fixed charge associated with loading, unloading, insurance, and so on, that is irrespective of volume or distance traveled. There is also a variable charge that is associated with the cost of transportation that does depend both on volume and distance traveled. Taken together, Tomek and Robinson (1990) argue that transfer cost is usually increasing at a decreasing rate in distance traveled. That is, each additional mile adds more to the transfer cost, but does not add as much as the previous mile.

Table 6.1 Per mile and per ton transfer costs for a high-speed catamaran vessel

From Tampa, FL, to:	Rio de Janeiro, Brazil	Port au Prince, Haiti
Total fixed cost	$216,367.05	$54,367.33
Trip variable costs		
At-sea fuel	$427,952.08	$89,313.67
Port expenses		
Port fuel	$1,216.69	$1,216.69
Port tariffs	$1,624.00	$1,624.00
Handling	$4,646.40	$4,646.40
Brokerage	$52,412.30	$23,628.10
Total trip cost	$704,218.56	$174,796.16
Container cost per trip	$20,006.21	$4,965.80
Trip cost per metric ton	**$1,379.74**	**$342.47**

Fuentes (2002) provides an example of transfer costs using a high-speed catamaran vessel from Tampa, FL, to alternative sites in the Carribbean and South America (Table 6.1).

Table 6.1 shows that the transfer cost per metric ton increases with distance, as would be expected. Thus, it is more costly to transfer one metric ton of produce to Brazil than it is to transport that same metric ton to Haiti. As you can see, however, there is more to the transfer cost than just the simple transportation cost. There are fixed expenses, port tariffs, handling, and brokerage costs. In fact, the actual transport cost (at-sea fuel) is only roughly half of total transfer costs in this example. The ratio of transport to other costs will depend on the transportation mode (truck, rail, ship, air, etc.), distance traveled, and other factors.

The concept of transfer costs leads to another important concept in spatial price relationships: **market boundaries**. Quite simply, a market boundary is a point beyond which it is no longer economically feasible to ship produce (Paul, 1979). Either another production region will ship to that area or consumers will not have access to the produce. Consider the situation for sweet potatoes in Figure 6.1. The major producing regions in the U.S. are California, Louisiana, Mississippi, and North Carolina. There is an effective market boundary as labeled on the map that roughly corresponds with the eastern edge of the Rocky Mountains. On the western side of the Rockies, California can deliver sweet potatoes at a lower price than any of the eastern states, and vice versa.[1]

If we were to treat the eastern and western regions as separate markets, would you expect to see a difference in price that exceeded transfer costs? Perhaps in the short run. But, in the longer term, we would not expect to see the prices exceed the transfer

---

[1] It is important to note that there are a variety of reasons why market boundaries arise. Natural boundaries such as rivers or mountains are obvious obstacles. However, political lines, such as national boundaries, or legal constraints, such as laws prohibiting transport or quarantines, may give rise to market boundaries as well.

Effective market
boundary

Figure 6.1   Sweet potato production regions and the effective market boundary.

costs, because arbitrage would force those two prices back into line with one another. Nevertheless, the transfer cost does create a natural boundary between markets.

6.1.3   Spatial Markets

Figure 6.2 shows a hypothetical market for wheat. There are two consuming regions (US and THEM) and two production regions (Farmer X and Farmer Y). The figure shows the transfer costs between each of the producing regions, and consuming regions, as well as between the consuming regions. Assume that the prevailing price for wheat at US is $4.00 per bushel. Wheat could be shipped from US to THEM at a cost of $0.50 per bushel, for a maximum price of $4.50 per bushel. However, from Figure 6.2, it is clear that someone could just as easily purchase wheat from Farmer X and deliver it to THEM at a cost of $3.90 + $0.40 = $4.30 per bushel. Likewise, someone could purchase from Farmer Y and ship to THEM at a cost of $4.10 + $0.20 = $4.30 per bushel. Thus, the *least-cost* mode would be to purchase from either Farmer X or Y and ship to THEM, and not ship from US to THEM, and the price of wheat at THEM is then $4.30 per bushel. Likewise, someone could purchase wheat from Farmer X and ship to US for $0.10, leading to a total price of $4.00. Or, someone could ship from Farmer Y for $0.30 per bushel for a total cost of $4.40. Clearly, US would prefer to purchase from Farmer X because of the lower net price. This leads to one important conclusion about spatial markets:

- The price in the deficit (consuming) market is determined by the lowest-cost source of supply.

Similarly, Farmer Y has the choice of marketing wheat to either US or THEM. If Y markets to US, the price would be $4.00 less the transfer cost of $0.30, or $3.70. If Y markets to THEM, the price would be $4.30 per bushel less $0.20 transfer cost, or $4.10 per bushel. Clearly, then, it is more profitable for Y to market to THEM. This leads to another important conclusion:

- Producers sell to whichever market yields the highest net return.

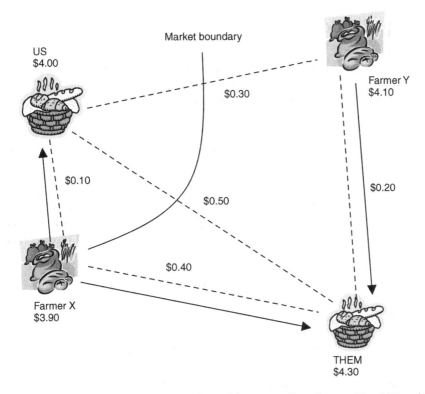

Figure 6.2 The hypothetical market for wheat with two suppliers (farmers X and Y) and two markets (*US* and *THEM*).

Farmer X presents a special case. The net price to Farmer X is the same in either market. This is because Farmer X lies on the market boundary, and is therefore indifferent to the market in which wheat is sold. Farmer Y is clearly in THEM's market area, and therefore will only ship to THEM because it generates the highest net price. In cases such as the ones discussed above, the concept of a market boundary is easy to visualize. Potential arbitrage forces the product to be allocated in the least-cost manner. The transfer cost clearly dictates much about how spatial markets are organized. However, in practice, there are many regions or areas of production shipping to many possible destinations. In these more complex cases, it is difficult to easily visualize the pattern of trade. Individual decisions of whether to ship to point A or point B are still clear. They are dictated by transfer cost. But, an overall picture of the pattern of prices and patterns of trade are difficult to discern or predict.

Key Questions

1. What is the law of one price?
2. What is arbitrage?
3. What is the driving force behind spatial markets?
4. What is a transfer cost and how is it different than transport costs?
5. What is a market boundary and how is it determined?

6.2 Spatial Equilibrium Models

We can generalize these spatial price relationships using a spatial equilibrium model.[2] We will begin by formalizing this model and then return to the graphical analysis. Assume there are two markets—a surplus market (1) and a deficit market (2)—each having a demand function:

$$Q_1^d = a - bP_1, \tag{6.1}$$

$$Q_2^d = c - d(P_1 + TC), \tag{6.2}$$

where P_1 is the equilibrium price in the surplus market with trade and TC is the per unit transfer cost to move the product from the surplus to the deficit region. For simplicity, we will assume that production in each region (Q_1^s, Q_2^s) is known and predetermined. Equilibrium is given by

$$Q_1^s + Q_2^s \equiv Q_1^d + Q_2^d.$$

Summing Equations 6.1 and 6.2 yields

$$Q_1^d + Q_2^d = a - bP_1 + c - d(P_1 + TC). \tag{6.3}$$

Equating 6.3 with the predetermined production, $(Q_1^s + Q_2^s)$, gives

$$P_1^* = \frac{a + c - dTC - (Q_1^s + Q_2^s)}{b + d} \tag{6.4}$$

which is the equilibrium price. Equation 6.4 indicates two key features that are apparent in the equilibrium price: supply and transfer cost. This result echoes the earlier discussion that transfer costs are a driving force behind arbitrage in spatial markets. That is, if transfer costs are zero, supply and demand are the only factors affecting price. If transfer costs are nonzero, transfer costs will have a direct impact on the equilibrium price. We can represent this situation graphically, as in Figure 6.3. In this figure, we relax the assumption of predetermined supply from above and do not include transfer costs. The surplus in the "surplus region" is given by $Q_1^s - Q_1^d$, and the deficit in the deficit region is given by: $Q_2^d - Q_2^s$.

Assuming that there are only two regions:

$$Q_2^d - Q_2^s \equiv Q_1^s - Q_1^d \equiv T,$$

where T is the quantity traded between the regions. Assuming no transfer costs, the result is an equilibrium price of P_1^*. We can focus attention on the center panel in Figure 6.3 (Trade) to examine the impact of transfer cost on price in Figure 6.4. The equilibrium

---

[2] You were introduced to this modeling approach in Chapter 5 in the analysis of international markets, so the concepts should be familiar.

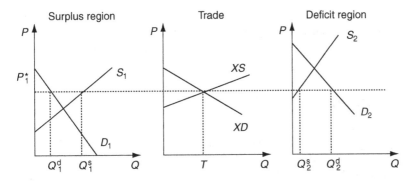

Figure 6.3 A graphical analysis of a spatial equilibrium model with no transfer costs.

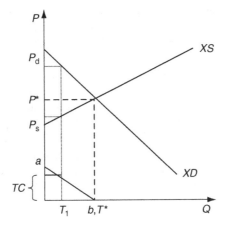

Figure 6.4 The impact of transfer costs on equilibrium trade volume prices.

price without transfer costs is P_1^*, as in Figure 6.3. We can introduce a **volume of trade** line, represented by the diagonal line *ab* in Figure 6.4. At a transfer cost equal to *a*, no trade between regions would occur. At a transfer cost of $b = 0$, full trade would occur, with an equilibrium price of P_1^*.

Assume that transfer costs are equal to *TC* in the figure. This would cause a reduction in trade equal to $T^* - T_1$. The result is a difference in equilibrium prices in the different regions. The result for the surplus region is a lower price than without transfer costs, while the deficit region pays a higher price. Thus, Figure 6.4 shows that the impact of transfer costs are generally felt by both suppliers and buyers. The distribution of the impact depends on the elasticities of excess demand and supply.

From a welfare perspective, the imposition of transfer costs decreases the welfare of both consumers and producers. That is, producers are receiving a lower price for their output and consumers are paying a higher price for consumption than would be the case with no transfer costs. Thus, there is a welfare loss to these groups. However, that "welfare" is not lost. Companies that provide the transfer services receive a benefit equal to $TC * T_1$. Clearly, then, there is some benefit to lowering transfer costs. The government attempts to lower transfer costs by building highways, bridges, and navigation channels in rivers. Transport companies attempt to lower costs through adoption of new technology. From Figure 6.4, it is clear that any reduction in transfer costs, other things being equal, will increase the price to producers and decrease the price to consumers.

6.3   Summary

This chapter has addressed the issues of price differences across space. The concept of arbitrage was introduced and discussed as the binding link between spatially dispersed markets. The examples show that the profit motive of individual traders will tie spatial markets together, with the difference in prices between markets being the transfer cost of moving product between markets. However, the power of arbitrage is not absolute.

Transfer costs are critical in determining both arbitrage relationships and establishing market boundaries. While the concept of market boundaries is simple, boundaries and patterns of trade in practice are difficult to visualize because of the large number of supply sources and destinations for produce. We have seen that we can generalize this relationship through the use of spatial equilibrium models that explicitly take into account supply and demand factors in different markets to determine the equilibrium price.

The conclusion we reach in this presentation is that transfer costs are crucial determinants of patterns of trade, whether we are using simple market boundary approaches or more sophisticated spatial equilibrium models. This result implies that research into transportation and transfer costs is a critical area of inquiry for physical scientists engaged in technology investment, practitioners and professionals in business, and economists. It is clear from our presentation here that transfer costs affect producer and consumer welfare and the pattern of trade.

Exercises

Problem 6.1   *Assume that there are two farmers (X and Y) and two marketing centers (US and THEM). The prevailing price at US is $5.00 and the prevailing price at THEM is $5.20. It costs $0.60 to transport products between US and THEM. It costs $0.10 to for Farmer X to transport products to US and $0.30 to transport to THEM. It costs $0.30 for Farmer Y to transport to US and $0.10 to transport to THEM. Construct a market boundary diagram representing this situation and indicate which farmer transports to which market center.*

Problem 6.2   *Assume that the demand in the surplus country is given by $Q_1^d = 20 - 2P_1$, and the demand in the deficit country is given by $Q_2^d = 17 - 3(P_1 + 0.5)$, where the 0.5 represents the per unit transfer cost. Also assume that the total supply $(Q_1^s + Q_2^s)$ is equal to 20. Based on this information, what is the equilibrium price between the two countries? If production is split evenly between the regions (that is, 10 units in each region), what is the amount traded between regions?*

Problem 6.3   *In the problem above, what happens to the equilibrium price if the total supply increases to 30, or if it decreases to 15?*

Problem 6.4   *Assume that a new loading technology has been introduced into ports that will lower the per unit cost of transferring products from ships to rail cars. What impact will this technology have on the market price in exporting and importing countries? Analyze this problem graphically and verbally.*

References

Brorsen, B., J. Chavas, and W. Grant. "Market Structure and Spatial Price Dynamics." *Southern Journal of Agricultural Economics*, 23(1991): 65–73.

Carter, C. *Futures and Options Markets: An Introduction*. Prentice Hall, Upper Saddle River, NJ, 2003.

Faminow, M. and B. Benson. "Integration of Spatial Markets." *American Journal of Agricultural Economics*, 72(1990): 49–62.

Fuentes, P. *An Economic Evaluation of Fast Displacement Vessels for Ocean Transportation of Perishables and High Value Commodities: A Spatial Equilibrium Approach*, Unpublished Ph.D. Dissertation, Department of Agricultural Economics, Mississippi State University, May 2002.

Fuller, S., L. Fellin, and K. Erikson. "Panama Canal: How Critical to U.S. Grain Exports?" *Agribusiness: An International Journal*, 16(2000): 435–455.

Kawaguchi, T., N. Suzuki, and H. Kaiser. "A Spatial Equilibrium Model for Imperfectly Competitive Milk Markets." *American Journal of Agricultural Economics*, 79(1997): 851–859.

Paul, A. "Some Basic Problems of Research into Competition in Agricultural Markets." *American Journal of Agricultural Economics*, 61(1979): 170–177.

Tomek, W. and K. Robinson. *Agricultural Product Prices*, third edition. Cornell University Press, Ithaca, NY, 1990.

Chapter 7

Price Variation Through Time

~

Price changes through time are a matter of interest to businesses, policy-makers, and economists. Price changes tell us something about changes in supply and demand, farm income, and other economic relationships. In addition, prices may also be used to gain some insight on further changes in price. Many factors, including expectations, may change price as time progresses. Economic agents would like to have a "crystal ball" to see into the future. Despite their relatively large supply, fortune tellers are largely unsuccessful (hence, relegated to sideshows and seedy dark alleys). Thus, we are forced to rely on past price behavior and expectations about future events to develop predictions about future prices. In this chapter, we will explore temporal price changes and discuss methods of analyzing these changes. We will focus on trends and seasonality and discuss strengths and weaknesses of forecasting methods.

7.1 Trends

Prices may exhibit trends (up, down, or sideways), which are consistent movements in price in a particular direction. Figure 7.1 shows a three-year trend in monthly corn price over the 1997–1999 period. As can be seen, prices were moving downward over the period. However, as can also be seen, prices did not constantly move downward. There are fluctuations about the linear trendline, which are short-term fluctuations in price.

Short-term fluctuations in price arise from such things as changes in expectations about future demand, weather events, political events, temporary disruptions in transportation, and so on. These short-lived events cause short-term disturbances in price that manifest themselves in fluctuations such as those observed in Figure 7.1. Trends, by contrast, are a manifestation of longer-term, more permanent changes in economic variables. For example, high levels of inflation in the economy lead to general increases in price levels.

The time period covered in Figure 7.1 was marred by the Asian financial crisis, where currencies of several major Asian countries collapsed, leading to rapid decreases in U.S.

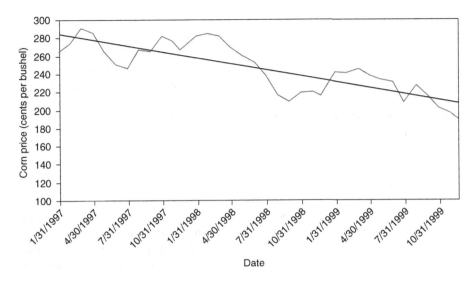

Figure 7.1   Monthly average corn prices (1997–1999) and the associated linear trend in price.

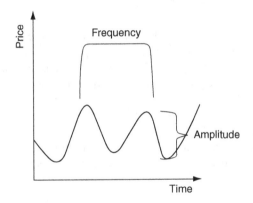

Figure 7.2   The frequency and amplitude of a price cycle.

agricultural exports to that region.[1] As we saw in Chapter 5, a decline in currency value in Asia leads to a leftward shift in demand, thus decreasing price in the U.S. The downward trend in Figure 7.1 is due, at least in part, to the Asian financial crisis.

Trends are not to be confused with cycles. A true price cycle is a situation in which the price moves up and down through a regular pattern, with varying degrees of frequency and amplitude (you just thought your high-school physics class would be useless!). The frequency refers to the number of times the price moves through an entire cycle over a given period of time. The amplitude refers to the size of the peaks and troughs of a cycle (Figure 7.2).

---

[1] Data from the U.S. Department of Agriculture suggest that total U.S. agricultural exports declined about 15% over the 1997–1999 period.

There is considerable debate whether price cycles natually exist in agriculture. Tomek and Robinson (1990) note that there is some evidence that a cycle in the cattle market lasts about 10–12 years. That is, it takes about 10–12 years for cattle prices to move from higher prices to lower prices and back to higher prices again. However, cyclical behavior may be a spurious reflection of changes in supply and demand which manifest themselves over long time periods as cycles.[2] Given the controversy over whether cycles actually exist or are a product of external forces, we will note their possibility and move on to more pressing matters.

7.1.1   Trend Analysis

The purpose of analyzing trends is not just to provide a graphical representation of what we already know. That is, we don't need a trendline in Figure 7.1 to know that prices are moving downward. Rather, we use trends to help us develop an expectation about what *may* happen in the future. The trendline in Figure 7.1 is a simple linear trend, which can be represented by the regression equation

$$P_t = \alpha + \beta t + \varepsilon, \tag{7.1}$$

where t is time ($t = 1, 2, 3, \ldots, n$) and ε is the random error term.[3] The linear trend is intuitive and visually easy to understand, hence its popularity with practitioners. However, consider the situation in Figure 7.3. We see a relationship where the linear trend (marked T in the figure) would lead to an expectation that prices would continue higher (that is, the linear trend overpredicts price in later time periods). However, a logarithmic trend[4] provides a more accurate picture of the price trend. As important as the predictive power is the interpretation of the two trends. As mentioned, the linear trend suggests prices are trending upward at a constant rate. The logarithmic trend, by contrast, suggests prices are increasing at a decreasing rate. Would your management decision be different if you thought prices were increasing constantly rather than if they were increasing at a decreasing rate?

The primary advantage of trend analysis of this type is that it is easy to implement. It is objective in the sense that the most appropriate trend is determined by the data.[5] That is, as in Figure 7.3, the logarithmic trend better describes the price behavior than the linear trend, the difference in explanatory power being a function of the price behavior, not the researcher's judgment.[6] The reported trends do not, however, provide us with a decision

---

[2] Some use a "cobweb" model of the farm sector to explain potential cyclical behavior (Tomek and Robinson, 1990). However, the cobweb model has generally been dismissed as too simplistic to adequately represent economic behavior. Nevertheless, the cobweb model is still a popular model. See Tomek and Robinson (1990) for a discussion.

[3] Many popular spreadsheet programs will plot linear and other forms of trendlines automatically. While convenient, it is useful to know the mechanics of trend estimation.

[4] A logarithmic trend is $P_t = \alpha + \beta \ln t + \varepsilon$.

[5] Other examples of functional forms for trends are power functions, exponential functions, and polynomials.

[6] Recall that a regression model attempts to minimize the sum of the squared errors between the prediction and the actual data. Comparison between the linear and logarithmic trends would reveal a higher R^2 value

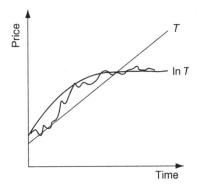

Figure 7.3 The difference between a logarithmic and a linear trend.

rule about how to evaluate the price movements. That is, where on the logarithmic trend should one sell the crop?

7.1.2 Moving Averages

Another popular method of analyzing trends is through moving averages. Moving averages get their name because they are averages of price series for a given period of time that "rolls" forward through time. Consider the following three-period average in Figure 7.4:

$$\bar{x}_1 = \frac{x_1 + x_2 + x_3}{3}. \tag{7.2}$$

Now, we can roll the average forward one period:

$$\bar{x}_2 = \frac{x_2 + x_3 + x_4}{3}. \tag{7.3}$$

Note the difference between Equations 7.2 and 7.3. In Equation 7.2, the average covers periods 1, 2, and 3, while in Equation 7.3 the average covers 2, 3, and 4. Thus, each successive period reflects the information contained within the three most recent prices. Figure 7.4 shows the construction of a three-month average from the monthly corn price data found in Table 7.1 in a spreadsheet environment. Equations used in the spreadsheet are noted in the table.

Length of Average

There are different lengths of moving averages, each providing different information. First, there are short-term moving averages such as the three-month moving average

---

and lower root mean square percentage error for the logarithmic trend relative to the linear trend. Thus, the conclusion that the logarithmic trend is a better representation of the data is made on statistical (objective) rather than subjective grounds.

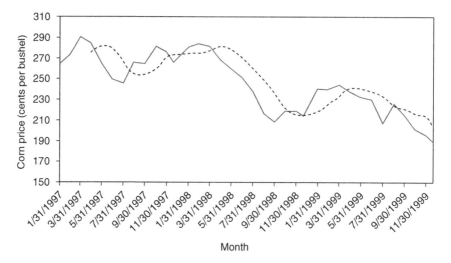

Figure 7.4 The monthly corn price and the three-month moving average corn price, 1997–1999.

Table 7.1 A spreadsheet calculation of a three-month moving average of corn prices

Date	Price	Three-month average
1/31/1997	264.205	
2/28/1997	272.934	
3/31/1997	290.237	
4/30/1997	284.58	275.79 ″=(264.205+272.934+290.237)/3
5/30/1997	264.44	282.58 ″=(272.934+290.237+284.58)/3
6/30/1997	249.488	279.75 ″=(290.237+284.58+264.44)/3
7/31/1997	245.5	266.17 ″=(284.58+264.44+249.488)/3
8/29/1997	265.94	253.14 ″=(264.44+249.488245.5)/3
9/30/1997	264.214	253.64 ″=(249.488+245.5+265.94)/3

shown in Figure 7.4 (the three-month average is the dashed line in the figure).[7] Because the length of the average is short, the average changes relatively quickly as price changes. Thus, the short-term average is ideal for rapidly identifying shifts in the direction of movement of price. However, because the short-term average is more sensititive to price changes, it is more prone to identifying random fluctuations, which can mask longer-term trends.

One can also use longer-term moving averages as well. For example, Figure 7.5 shows a three- and six-month moving average (the three-month is the small dashed line and the six-month is the larger dashed line). Because the six-month average is over a longer

---

[7] "Short-term" is subjective and relative to the interval of measurement of the data. For example, the interval of measurement in Figure 7.4 is monthly, so a short-term average is presented as a three-month average. If the data were daily, we might be interested in a three-day moving average.

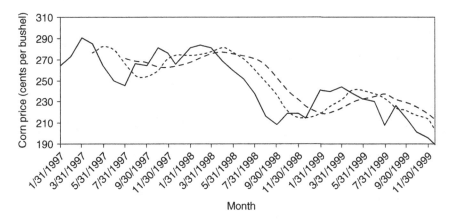

Figure 7.5 The monthly corn price and the three- and six-month moving average corn prices, 1997–1999.

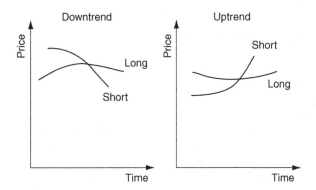

Figure 7.6 Analysis using the intersection of long- and short-term trendlines.

period, it is less responsive to short-term changes in price. It does, however, detect the more general movement of prices. Because these two averages provide different types of information about price changes, we can use them in conjunction with one another to make predictions about price changes over time.

Analysis Using Moving Averages

The relationship between the short- and long-term trendlines may be useful in gathering information about potential shifts in the direction of movement of prices. We analyze these situations based on the intersections of the short- and long-term moving averages. Recall that the short-term average is more sensitive to random fluctuations in price. However, when a short-term average crosses a longer-term average, it is more likely that a shift in the trend has occurred. Consider the situations depicted in Figure 7.6.

In the first panel, the short-term moving average is intersecting the long-term moving average from above. Because the short-term average is more responsive to price, it will begin to move downward as prices move downward before the longer-term trend. If the

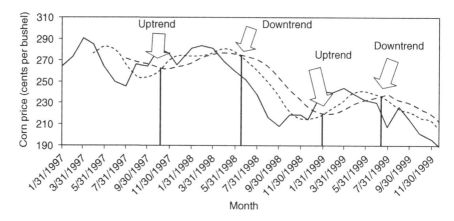

Figure 7.7   Using trend analysis to evaluate changes in monthly corn prices, 1997–1999.

short-term average intersects the longer-term average from above, the result is a signal that the market price is making a significant downward movement. The opposite is true for when the short-term trend intersects that longer-term trend from below (the second panel). In this case, the market is on an uptrend.

Thus, we can use the same data as in Figure 7.5 to analyze changes in price using our trend analysis as in Figure 7.7. The first intersection occurs in October 1997 and the short-term average is intersecting the long-term average from below, signalling an uptrend in prices. As you can see, the underlying monthly prices were on an uptrend and continued on an uptrend after the point of intersection. Then in May 1998, the short-term average intersected the long-term average from above, indicating that a downtrend was in progress. Again, the downtrend did occur and continued beyond the point of intersection. Then, the market turned around and began an uptrend and relatively quickly turned back into a downtrend. Both of these changes in trend were signaled by the moving averages.

Figure 7.7 does point to two relative weaknesses in trend analysis. First, in all cases, the moving averages did not indicate a change in the direction of movement in prices until after the changes had occurred. This result arises from the fact that we are using averages of past prices to get an indication of current price. Thus, the moving average naturally "lags" behind actual price movements. Second, when the price frequently changes direction, as occurred in the later part of the period in Figure 7.7, the moving averages will indicate a frequent change in direction. Thus, when markets move "sideways" (that is, often change direction, but do not move in one direction or the other by large amounts or for long periods of time), trend analysis does not help us predict price changes well. Finally, trend analysis is useful in providing an indication of the direction of change of prices, but tells us little about the duration of the likely trend or the magnitude of potential price changes. We will return to the issue of price forecasting later in the chapter and examine methods of deriving more quantitative predications about price changes through time.

Key Questions

1. What factors contribute to the formation of trends in prices?
2. What is the difference between a trend and a cycle?

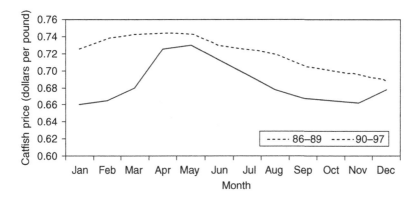

Figure 7.8 The seasonal variation in farm-level catfish prices for two different periods, 1986–1989 and 1990–1997.

3. How do you analyze trends?
4. How can trend analysis be used to predict price changes?

7.2 Seasonality

Seasonality is a type of trend that occurs in agricultural products that emanates, at least in part, from the fact that agricultural production is a biological process. That is, for many products, there are discrete planting times and harvest times, with lags between the time the crop is harvested and consumed. In livestock and other live animal products, seasonality may also be present because of peaks in production due to biological processes such as calving seasons or harvest times for fish (Buguk, Hudson, and Hanson, 2003). For example, Figure 7.8 shows the seasonal patterns in U.S. catfish prices. The figure shows two distinct time periods: 1986–1989 and 1990–1997. Consider first the time period 1986–1989. Price begins to rise, on average, in early spring and summer. This increase in price is due primarily to two factors. First, early spring is important for religious holidays such as Lent, where fish is the primary source of food protein for consumption. At the same time, in the earlier years of catfish production, late spring and summer were the periods with the least amount of harvest because of the growth period for the fish. Thus, the seasonal pattern is pronounced and easily detected.

Technological and genetic development, however, has allowed catfish to become more or less continuously harvested, thus dampening the seasonal variation in fish harvest. In addition, catfish consumption has grown from a regional basis (the Southeast) to a national basis, which changes the dynamics of the consuming population. Thus, an examination of the second time period (1990–1997) reveals that while the general peak in prices in the spring is still apparent, the seasonal trend has flattened out and is less pronounced.[8] The results in Figure 7.9 show that while seasonal trends are persistent,

---

[8] It is important to note that the average prices over the 1990–1997 period were higher than the average prices over the 1986–1989 period, which leads to the average price line being higher for the former than the latter period. This is not a result of seasonality, but a difference in the overall price level.

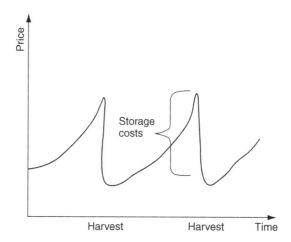

Figure 7.9 The seasonal price pattern and storage costs for seasonally produced, storable products.

the magnitude of the seasonality may change through time as a result of technology or shifts in consumption patterns.

7.2.1   Normal Backwardation

For storable commodities that are seasonally produced, there is a normal pattern of prices over time, called **normal backwardation**. Normal backwardation occurs when, after harvest, the price of the product increases through time until the next harvest, but the price differences between successive periods are insufficient to cover the cost of storage (Carter, Rausser, and Schmitz, 1983; Kolb, 1992). It is often thought that in the case of normal backwardation hedgers must pay speculators a premium for the risk of price changes over time, leading to price differences over time that are slightly below the cost of storage. For a "well functioning" [9] market, the difference between the price at any point in time after harvest and the harvest time price should equal the storage cost from harvest to that point in time (Figure 7.9). This type of market is called **contango** (sounds like a dance!) (Keynes, 1930). For example, assume that corn is harvested in August. The price of corn in November is likely to be higher than in August, but only by the amount of the cost to store the corn from August to November if the market is exhibiting contango. Why is this likely to be so?

Example 7.1 *Assume that the price of corn in August is $2.30 per bushel. The cost of storage is $0.10 per bushel per month. Someone is offering a contract for delivery of corn in November at $2.80 per bushel. What do you do?*

---

[9]"Well functioning" is taken to mean that markets efficiently and accurately reflect the supply and demand conditions in the market and that there are no structural or informational barriers to the efficient determination of prices (a heroic assumption by some standards).

If the cost of storage is $0.10 per bushel per month, you could purchase corn in August and hold it to November at a cost of $2.30 + ($0.10 * 4) = $2.70 per bushel and sell it for $2.80 per bushel. With this price available in the market, others would arbitrage this market until there were sufficient supply being contracted for delivery in November, and the offered price would be lowered to $2.70 per bushel (in order not to attract any more suppliers). Thus, the arbitrage would force the price for later months to equal the harvest time price plus storage costs.

In some cases, the price for future delivery is less than the current price, or an **inverted market**. Why would the market signal that is prefers current consumption to storage? One reason might be that current supplies are insufficient to cover current consumption. In this case, the market would prefer that no product be stored for future consumption. Also, the market may expect a large crop in the next period. In that case, there would be little need to carry stocks forward in time. Expectations about the relationship between current and future prices (inverted market, normal backwardation, or contango) have important implications for decision-making and can be used to determine potential storage and marketing decisions (Isengildina et al., 2000).

Key Questions

1. What is seasonality and what causes seasonality?
2. Can seasonal patterns change? Why?
3. What is normal backwardation? What is contango? What is an inverted market?

7.3   Price Forecasting

The "crystal ball" mentioned at the beginning of this chapter is a matter of intense interest to most economic agents. You might even find yourself anxiously awaiting to read the secrets to the road to the city of gold (yeah, right!). But, alas, as you will see below, there is no magic recipe for success.[10] However, we will see that there are systematic procedures for developing quantitative forecasts.

7.3.1   Forecasting Basics[11]

There are several important points to remember when considering forecasting models and as you proceed through the following sections. First, you are attempting to construct a forecast, not an explanatory model. That is, an explanatory (or structural) model is

---

[10]This, of course, is excluding Hillary Clinton, who purportedly turned $10,000 into $100,000 in the cattle futures market in just 10 months! Anderson and Jackson (1994) reported the probability of such a windfall at about one in 31 trillion!

[11]In this section, we are not going to address the time series properties of forecasting models, such as the order of integration or autocorrelation. However, if one intends on actively pursuing forecasting models, careful additional study of time series properties is necessary. See Greene (2000) or any other standard econometrics textbook for a discussion of these types of models and statistical properties.

Table 7.2   OLS estimates of catfish price forecasts ($R^2 = 0.9332$)

ANOVA	df	Sum of squares	Mean square	F-value
Regression	1	0.719598	0.719598	2039.638*
Residual	146	0.051510	0.000353	
Total	147	0.771108		
	Coefficient	Standard error	t-value	
Intercept	0.024197	0.015311	1.58	
P_{t-1}	0.966023	0.021390	45.16*	

*Statistically significant at the 0.01 level.

contructed as follows:

$$Y_t = f(X_t).$$

If Y and X occur at the same point in time, t, is it possible to forecast the value of Y from the value of X? The answer, of course, is no. You do not know what the value of X is until after Y has been established. Thus, you cannot use X to predict the value of Y ahead of time. Thus, in order to develop a usable forecasting model, we must use past values of the independent variables (X's) to forecast the value for Y. In terms of prices, the simplest form of a forecast is a naive expectations model:

$$P_{t+1} = \alpha + \beta P_t + \varepsilon \tag{7.4}$$

or

$$P_t = \alpha + \beta P_{t-1} + \varepsilon. \tag{7.5}$$

Equations 7.4 and 7.5 (which are essentially equivalent) suggest that the price in the next period will be a function of the price in the previous period.[12] This is called "naive" because it is relying solely on the previous period's price to establish an expectation about the next period's price. However, the real strength of this type of model is that it is simple to execute and requires only the price series for which you are interested.

A simple example using monthly catfish farm-level prices from 1986 to 1998 will help illustrate this concept. Equation 7.5 was estimated using ordinary least squares and the results are shown in Table 7.2.

As can be seen, the coefficient on the lagged price is statistically significant, suggesting that current price is related to past prices, as would be expected. In fact, given the magnitude of the estimated coefficient (0.966), the relationship between current and past price is very close to a one-for-one relationship. If we plot the forecasted price against

---

[12] A special case of this model forms what is known as the Efficient Market Hypothesis (EMH) (Fama, 1970). In this case, today's price is an unbiased forecast of tomorrow's price. For this to be true, the condition of $\alpha = 0$, $\beta = 1$, and $\varepsilon \sim N(0, \sigma^2)$ would have to be true, and prices would follow a "random walk." That is, there is no effective way to predict tomorrow's price from today's price because movements from today's price, ε, are random. We will use the concept of unbiasedness below to test our forecasts.

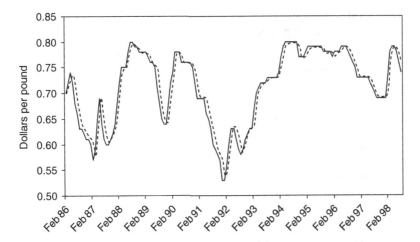

Figure 7.10 The actual (solid line) and forecasted (dashed line) monthly farm-level catfish prices, naive expectations model, 1986–1998.

the actual price (Figure 7.10), we see that the forecasted price closely resembles the actual price. The figure shows that the naive expectations model does a reasonable job of predicting the movements in catfish prices. However, the forecast (dotted line) appears to be a reflection of the actual prices, with the line appearing to predict changes one period after it has happened. This is because of the simple one-period lag structure in the model. However, as is evidenced from Figure 7.10, the forecast created by the model is a reasonable predictor of actual price changes.[13]

7.3.2   Distributed-Lag Models

A weakness of the naive expectations model is that, as we have seen in earlier chapters, the biological nature of agricultural production creates lags in production response, and thus, price. In addition, one may argue that the impacts of a change in a supply or demand variable are not immediately reflected in price due to inventories and processing lags. These potential impacts on price determination processes might be useful in predicting future price changes. Yet, the naive model only utilizes the price from the immediately prior period to predict future price.

An alternative to the simple naive model is a **distributed-lag model**, which includes multiple past prices as explanatory variables:

$$P_t = \alpha + \beta_i \sum_{i=1}^{n} P_{t-i} + \varepsilon. \qquad (7.6)$$

---

[13] It is important to note that this is a within-sample forecast. That is, this model has not been used to predict future price changes. We will return to the issue of out-of-sample forecasts later in the chapter.

Table 7.3   An example spreadsheet construction of three lags of catfish prices

Date	Farm price	Lag 1	Lag 2	Lag 3
Jan 86	0.7			
Feb 86	0.7	0.7		
Mar 86	0.72	0.7	0.7	
Apr 86	0.74	0.72	0.7	0.7
May 86	0.72	0.74	0.72	0.7
Jun 86	0.68	0.72	0.74	0.72
Jul 86	0.66	0.68	0.72	0.74
Aug 86	0.63	0.66	0.68	0.72
Sep 86	0.63	0.63	0.66	0.68
Oct 86	0.62	0.63	0.63	0.66
Nov 86	0.61	0.62	0.63	0.63
Dec 86	0.61	0.61	0.62	0.63
Jan 87	0.6	0.61	0.61	0.62
Feb 87	0.57	0.6	0.61	0.61

Table 7.4   OLS estimates of the distributed-lag model of catfish prices ($R^2 = 0.9575$)

ANOVA	df	Sum of squares	Mean square	f-value
Regression	3	0.739036	0.246345	1,087.643*
Residual	145	0.032842	0.000226	
Total	148	0.771878		

	Coefficient	Standard error	t-value
Intercept	0.030293	0.012786	2.36*
P_{t-1}	1.649002	0.080739	20.42*
P_{t-2}	-0.904910	0.139793	-6.47*
P_{t-3}	0.213336	0.081240	2.63*

* Statistically significant at the 0.01 level.

For example, a model with three lags is

$$P_t = \alpha + \beta_1 P_{t-1} + \beta_2 P_{t-2} + \beta_3 P_{t-3} + \varepsilon. \tag{7.7}$$

Equation 7.7 suggests that prices from two and three periods ago affect current price as well as the price from the immediate past period. We can construct data on catfish prices used in the previous example to estimate a distributed-lag model as in Table 7.3. "Farm price" in the table represents the farm-level monthly catfish price. Modern spreadsheet programs allow fast and simple control and construction of data sets.

Using these data (for the 1986–1998 period), Equation 7.7 was estimated using ordinary least squares, and the results are shown in Table 7.4.

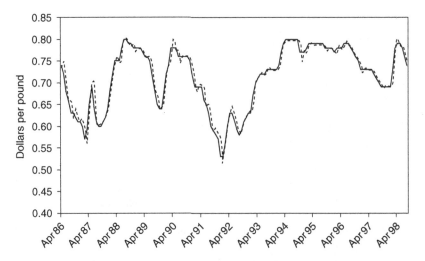

Figure 7.11   The actual (solid line) and forecasted (dashed line) monthly farm-level catfish prices, distributed-lag model, 1986–1998.

As can be seen, all the coefficients on the lagged prices are statistically significant, suggesting that previous lagged prices are affecting current price. This confirms the hypothesis that more than the previous period's price impacts the current price. The R^2 value of 0.9575 suggests that about 95% of the variation in current price is explained by past prices, which is higher than the R^2 observed for the naive model.[14]

Note that the magnitude of the coefficients (in absolute value) decline with successively longer lags. This result suggests that the immediately past period price has the largest impact on current price, with a declining effect as one moves backwards in time. This relationship between the magnitude of the coefficients and the length of the lag is common, but certainly not always the case. Figure 7.11 shows the relationship between actual and forecasted (predicted) prices. The figure shows a similar relationship to that found in Figure 7.10 in that the forecasted prices closely resemble the actual prices. However, in contrast to the naive model, the forecast of the distributed-lag model does not appear as simply a "blurry reflection" of actual prices as with the naive model. Rather, the distributed-lag model tends to more accurately predict changes in direction of prices as they happen as opposed to one period after it happens as in the naive model. Thus, the results shown in Figure 7.11 are a demonstration of the greater explanatory power of the distributed-lag model observed in the higher R^2 value.[15]

In addition to the standard measure of goodness of fit, R^2, there are other tools available to evaluate the effectiveness of the forecast. Implicitly, we have been evaluating our forecasts to this point by looking at **turning points**. That is, we are examining whether

---

[14] The adjusted R^2 for the distributed-lag model is higher as well, which accounts for the added explanatory variables. Three lags are used here in this model. However, there are specific procedures for determining optimal lag length. See Greene (2000) for an introduction.

[15] It is important to note here that we are making a qualitative judgment based on the visual evidence. There are specific econometric tests to analyze whether the distributed-lag model actually produces statistically superior results. We will not address those here, but those of you who wish to employ forecasting techniques in practice should explore those testing methods.

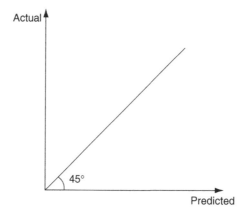

Figure 7.12   The relationship between unbiased predicted and actual prices.

a change in direction of the actual price is effectively predicted by the forecast. While visual inspection of this type gives us an intuitive feel for how the forecast model is performing, turning points do not give us a solid statistical conclusion about whether the forecast is accurate.

A key test of whether a forecast model is performing well is whether the forecast is an unbiased predictor of the actual price. **Unbiasedness** is a statistical term with a very specific meaning. In general, it means that the predicted and actual price are equal, on average. Mathematically:

$$E\left(P_t - \hat{P}_t\right) = 0,$$

or the expected[16] difference between the actual and predicted price is zero. In Figure 7.12, at any level of price, the predicted is equal to the actual price, resulting in a 45° line between the two prices indicating unbiasedness. That is, in the equation

$$P_t = \alpha + \beta \hat{P}_t + \varepsilon, \tag{7.8}$$

the $\alpha = 0$ and $\beta = 1$ results in a 45° line. Thus, if we were to regress the forecasted price on the actual price and the resulting coefficient for the intercept, α, were equal to zero and the coefficient on the slope, β, were equal to one, we could conclude that the forecasted price was an unbiased predictor of the actual price.

Using the predicted prices from the distributed-lag model, this test for unbiasedness was conducted and the results are shown in Table 7.5. Clearly, the intercept term, α, is not significantly different from zero. One may be tempted to conclude that β is significantly different from one, because it is statistically significant in Table 7.5. However, that t value is based on the null hypothesis that $\beta = 0$. To test for significant difference from one, the following formula is used:

$$t = \frac{1 - 0.999998}{0.017387} = 0.000115.$$

---

[16]Recall that in mathematics/statistics, the expectations operator, E, refers to the average.

Table 7.5 A test for unbiasedness of the distributed-lag forecast ($R^2 = 0.9575$)

ANOVA	df	Sum of squares	Mean square	f-value
Regression	1	0.739036	0.739036	3,307.934*
Residual	147	0.032842	0.000223	
Total	148	0.771878		

	Coefficient	Standard errpr	t-value
Intercept	−0.0000006	0.012446	−0.00005
$\hat{P}_t$	0.999998	0.017387	57.51464*

*Statistically significant at the 0.01 level.

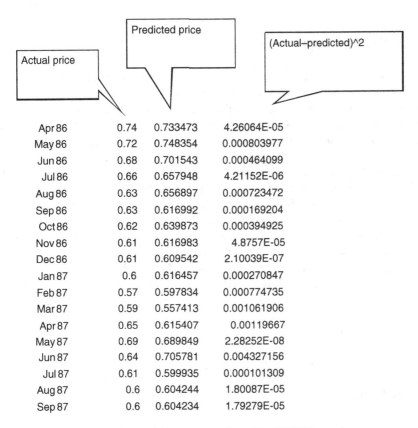

	Actual price	Predicted price	(Actual−predicted)^2
Apr 86	0.74	0.733473	4.26064E-05
May 86	0.72	0.748354	0.000803977
Jun 86	0.68	0.701543	0.000464099
Jul 86	0.66	0.657948	4.21152E-06
Aug 86	0.63	0.656897	0.000723472
Sep 86	0.63	0.616992	0.000169204
Oct 86	0.62	0.639873	0.000394925
Nov 86	0.61	0.616983	4.8757E-05
Dec 86	0.61	0.609542	2.10039E-07
Jan 87	0.6	0.616457	0.000270847
Feb 87	0.57	0.597834	0.000774735
Mar 87	0.59	0.557413	0.001061906
Apr 87	0.65	0.615407	0.00119667
May 87	0.69	0.689849	2.28252E-08
Jun 87	0.64	0.705781	0.004327156
Jul 87	0.61	0.599935	0.000101309
Aug 87	0.6	0.604244	1.80087E-05
Sep 87	0.6	0.604234	1.79279E-05

Figure 7.13 An example of spreadsheet construction of the RMSPE equation.

Thus, because $0.000115 < 1.96$, we would conclude that β is not significantly different than one. Given that $\alpha = 0$ and $\beta = 1$, we conclude that the forecast created by the distributed-lag model is an unbiased predictor of the current farm-level catfish price.

In addition to the unbiasedness of the forecast, we should also be concerned about the relative error in the forecast. There are a number of statistical tests and measures that can be used to examine forecast error, but a relatively common and simple test is the **root**

mean square percentage error (RMSPE), which is given by the following equation:

$$RMSPE = \sqrt{\frac{1}{n} \sum_{i=1}^{n} \left(\frac{\hat{P}_t - P_t}{P_t}\right)^2} * 100, \tag{7.9}$$

where n is the number of observations in the data set. The formula looks complicated, but is surprisingly easy to calculate in a spreadsheet. After constructing the $((\hat{P}_t - P_t)/P_t)^2$ portion, you would simply sum that column and take the square root.[17] Applying the RMSPE formula to our distributed-lag model indicates that the distributed-lag model exhibits 1.486% error, on average. There is no magic number for the RMPSE, but certainly a number closer to zero indicates lower forecast error. An example of the spreadsheet calculation is shown in Figure 7.13.

7.3.3   Out-of-Sample Forecasts

To this point, we have been utilizing the entire series of data to develop a forecasting model. However, this approach does not tell us how well our forecasting model will perform in the future. To accomplish this, we use a technique called **out-of-sample forecasting**. That is, we have a sample of data (our time series). However, we have no real means of assessing whether our model will effectively predict prices tomorrow (a data point that is not in our sample).

To accomplish this test, we can simply divide our data in half. We use the first half of the data to estimate our forecasting model, "pretending" that the second half of the data has not occurred yet (that is, we are acting as if we are standing at a point in time that is halfway through our time series). We then use our forecasting model to predict the second half of the data set and evaluate how well the forecasting model performs.

Continuing with our catfish example, the data were divided in half and the distributed-lag model was estimated using the first half of the data (Table 7.6).

The results look similar to those found in Table 7.4, but the explanatory power of the model is lower, which would be expected with fewer observations. Now, using the estimated equation in Table 7.6, we can forecast the second half of the data set, which appears in Figure 7.14. Note that in Figure 7.14 the forecast line (the dotted line) does not start until halfway through the period in the figure. As can be seen, the same general relationship exists between the forecasted and actual price as seen in previous figures, suggesting that the forecast performed well in predicting the future prices *out of sample*. This result suggests that this forecast model would perform well in predicting future prices.[18]

Key Questions

1. What are the weaknesses of price forecasts?
2. What are naive expectations?

---

[17]Note that the calculation is the actual minus the predicted in Figure 7.13. It does not matter which term is subtracted from which, because the resulting difference is squared.

[18]In a complete analysis, we would need to perform the test for unbiasedness and the RMSPE on the out-of-sample forecast to examine forecasting effectiveness.

Table 7.6 OLS estimates of the distributed-lag model of catfish prices (half sample) ($R^2 = 0.9397$)

ANOVA	df	Sum of squares	Mean square	f-value
Regression	3	0.361182	0.120394	342.568*
Residual	66	0.023195	0.000351	
Total	69	0.384377		
	Coefficient	Standard error	t-value	
Intercept	0.032638	0.023842	1.37	
P_{t-1}	1.617409	0.120478	13.42*	
P_{t-2}	-0.852920	0.211099	-4.04*	
P_{t-3}	0.186275	0.126370	1.47	

*Statistically significant at the 0.01 level.

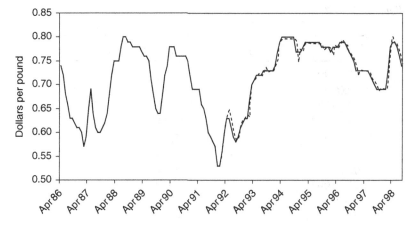

Figure 7.14 Actual (solid line) and forecasted (dashed line) monthly farm-level catfish prices, distributed-lag model, out of sample forecast, 1986–1998.

3. What is a distributed-lag model?
4. How do we evaluate forecasts?
5. What is out-of-sample forecasting?

7.4 Summary

As can be seen by the length and complexity of this chapter, price variation through time is of considerable interest to economists. The information contained within price changes through time can be used to develop expectations about future changes in price. In addition, the price changes themselves tell us something about the underlying economic variables of supply and demand. Seasonal patterns in price are a function of the biological production process and the ability to store (or not store) a commodity through time. While seasonal patterns are generally predictable, the prices through time generally reflect storage costs, implying that profiting (in an economic sense) from that predictability is generally not possible.

Understanding trends and cycles leads to an understanding of price dynamics, which can be employed in developing forecasting models. As we have seen, forecasting models can be developed that perform well in forecasting price changes in markets. Increasing the complexity of the model (e.g., a naive expectations model versus a distributed-lag model) *generally* leads to more accurate estimates. However, with increasing accuracy, there is increasing statistical complexity and the requirements on access to data are heavier. This chapter has only broached the subject of forecasting. There is a vast literature on forecasting methods that you are encouraged to explore.

Exercises

Problem 7.1 *Using the following set of data, construct a linear trendline and a logarithmic trendline.*

Date	Monthly average corn price (cents per bushel)
1/31/1997	263.75
2/28/1997	271.776
3/31/1997	289.413
4/30/1997	285.205
5/30/1997	265.524
6/30/1997	249.976
7/31/1997	243.33
8/29/1997	265.929
9/30/1997	264.631
10/31/1997	280.022
11/28/1997	276.211
12/19/1997	267.217
1/30/1998	280.45
2/27/1998	283.684
3/31/1998	280.989
4/30/1998	269.333
5/29/1998	260.275
6/30/1998	250.295
7/31/1998	238.648
8/31/1998	217.024
9/30/1998	207.631
10/30/1998	217.841
11/30/1998	218.762
12/21/1998	215.333

Problem 7.2 *Using the data above, calculate three-month and six-month moving averages and plot them against the original data. Identify signals for up- and downtrends on the basis of the moving averages.*

Problem 7.3 *Using the data above, estimate naive expectations and distributed-lag (two lags) models. Test for the unbiasedness of the forecasts of both models and calculate the RMPSE for both models. Be sure to plot the actual results and forecasts on graphs and examine turning points.*

References

Anderson, S. and J. Jackson. "A Note on the Odds in the Cattle Futures Market." *Journal of Economics and Finance*, 18(1994): 357–365.

Buguk, C., D. Hudson, and T. Hanson. "Price Volatility Spillover in Agricultural Markets: The Case of U.S. Catfish Markets." *Journal of Agricultural and Resource Economics*, 28(2003): 86–99.

Carter, C., G. Rausser, and A. Schmitz. "Efficient Asset Portfolios and the Theory of Normal Backwardation." *Journal of Political Economy*, 91(1983): 319–331.

Fama, E. "Efficient Capital Markets: A Review of Theory and Empirical Work." *Journal of Finance*, 25(1970): 383–417.

Greene, W. *Econometric Analysis*, fourth edition. Prentice Hall, Upper Saddle River, NJ, 2000.

Isengildina, O., D. Hudson, O. Cleveland, and B. Herndon. "Using a Cotton Options Strategy to Increase Revenues." *Proceedings of the Beltwide Cotton Conferences*, Volume I, 2000, pp. 315–319.

Keynes, J. *A Treatise of Money Volume II: Applied Theory of Money.* Macmillan, London, 1930.

Kolb, R. "Is Normal Backwardation Normal?" *Journal of Futures Markets*, 12(1992): 75–91.

Tomek, W. and K. Robinson. *Agricultural Product Prices*, third edition. Cornell University Press, Ithaca, NY, 1990.

Chapter 8

Product Quality

~

In the preceding chapters, we have operated under the assumption that the product under question was of homogeneous quality. However, casual observation tells us that quality is not homogeneous. Every steer in a pen of cattle, every steak, every tomato, and so on, has quality differences. Some of these differences are minute and unobserved, making one specimen of a product virtually indistinguishable from any other specimen. Many quality attributes are observable, however, making each specimen different. For example, some steaks have more marbling[1] than others, which leads to taste differences in the steaks. Also, some cotton has longer fibers, called staple length, which affects the textile processing of cotton into yarns and fabrics. This theory of demand based on quality is called **hedonic price theory**. From an empirical perspective, there is ample evidence to suggest that consumers factor product quality into consumption decisions and, therefore, quality has an impact on price. However, from a theoretical perspective, there is some inconsistency between hedonic and neoclassical theory. The most important distinction is that neoclassical theory is based on quantity while hedonic theory is based on quality. While the two theories are not mutually exclusive, they are not easily combined.

In this chapter, we explore how product quality affects prices, and therefore demand, for a product. We begin by exploring hedonic price theory and present the basic distinctions between the neoclassical model and the theory of the impacts of quality. Then, we explore the tools used to estimate the effects of quality on price.

8.1 The Impacts of Quality on Price

8.1.1 Observability

A core concept related to product quality is the observability of the product quality. That is, can the consumer recognize the quality difference between two products?

---

[1]Marbling is the intramuscular fat in the meat, not the fat that is around the steak.

Example 8.1 *Assume that a consumer is examining two tomatoes. Both tomatoes appear to be plump, red, ripe, and of equal size. However, one tomato is of a variety in which the amount of seeds is reduced and the amount of tomato meat is increased, while the other is of an ordinary variety. If the consumer has no information about the varieties (and cannot examine the interior of the tomato), there is no way for the consumer to know the difference until after the good has been purchased.*

By contrast, there are situations in which the differences are obvious:

Example 8.2 *Assume that a consumer is examining two automobiles. The consumer can observe the characteristics of the size of engine, number of doors, color, and so on. In this case, the consumer can easily distinguish between the automobiles and make a choice as to which one is preferred.*

In many cases, consumers of agricultural products cannot distinguish between different products easily. We may be able to try the tomato out or search out additional information, but these activities come at a cost. That is, there is a *transactions cost* associated with either purchasing and trying it or searching out additional information. To counter this cost, many agricultural products have "grades," or official indications of quality. For example, most consumers are not aware of how to evaluate meat quality. The U.S. Department of Agriculture posts grades for each cut of meat found in the grocery store. The consumer can examine the quality grade—Standard, Choice, Prime—and make a decision about the preferred quality grade without having to have extensive knowledge of the grading system. This lowers the transactions cost of purchasing goods of different qualities and allows a refinement in the consumer's decision about quality that was not previously present.

Another method of conveying information about product quality is labeling (Nimon and Beghin, 1999; Kim, Nayga, and Capps, 2001). Labels identify key features of a product that may or may not be observable. For example, nutritional labels provide information on calories, vitamins, minerals, fat content, and so on. To the extent that people are concerned about health effects, the nutritional content will affect an individual's willingness to purchase a product at a given price. Labels may also convey information about how a product is produced. "Nongenetically modified product" or "dolphin-safe tuna" are examples. These types of labels do not convey information about the product, *per se*, but do provide information relating to the product that consumers may value.

Whatever the method of conveying the information—direct observation, grades, or labels—the consumer must be able to recognize a difference in quality before any price differential associated with quality will arise. If the difference is not observable, it becomes a situation of a distinction without a difference. That is, if the consumer cannot observe a difference, he or she will not be willing to pay for that difference. The second criterion that must be met for a difference in price is a difference in the level of consumer satisfaction arising from the different qualities.

8.1.2 Utility Differences

Suppose now that there are observable differences in quality. The question then becomes "Given quality differences, do consumers derive different levels of utility from those different qualities?" This is consistent with asking whether consumers are willing to pay different prices for different qualities. The concept of deriving utility from the attributes or qualities of a good was formalized by Lancaster (1966) and later extended by Rosen (1974). We begin by assuming that each product has a quoted market price and is composed of a set of quality characteristics, z, such that the good has a market price function:

$$p(z) = p(z_1, \ldots, z_n), \qquad (8.1)$$

which relates the price of the good to its characteristics. The price represents the hedonic (or implicit) price function (we will show this graphically in a moment). Following Rosen (1966) we define utility as follows:

$$U(x, z_1, z_2, \ldots, z_n). \qquad (8.2)$$

We assume that consumers purchase one unit of a good with a particular value, z, and that x is all other goods consumed.[2] We maximize utility subject to a budget constraint, which requires choosing x and $(z_1, z_2, \ldots, z_n)$ to satisfy the budget and the first-order conditions:

$$\frac{\partial p}{\partial z_i} = p_i = \frac{U_{z_i}}{U_x}, \quad i = 1, \ldots, n. \qquad (8.3)$$

Maximum utility is derived by purchasing a product offering with the desired combination of characteristics. We can define a family of indifference curves, $\theta(z; u)$, which identifies the trade-offs the consumer is willing to make between income (or money forgone) and a particular attribute (while holding the level of utility, u, constant). We note that the producer faces a symmetrical problem of chosing which attributes to produce, called $\phi(z; \pi)$.[3] Given the consumer and producer's indifference curves (called bid and offer curves), we can visualize the interaction in the marketplace as in Figure 8.1. The consumers and producers interact in the marketplace to establish the market price for a given quality attribute, z (the implicit price function). It is important to note that this price is often not observed in the market. That is, the market price for a good in the market is a *composite* of the implicit prices.

Example 8.3 *Assume that consumers value a V6 engine at $6,000, but value a V8 engine at $9,000. We do not observe either the $6,000 or $9,000 in the marketplace. Rather, we observe that a car with a set of attributes and a V6 engine costs $22,000 and a car with the same attributes except that it has a V8 engine costs $25,000.*

Based on the above example, then, we would conclude that the implicit price function defines the *difference* in prices between two goods. From this, we gather two important

---

[2] Herein lies part of the distinction between the neoclassical model and the hedonic model—the consumer is purchasing only one unit. Rosen extends his model to a "second stage," which represents the general supply and demand for characteristics. However, a more cohesive combination of hedonic and neoclassical theory remains elusive.

[3] We are skipping the producer's decision here to preserve clarity and maintain focus on the consumer. However, the producer's decision is equally important. You should examine Rosen (1974) for the underlying theory and/or Hudson, Ethridge and Segarra (1998) for a practical application.

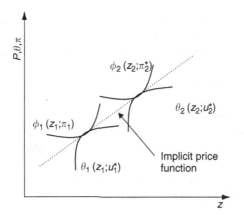

Figure 8.1 The derivation of the implicit price function from bid and offer curves for quality.

pieces of information. First, we are able to understand the marginal value that consumers place on different quality attitudes. Second, we are able to make predictions about the difference in price between two goods based on their quality.

8.1.3 Product Marketing and Quality

Given the above, it should be obvious that product quality will be an issue in the marketplace. On the consumer level, we can clearly see that product quality affects how consumers value products by their attributes, and so marketers attempts to fill those demands with products of different quality and with different prices. Fresh, vine-ripened tomatoes generally cost more than "greenhouse" tomatoes, and choice steak generally costs more than select steak. This form of product marketing allows consumers to select the quality of goods that maximizes their utility subject to their budget constraint.

Less obvious, however, is the amount of quality differentiation that takes place within an agricultural supply chain before it even reaches the customer. For example, oranges may be sold fresh or processed into orange juice and other products. Processors will generally segregate oranges into those of higher quality for the fresh market, and those of lower quality for the processing market. Likewise, sweet potatoes are classified into those that will be sold in fresh markets and those that will be processed into canned goods and processed foods. You probably don't want to purchase a potato that is shaped like a human brain, do you? But this potato is just fine for processing because it tastes the same. In this manner, processors are making choices that you would *likely* make, thereby reserving the highest-valued products for the fresh market.

8.2 Estimation

8.2.1 Data and Model

Empirical investigation into the values consumers place on quality attributes has been wide and varied. Waugh first published an empirical piece on vegetable quality in 1928, but he did not identify it as hedonic price theory. Ethridge and Davis (1982) provide the first empirical application of hedonic price theory in an agricultural setting as it is commonly known today. Since then, there have been numerous applications of hedonics in cotton (Ethridge and Neeper, 1987; Bowman and Ethridge, 1992; Brown et al., 1995) as well as other agricultural commodities and natural resource and real estate applications (Hite et al., 2001).

Many of these applications have one thing in common—they are primarily focused on estimating the marginal implicit prices of the goods under question.[4] These applications can be quite data intensive, as they require individual transactions data on which to estimate the marginal implicit prices.[5] As such, these data sets tend to be quite large. In addition, they are most typically cross-sectional in nature.

The general marginal implicit price function begins with

$$P = f(z_i),$$
(8.4)

where P is the observed transactions price for the good in the market and z_i are the attributes of the good. These models are simply constructed and can often be estimated with ordinary least squares, although the choice of estimation technique is up to the researcher and the problem to be analyzed. The marginal implicit prices are

$$\frac{\partial P}{\partial z_i} = p_i,$$
(8.5)

where p_i is the marginal implicit price of attribute/quality i. These marginal implicit prices are often the ultimate goal of the empirical examination.

A brief empirical example is useful in illustrating this concept. Ethridge and Davis (1982) analyzed the impacts of quality attributes of cotton on cotton price. Cotton is purchased in lots, or groups of bales. Buyers are provided information about the quality of the cotton in the lot by the Agricultural Marketing Service of the U.S. Department of Agriculture, which is the official grader of cotton in the U.S. Ethridge and Davis collected individual transactions data of cotton sales in West Texas from 1976 through 1978. The price of each transaction was regressed against the quality characteristics as follows:

$$P = \beta_0 + \beta_1 G_1 + \beta_2 G_2 + \beta_3 L + \beta_4 M + \beta_5 M^2$$
$$+ \beta_6 LS + \beta_7 VM + \varepsilon,$$
(8.6)

where G_1 and G_2 were average grade codes in the lot, L was the average length of the cotton fiber in the lot, M was a measure of the average fineness and maturity of the fiber in the lot, LS was the number of bales in the lot, and VM was the standard deviation of M within the lot. Without dwelling on the specifics of the cotton market, higher levels

---

[4]A notable exception is the work of Bowman and Ethridge (1992). In this analysis, the authors estimated Rosen's "second-stage" model, which is the market supply and demand for goods with heterogenous qualities. By contrast, most other applications focus on the first-stage estimation of the marginal implicit prices of the attributes of the good.

[5]It is important to note that regression analysis is not the only method to derive marginal implicit prices. For example, linear programming models and simulation methods may also be used. The focus here is on regression analysis because it is the most common method of analysis in the literature.

Table 8.1 Regression results of cotton quality impacts on price[6]

Variable	Parameter estimate	*t*-value
Constant	0.513	NR
G_1	−0.960	−6.83
G_2	−2.270	−15.59
L	0.442	8.89
M	25.971	28.93
M^2	−2.975	−23.10
VM	−2.688	−6.32
LS	0.003	1.69
R^2	0.91	

of G_1 and G_2 are associated with lower-quality cotton. Higher levels of L are associated with higher-quality cotton, and the impact of M on quality depends on the level of M. Thus, M is specified as a quadratic. Larger lot sizes (LS) should increase price, and more variability of quality within the lot (VM) should reduce price.

Table 8.1 shows that all signs are consistent with expectations. For example, the coefficient on G_1 was −0.960, suggesting that increases in the average of that grade code lead to decreases in price. Recall that the marginal implicit price is $\partial p/\partial z_i$, so that the marginal implicit price for G_1 is −0.960.[7] This result suggests that a one unit increase in this grade code will reduce the price of cotton by nearly one cent per pound, on average. You should consider what is the marginal implicit price for M.

8.2.2 Functional Form

As with ordinary demand and supply functions, choice of functional form is important and should be based on both theoretical and statistical foundations. Consider the following. Assume that you are attempting to examine the impact of fiber length and fiber strength on the price of cotton. From a theoretical perspective, there are anticipated impacts of these attributes on the efficiency of textile processing and, thus, the willingness of the textile mill to pay for these qualities. These relationships are depicted in Figure 8.2. What can be seen is that fiber length and strength both provide positive marginal value to textile mills in processing of cotton into yarns and fabrics. This is because increases in both attributes make processing machinery more efficient and, thus, reduce the cost of processing. However, the marginal value decreases as the fiber strength and length increase. That is, the marginal increases in processing efficiency (and cost reduction) decline as these quality attributes increase. Textile mills will be

[6]Results reported are for a generalized least squares model, which was used to correct for autocorrelation. See Ethridge and Davis(1982) for computational details.

[7]As with all regression models, the estimated coefficient and, in this case, the marginal implicit price, is the average marginal implicit price within the sample.

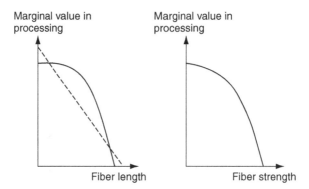

Figure 8.2   Marginal value in processing of cotton to textile mills of cotton fiber length and strength.

willing to pay higher amounts for higher levels of strength and length, but the differential in willingness to pay declines as the level of the attribute increases. Thus, for example, the mill may be willing to pay an extra two cents per pound for a staple length of 34/32nds of an inch relative to 32/32nds of an inch, but would only be willing to pay one cent per pound more for a staple length of 36/32nds of an inch relative to 34/32nds of an inch.

More importantly, this theoretical reasoning indicates that the marginal implicit price functions for fiber strength and length are nonlinear, so a choice of a linear-additive function would be inappropriate in this case. Reseachers must carefully consider these type of theoretical motivations for functional forms if they are to arrive at realistic estimates of marginal implicit prices.

The statistical properties of the functional form are a second set of criteria. We are, of course, concerned with the standard statistical measures such as the goodness of fit. However, Brown and Ethridge (1995) outline a more rigid statistical criteria for functional form choice. In this case, these authors use partial regression analysis of the error terms from the estimated equations to examine functional form choice. By examining the error term, one can tell if there remains a systematic pattern to the error term. If a systematic error exists, this suggests that the model is misspecified. If all theoretically important quality attributes are included in the model, then a systematic pattern in the error term suggests that the functional form of the model is not adequately identifying the patterns within the data.

Using Figure 8.2 as an example, we can see that choosing a linear approximation (the dashed line in the figure) of the nonlinear relationship will result in an error term that underpredicts the marginal implicit price of fiber length in the mid-range of length, and over-predicts the price at high and low levels of length. Using the technique of Brown and Ethridge (1995), we would identify this systematic pattern in the error term and would suggest that we utilize a nonlinear functional form.

8.2.3   Other Issues

Transactions do not typically occur at one point in time. Thus, there is a time dimension to these data. Although this time dimension is often ignored by researchers, there is a fundamental problem that the overall market price level for a particular good changes over time. For example, you may wish to analyze the impacts of beef quality on consumer demand, thereby deriving the marginal implicit prices for beef qualities. However, your transactions data may span a period of several weeks. What happens if the overall price of beef declines or increases over that period? Chen, Ethridge, and Fletcher (1997) demonstrate a method of accounting for these price-level changes in marginal implicit price estimation. By including an overall price of cotton in their model, they captured the effect of the price-level changes, allowing for a more consistent estimation of the marginal implicit prices of cotton quality attributes for textile mills.

8.3   Summary

Hedonic price analysis is a growing field in economics. There is a wide range of potential applications that lend themselves directly to this form of empirical analysis. Agricultural markets are being increasingly characterized by product heterogeneity, as consumers place a greater demand on markets to produce products with specific qualities. Thus, hedonic price analysis will continue to be an important tool in understanding the operation of agricultural markets. We have omitted much of the theoretical subtleties that exist in hedonic price theory and its relationship to the standard neoclassical model. Practitioners should delve into this body of literature to acquaint themselves with the theoretical issues, so that empirical applications produce the most applicable results.

References

Bowman, K. and D. Ethridge. "Characteristic Supplies and Demands in an Hedonic Framework: U.S. Market for Cotton Fiber Attributes." *American Journal of Agricultural Economics*, 74(1992): 992–1,002.

Brown, J. and D. Ethridge. "Functional Form Model Specification: An Application to Hedonic Pricing." *Agricultural and Resource Economics Review*, 24(1995): 166–173.

Brown, J., D. Ethridge, D. Hudson, and C. Engels. "An Automated, Econometric Approach for Estimating and Reporting Daily Cotton Market Prices." *Journal of Agricultural and Applied Economics*, 27(1995): 409–422.

Chen, C., D. Ethridge, and S. Fletcher. "Textile Manufacturers' Market Valuation of Cotton Fiber Attributes." *Journal of Agricultural and Applied Economics*, 29(1997): 185–195.

Ethridge, D. and B. Davis. "Hedonic Price Estimation of Commodities: An Application to Cotton." *Western Journal of Agricultural Economics*, 7(1982): 293–300.

Ethridge, D. and J. Neeper. "Producer Returns from Cotton Fiber Strength and Uniformity: A Hedonic Price Approach." *Southern Journal of Agricultural Economics*, 19(1987): 91–97.

Hite, D., W. Chern, F. Hitzhusen, and A. Randall. "Property Value Impacts of an Environmental Disamenity: The Case of Landfills." *Journal of Real Estate Finance and Economics*, 22(2001): 185–202.

Hudson, D., D. Ethridge, and E. Segarra. "Incorrect Price Information for a Heterogeneous Commodity: A Conceptual Synthesis." *Review of Agricultural Economics*, 20(1998): 363–374.

Kim, S., R. Nayga, and O. Capps, Jr. "Health Knowledge and Consumer Use of Nutritional Labels: The Issue Revisited." *Agricultural and Resource Economics Review*, 30(2001): 10–19.

Lancaster, K. "A New Approach to Consumer Theory." *Journal of Political Economy*, 74(1966): 132–156.

Nimon, W. and J. Beghin. "Are Eco-Labels Valuable? Evidence from the Apparel Industry." *American Journal of Agricultural Economics*, 81(1999): 801–811.

Rosen, S. "Hedonic Prices and Implicit Markets: Product Differentiation in Pure Competition." *Journal of Political Economy*, 82(1974): 34–55.

Waugh, F. "Quality Factors Influencing Vegetable Prices." *Journal of Farm Economics*, 19(1928): 185–196.

Chapter 9

Futures Markets

~

To this point, we have been examining markets for physical products at a particular place or time, or in a particular form. Many basic commodities and products also have markets for *future delivery* of the product at a particular price or place, or in a particular form. These are called **futures markets**. At its most basic level, futures markets are composed of economic agents (individuals or firms), some of whom are willing to purchase today at current prices a product for delivery to them at some defined point in the future, and others who are willing to sell today at current prices the same product for delivery at that same point. Imagine yourself as a feedlot manager somewhere in the Midwest. For management purposes, you would like to know the cost of your feed (primarily, corn) for the next 12 months so that you can plan your business. Would it not be nice if you could purchase corn today, at today's prices which you know with certainty, for delivery in 12 months? Now imagine yourself as a corn farmer in the Midwest. Would it not be nice to be able to sell your crop today before you plant it, so that you will know for certain what price you are going to receive? Both parties would like some degree of certainty about future prices and supply and/or demand. They could develop a contract with one another if they knew each other, but more than likely, they do not. The futures market allows these individuals and many others to participate in a market to accomplish their goals. This chapter will explore the structure and institutions of futures markets, develop basic ideas on the uses and benefits of futures markets, and discuss basic trading principles depending on circumstances.

9.1 Futures Markets and Exchanges

9.1.1 A Brief History

Current futures markets had their beginnings in 1848 with the Chicago Board of Trade, although there is evidence of earlier futures trading in Japan and Europe. Chicago's proximity to the grain-producing areas of the Midwest and the major shipping routes on the Great Lakes made it a prime location to trade grain. As we have seen in previous chapters, cash prices tend to be lowest right after harvest, due to the large supply on the market at that time, and then increase over time as supply is used. In Chicago in the 1800s, there were insufficient storage facilities to hold all the grain from harvest. To encourage storage, traders began offering contracts that guaranteed a price for future delivery of grain to Chicago in order to smooth delivery of grain over longer periods of time (Carter, 2003).

While these contracts were generally well received, many traders were reluctant to trade them because each contract was different, thereby making it difficult to compare contract terms. The Chicago Board of Trade standardized contracts by providing consistency in quantity, quality, and delivery time and location. At this, modern futures trading was born. Today, futures contracts are traded on basic commodities such as corn, cotton, beef, and timber, as well as energy products, metals, financial instruments, and even individual stocks.

Futures contracts are traded on **futures exchanges**, which are organized markets. These exchanges are located around the world. Major exchanges in the United States are in Chicago (the Chicago Board of Trade, or CBOT, and the Chicago Mercantile Exchange, or CME) as well as New York (the New York Mercantile Exchange, or NYMEX, and the New York Board of Trade, or NYBOT), with smaller exchanges in Philadelphia, Kansas City, and Minneapolis. While futures markets have their roots in agricultural commodities, financial futures have far outstripped agricultural futures in terms of volume and growth. Thus, while these exchanges still maintain their presence in agricultural markets, their major focus has changed to financial markets.

9.1.2   The Roles of Futures Markets

Futures markets play several important roles in the economy (Tomek and Robinson, 1990). First, and perhaps most obvious, is **price discovery**. Think about all the times you have heard about the "price" of corn. Often, you are hearing what the price is currently on the futures markets. Because futures markets are fluid, with many buyers and sellers, the prices observed on those markets are used as "the" price. Although we will not discuss the technical details here, you should be aware of something called the **Efficient Market Hypothesis** (or EMH) (for a detailed discussion, see Fama, 1970). This hypothesis holds that all available information about supply, demand, and so on, are reflected in current market prices. As such, today's price on the futures market is the best predictor of future prices and traders cannot earn above a *normal rate of return* from trading. Given the EMH, then, individuals rely on futures markets to "discover" what the potential prices for their products are for future delivery.

A second critical role of futures markets is **risk shifting**. Imagine yourself as a corn farmer in Iowa. You are going to plant a crop in the spring, to be harvested in the fall. You know that the price today is $2.80 per bushel, but what will it be at harvest time? The possibility that the price will change (either positively or negatively) is known as price risk. But, what if you could sell your crop today at $2.80, thereby guaranteeing yourself a price for your crop at harvest?[1] Because futures markets allow you to sell your crop in

---

[1] We are abstracting here from something called "basis," which we will address it a later section.

advance for future delivery, you have shifted the risk of price changes from yourself to the person buying the corn. If the price goes down over the growing season, you have already sold your crop, so you are protected. Of course, the price could go up as well, but by selling early, you have forgone the opportunity for price increases in order to protect against price decreases.[2]

Finally, the ability to shift risk leads to the third primary role of futures markets, which is **facilitating financing**. Now imagine yourself as the banker that will loan the corn farmer above the money to plant their crop. If the farmer does not sell his or her product forward in the futures market, there is no guarantee of the price he or she will receive at harvest, and therefore, no guarantee the farmer will be able to repay you at the end of the year. Would you not feel more comfortable making that loan if you knew the farmer already had guaranteed him- or herself a price? The existence of futures markets has allowed farmers to guarantee prices, thereby opening greater access to capital for operating.

Of course, the use of futures markets is not limited to farmers. Suppose you are a cereal company such as Kellogg's® or General Mills. Would you not like to guarantee your purchase price of wheat or corn for future delivery to your processing plants? In fact, there are many players in a market that, at some point, actually own the underlying commodity, such as farmers, merchants, storage facilities, transportation firms, processors, and retailers. When these agents take a position (either buying or selling) that is the opposite of their position in the underlying cash or spot market, they are **hedging**, or attempting to shift price risk from themselves to another party. At the same time, **speculators**, who do not own the physical commodity, are willing to take on that risk of price changes in hopes of making a profit. We will discuss hedging and speculating in more detail later in this chapter.

Key Questions

1. What are futures exchanges?
2. How long have futures contracts been traded?
3. What is the Efficient Market Hypothesis?
4. What is price discovery?
5. What is risk shifting?
6. What is the difference between a hedger and speculator?

9.2 Basic Institutions and Mechanisms

9.2.1 Institutions and Governance

Although each futures exchange maintains its own unique structure, all are commonly member- or shareholder-owned institutions. Each exchange has a **board of governors** that is elected from the membership or shareholders. This board oversees the daily operation of the exchange, and enforces the exchange's bylaws and regulations. Because

---

[2]The advent of options on futures contracts, simply called "options," has changed this statement a bit. We will briefly introduce the idea of options later in the chapter.

Table 9.1   The Chicago Board of Trade (CBOT) corn contract specifications

Contract size	5,000 bushels
Deliverable grades	No. 2 Yellow at face value; No. 1 at $0.015 per bushel premium; No. 3 at $0.015 per bushel discount
Tick size	$0.0025 per bushel or $12.50 per contract
Price quote	Cents and quarter cents per bushel
Delivery months	December, March, May, July, and September
Last trading day	One business day prior to the 15th calendar day of the delivery month
Last delivery day	Second business day following trading day
Daily price limit	$0.20 per bushel or $1,000 per contract

futures trading is a zero-sum game,[3] if one trader attempts to manipulate the market, another trader is harmed and it is in their best interest to complain (Carter, 2003). Thus, for most of their history, futures exchanges have been self-regulated. In 1974, however, the Commodity Futures Trading Commission (CFTC) was established to oversee the orderly operation of the exchanges. The CFTC works with exchanges to prevent fraud and abuse, and also monitors trading activity to prevent market manipulations and financial crimes. The industry also has a self-regulatory body called the National Futures Association, established in 1981, which works with the CFTC to register all firms and individuals that trade futures and options, and that has an arbitration program to handle complaints filed against traders or brokers.[4]

A second major component of the futures exchange is called the **clearing house**. A clearing house consists of a subset of the members of the exchange that provide financial backing and guarantees for all futures contracts and handle all the financial transactions that take place on the exchange (Carter, 2003). Despite the many years of bankruptcies, closures, and defaults on the part of major banks, there has never been a default at a clearing house on a U.S. exchange. This is a remarkable fact, given the billions or trillions of dollars worth of contracts that are traded annually, and it is a testament to the strength of the self-regulatory rule of exchanges.

9.2.2   Trading Mechanisms and Definitions

Before delving into the specifics of hedging and speculating, it is useful to provide some basic definitions of the trading mechanims used in futures markets. First, the **contract** is a written document that specifies the terms of delivery for the product being traded. Table 9.1 shows the contract specifications for the CBOT corn contract. As can be seen, the contract specifications outline quantity, quality, and delivery time as well as other features of the contract trading, such as **tick size**, which is the minimum amount by which the contract price can change, and the **daily price limit**, which is the maximum amount by which the price can change from the previous day of trading. You may occasionally

---

[3]That is, the nature of futures trading is such that when one trade wins, another must lose.

[4]A broker is a registered individual or firm that trades futures and options contracts on behalf of individuals in the public.

hear terms like "limit up" or "limit down," which means that the futures contract price has moved the maximum amount allowed by the contract trading rules.

The **delivery month** is the month in which the 5,000 bushels in the contract are to be delivered. There will be different markets for different months of delivery. That is, you will observe in the price quotes on the news or in the newspaper (or on the Internet), different prices for different delivery months. For example, if you were to go to the website for CBOT (www.cbot.com) and click on the corn futures contract, you would see current price quotes for December, March, May, July, and September, and depending on what month you are in, a quote for some of those contracts a year further out.[5] There are also specific delivery locations contained within the contract, called **delivery points** (which are not shown in the table).

Given this contract, individuals may choose to purchase the product for future delivery, which is called taking a **long position**. Taking a **short position** means selling a product for future delivery to someone else. An individual, such as a farmer, who already owns the physical commodity (or is about to plant it) is said to be in a long position in the cash market. Therefore, to shift risk, he or she would like to sell the product for future delivery, of take a short position in the futures market. By taking an opposite position in the futures and cash markets, this individual has created a **hedge**. Likewise, a processor who wishes to purchase the physical commodity at some point in the future is said to be in a short position in the cash market. To create a hedge, this processor would take a long position in the futures market. Speculators, by contrast, do not, nor do they wish to, own the underlying physical commodity. They can still take long or short positions in the futures markets, but these trades are called **uncovered**, because they do not have an offsetting position in the cash market. We will address these positions in more detail in the next section.

At contract expiration, or the end of trading for that contract, some form of **settlement** must occur. There are a number of way to settle a futures contract. First, and most obvious, is that those people holding short positions deliver the product to the specified location. Those holding long positions must take delivery of the product and then dispose of the product on the cash market. Thus, **delivery** of the product to satisfy the terms of the contract is one way to settle, but is, by far, the least common method. Some futures contracts allow for **cash settlement**, which is simply settling the value of the contracts on a cash basis. By far, the most common method of handling contract expiration is through **contract liquidation, offsetting,** or **lifting the hedge**[6] prior to the expiration of a contract.

Example 9.1 *Assume that you took a short position in the corn futures market for July delivery. You could wait until contract expiration and then deliver the corn to the specified location, but that would mean that you would have to load the trucks and haul the grain to that location. Alternatively, at some point during the trading period, you could also simply take a long position in the futures market, thereby offsetting your short position, and then sell your grain in the cash market to your local elevator.*

---

[5] That is, for example, if it is February 2006, you will see March through December 2006 contract prices as well as March 2007. That's right: you as a farmer could not only sell this year's crop before you plant it, but you could also sell next year's crop as well!

[6] All of these terms mean the same thing, but different people will use different terms in practice.

Offsetting is often difficult for students to understand at first, probably because we envision having sold the contract to a particular individual in the futures market. So how are we going to track that person down, and even if we did, what if they don't want to sell that contract back? Well, let's continue with that analogy for a moment. Let's say that we did sell our contract initially to a person and that, later, we tracked this person down and they did not want to sell it back to us. Could we not just purchase a contract for delivery for the same month and then hand it to this person and say: "Well, I've decided not to deliver my corn, but I have purchased some from someone else and here is their contract to deliver"? By doing this, we have satisfied our agreement to deliver this person 5,000 bushels of corn … it's just not our corn. Fortunately, the market does not function this way. When we take a short position, we are considered to have an **open position**. If we then take a long position in the same commodity and contract month, we have offset the short position and closed our open position. We are no longer obligated to deliver corn against our original short position. So, the fact is that most futures contracts are never actually delivered. They are simply offset in the market.

A logical question to ask is "Well, if products are not delivered against contracts, why is there any relationship between cash and futures prices (the price discovery role of futures markets)?" The answer was addressed previously when we talked about spatial markets and arbitrage. The fact that we *can* deliver a product against a futures contracts makes the markets behave *as if* delivery actually occurred.

Example 9.2   *Assume that you are a corn farmer in Iowa. You have taken a short position in the futures market for September delivery for $2.80 per bushel. Currently, the cash market in your local area is offering $1.25 per bushel, but the futures market is trading at $2.60 per bushel. It would not make sense for you to take a long position in the futures market to offset and then sell in the local cash market. Rather, it makes sense for you deliver your corn against the futures contract.*

Now, if you are a speculator that has taken a long position opposite of this farmer, you certainly don't want to take delivery of 5,000 bushels of corn. Where would you store that in your New York townhome? Because all traders in the market are cognizant of the market conditions, and almost all of them would prefer not to deliver or take delivery, the futures markets behave *as if* delivery was taking place, thus linking them directly to the cash market.

Just as we discussed in the chapter on spatial price variation, the above fact does not mean that futures prices and cash prices will be equal. Differences arise due, primarily, to transportion costs, but also reflect quality differences and local supply/demand conditions. The difference between the local cash price and the futures price is called the **basis**. The basis can be positive (cash price minus futures price) or negative. For example, California cotton regularly sells at a premium in the cash market relative to the futures market. This is due in part to the fact that the California cotton crop is, on average, of much higher quality to the futures contract specifications. Most typically, however, the basis is negative for locations that are away from delivery points due to transportation costs, and the basis becomes larger (in absolute value) as one moves farther away from a contract delivery point. As with spatial markets, arbitrage keeps the basis at or around transport costs, allowing for quality differences.

Table 9.2   An example of a short hedge in the corn futures market

Date	Futures price dollars per bushel	Basis dollars per bushel	Cash price dollars per bushel	Decision
December 1	3.00	0.25	2.75	Sell one May contract (short position) and purchase cash
April 15	2.50	0.30	2.20	Buy one May contract (offset) and sell cash
Gain/(loss)	0.50		(0.55)	

Key Questions

1. What is a clearing house?
2. What is a long position? What is a short position?
3. What is a hedge?
4. What is basis?
5. What is the CFTC?

9.3   Hedging

In this section, we will explore the basics of hedging. This section is not intended as a "trading strategies" manual. Rather, it is intended to acquaint you with the basic concept of hedging as a risk management tool. As discussed earlier, a hedge involves taking the opposite positions in the futures and cash markets.[7] Assume for a moment that you are a grain elevator operator in Iowa. You are going to take delivery from a farmer of 5,000 bushels of corn and pay that producer $2.75 per bushel. Table 9.2 outlines a storage hedge in the corn futures market. The first row shows that as of December 1, the futures price for May delivery of corn is $3.00 per bushel. The basis to your local market is $0.25 per bushel, yielding a local cash price of $2.75 per bushel, which you paid to the farmer. On that date, you decide to sell one contract for May delivery at $3.00 per bushel. Over the course of the next several months, the price of corn declines. On April 15, the futures price for May delivery has fallen to $2.50 per bushel and the local cash price has fallen to $2.20 per bushel. So, since the time you initially took possession of the corn in December, you have lost $0.55 per bushel in the cash market. Unhedged, this would be a loss to you. But, remember that you sold your contract on the futures market at $3.00 per bushel. To offset that position, you can now buy it back at a lower price ($2.50 per bushel), yielding a gain in the futures market of $0.50 per

---

[7] There is also something called a "Texas hedge," where the individual takes the same position in the futures and cash market (e.g., owns corn and takes a long position in the corn futures market). This is not really a hedge but, rather, a large speculative position. If the price of corn goes up, the individual doubles his or her profits. But, if the price of corn goes down, the losses are double.

bushel. Thus, by hedging, you have turned a $0.55 per bushel loss into a $0.05 per bushel loss.

Note that in the above example, there are two types of risk—price risk and basis risk. Price risk is related to changes in the level of the price of corn over the storage period. Basis risk is related to changes in the relationship *between* the futures market and the local cash market. Basis can change for any number of reasons, including changes in transportation costs and relative supply and demand in local markets. Nevertheless, the futures markets are an effective tool for managing price risk, but not basis risk. In the above example, if the basis had not changed over the time period, losses in the cash market would have been completely offset by gains in the futures market, or a **perfect hedge**. But, because the basis changed, the hedge did not perfectly protect you from price changes. While price risk is generally much larger and more important than basis risk and, therefore, futures markets are extremely useful, it is important to remember that basis risk is present and can sometimes be substantial.

The above example represents a direct hedge. That is, the hedge was placed in a futures contract that was the same as the underlying commodity—corn. However, for many products, a direct futures market does not exist.

Example 9.3   *You are a catfish farmer. Feed costs make up a substantial proportion of your overall production cost. You would like to protect yourself from adverse movements in catfish feed prices, but there is no futures market for catfish feed. However, catfish feed is comprised primarily of corn or soybean meal.*

In this example, there is no way to directly hedge catfish feed, but there may be a possibility to **cross-hedge** catfish feed by using corn and/or soybean meal futures contracts. The potential success of the cross-hedge depends on the correlation between cash market (catfish feed) prices and the futures market (corn and/or soybean meal) prices (Nalley et al., 2005). The higher the degree of correlation, the greater is the potential success of the cross-hedge. Cross-hedges have been investigated in a number of commodities and situations, each with varying results as to the potential success. Nevertheless, cross-hedging across commodities is a potential vehicle to address price risk for products that do not have a futures market.

Key Questions

1. What is a perfect hedge?
2. What is basis risk?
3. What is a cross-hedge?
4. What determines the potential success of a cross-hedge?

9.4   Options

9.4.1   Options Defined

Options are a relatively recent innovation in futures markets (compared with the age of futures markets themselves). At their most basic level, options are the *right, but not*

Table 9.3 Corn options premiums: 5,000 bushels (dollars per bushel)

Strike price	Call option	Put option
$1.80	$0.20125	$0.02500
$1.90	$0.11250	$0.12500
$2.00	$0.4750	$0.47500
$2.10	$0.1750	$0.11750
$2.20	$0.0625	$0.20625
$2.30	$0.0250	$0.30250

the obligation, to engage in a particular activity. For example, you are in college. Your successful completion of college will purchase you an option, with the right, but not the obligation, to pursue a career in your chosen field. After all, once you finish, you could choose to dig ditches the rest of your life if that is what you enjoy. Options are pervasive in life, and we likely engage in options trading regularly without even realizing it.

Options on futures contracts, however, have a very specific market and meaning. When on individual purchases an option on a futures contract, he or she is purchasing the right, but not the obligation, to exercise that futures contract at some point in the future. There are two basic types of options on futures (Hull, 2003). First, a **put option** is the right to take a short position (sell futures) at some point in the future. Conversely, a **call option** is the right to take a long position (buy futures) at some point in the future. Unlike the underlying futures contract which are traded on **margin**,[8] the purchaser of an option pays the full price of the option at purchase.

The price of an option is called its **premium**. The premium is some fraction of the underlying futures price. For example, the underlying price on a corn futures contract may be $2.00 per bushel, and a premium on an options contract may be $0.15 per bushel. In this case, the purchaser would pay the $0.15 per bushel for the options contract (or $750) for the right to take a position in the underlying futures contract. The premium is determined by a number of factors, the most important of which is the **strike price**. The strike price is the price at which the option holder can take a position in the futures market should he or she decide to do so. Table 9.3 shows both put and call option premiums for corn at various strike prices, where the underlying futures contract price is $2.00 per bushel.

There are a couple key features in Table 9.1 that should be noted. First, the premiums for puts and calls move in opposite directions across strike prices. This is because, of course, call options are the right to purchase futures, whereas the put is the right to sell futures, so their values must be the inverse of one another. The current futures price is $2.00 per bushel, so call options at strike prices below that amount are said to be **in-the-money**. Say, for example, you had previously purchased a call option on this contract at a strike price of $1.80 per bushel. Today, you could exercise this option, take a long position at $1.80 per bushel, and have an instant gain of $0.20 per bushel. Thus, the value of that option is roughly $0.20 per bushel, which is approximately the price.

---

[8] Purchasing on margin means that you only put up some fraction of the value in cash, with the contract itself serving as collateral. Because we typically offset our position in the futures market, the use of margins is justified.

Conversely, a put option with a strike price of $1.80 per bushel is said to be **out-of-the-money**. This is because if you had previously purchased a put option at a strike price of $1.80 per bushel, there would be no reason for you to exercise that option and sell futures today at $1.80 per bushel and then have to buy it back at $2.00 per bushel. Also note that at a strike price of $2.00 per bushel, the options premiums are the same, because that strike price is said to be **at-the-money**, or just equal to the underlying futures contract price.

You may ask why, if the put option is out-of-the-money at $1.80, it has any premium. The answer comes from two key variables. First is the **time to maturity**, which is basically the time left until the contract expires (Samuelson, 1965; Hudson and Coble, 1999). The longer the time left before maturity, the more possibility the underlying futures contract has of moving down (in the case of put options) or up (in the case of call options) to a point at which the strike price is in-the-money. Thus, as time to maturity approaches, the **time decay**, or loss in option values, increases, especially for options that are out-of-the-money. A second key variable is the **volatility** of the underlying futures contract price. Volatility is essentially the variance in prices over time. As you should recall from basic statistics, as the variance of prices increases, the probability of observing a price far from the mean goes up. So, for example, if the current price is $2.00 per bushel, but the volatility is high, there is a higher probability of the price dropping below $1.80 per bushel and the put option with a strike of $1.80 will go up compared to a situation in which the volatility is low. Thus, options premiums are positively correlated with the underlying volatility of the futures contract price.

9.4.2   Why Use Options?

Options have a number of advantages over simply using the underlying futures contracts. Recall in our discussion of heding that, while an excellent risk management tool, the hedged price was basically the final price received (plus or minus any changes in basis). Thus, while the hedge using futures is effective in shifting price risk, it does not allow individuals the opportunity to increase returns if the market moves favorably to them. For example, if a farmer initiates a short hedge using futures, he or she is protected if the price decreases. But what if the price increases? With a futures hedge, the farmer would gain in the cash market, but lose in the futures market.

With a put option, however, this is not the case. If the farmer purchased a put option and the price went down through the season, the value of the option would increase and could then be sold (or exercised) to capture that value, offsetting losses in the cash market. However, if the price of the product went up, the farmer would gain in the cash market and the option would expire worthless. The farmer would only be out the purchase price of the option, but would have captured the gains in the cash market. Thus, options provide flexibility not offered by standard hedging using futures contracts.

A second important advantage is financial exposure. Unlike futures contracts, which are traded on margin, options are purchased outright,[9] meaning that if the price moves against the trader, the trader is only out the value of the option. By contrast, if the price

---

[9] This discussion does not apply to those that sell, or write, options. Individuals that sell options are still exposed to considerable financial risks. But, as with most investments, there is a positive relationship between the level of risk and the level of returns.

moves against the trader in the futures market, the trader may be subject to margin calls and large financial losses.[10] It is important to realize, however, that options trading is not a panacea for risk management. Options trading can be significantly more complex and subject to a number of key variables that do not have direct impacts on the underlying futures contracts, such as time decay and volatility. Thus, careful study of these markets is needed before diving in.

Key Questions

1. What is a put option? What is a call option?
2. What is the strike price? What is the premium?
3. What are the key variables that affect options premiums?

9.5   Summary

This chapter has introduced the concept and operation of futures markets. Futures markets perform the important functions of price discovery, risk shifting, and facilitating financing. According to the Efficient Market Hypothesis, prices arising on futures markets are the best predictor of future prices for the underlying commodity, plus or minus the local cash basis. Market participants can use futures markets to hedge future price risk, thereby shifting price risk to speculators who are willing to take on risk in hopes of making a profit. While futures markets are effective at shifting price risk, hedgers are still exposed to basis risk, which can be substantial.

Options on futures contracts offer greater flexibility by providing the right, but not the obligation, to exercise the underlying futures contract. But purchasing that right requires an upfront cash outlay, called the premium. Nevertheless, options can be a useful addition to a risk management strategy by offering greater flexibility in decision-making.

Exercises

Problem 9.1   *Assume that you are a farmer who wishes to plant soybeans. The current cash price at planting time is $2.80 per bushel and the current futures price is $2.97 per bushel. (1) What is the current local cash basis? Assume that you take a short position in the futures market at planting time (current market). Over the course of the growing season, the price of soybeans at your local elevator declines to $2.65 per bushel and the futures price declines to $2.85 per bushel. Now assume that you offset your futures position and sell your soybeans to the local elevator. (2) Calculate your gains/losses from each position and your net gain/loss. (3) What would your gains or losses have been without the hedge?*

Problem 9.2   *In Problem 9.1, assume that instead of taking a short position, you could purchase a put option with a strike price of $2.97 per bushel at a price of $0.11 per*

---

[10] If the trader is hedging, however, he or she is presumably offsetting these losses in the cash market. But, even then, margin calls are occurring throughout the growing season, requiring him or her to put up larger sums of cash, which will not be recovered until the underlying product is sold in the cash market.

bushel. If a soybean contract is for 5,000 bushels, what is the total cost of the option? Now, assuming the same decline in prices as stated above, what would be your net gain/loss by purchasing the put option?

Problem 9.3   *In Problem 9.1, assume instead of price declines that the the price of soybeans in the local market increases from $2.80 per bushel to $3.25 per bushel and the futures price increases from $2.97 per bushel to $3.40 per bushel. (1) Calculate the gains and losses using the short hedge. (2) Calculate the net gains/losses from using the put option.*

References

Carter, C. *Futures and Options Markets: An Introduction*. Prentice Hall, Upper Saddle River, NJ, 2003.

Fama, E. "Efficient Capital Markets: A Review of Theory and Empirical Work." *Journal of Finance*, 25(1970): 383–417.

Hudson, D. and K. Coble. "Harvest Contract Price Volatility in Cotton." *Journal of Futures Markets*, 19(1999): 717–733.

Hull, J. *Options, Futures, and Other Derivatives*, fifth edition. Prentice Hall, Upper Saddle River, NJ, 2003.

Nalley, L., D. Hudson, J. Anderson, and T. Hanson. "Potential for Hedging Catfish Feed Prices." Paper presented to the 2005 Aquaculture America Conference, January 2005, New Orleans, LA.

Samuelson, P. "Proof that Properly Anticipated Prices Fluctuate Randomly." *Industrial Management Review*, 6(1965): 41–49.

Tomek, W. and K. Robinson. *Agricultural Product Prices*, third edition. Cornell University Press, Ithaca, NY, 1990.

Part II

Imperfect Competition, Market Structure, and Market Analysis

~

Chapter 10

Monopoly

~

Monopolies continue to be of interest in economics, despite the fact that pure, unregulated monopolies are rare. However, study of monopolies provides critical understanding of some pricing relationships that are present in modern economics. For example, a firm that develops a new product with patent protection may exhibit monopoly pricing power. Thus, understanding pricing mechanisms in a monopoly is important. We will examine monopoly pricing relationships and contrast the welfare implications of a monopoly with that of perfect competition. Finally, we will examine an important extension of the monopoly model—price discrimination.

10.1 Monopoly Structure and Pricing

It is useful to distinguish the overall structure of a monopoly from other market structures. In contrast to perfect competition, where there are many buyers and sellers, a monopoly only has one seller in the market.[1] As such, the supply function for the firm is the supply function for the market.[2] There are significant barriers to entry, so that entrance of competitors is unlikely.[3] The profit-maximizing condition for the monopolist is the same as for the competitive firm: $MC = MR$. However, unlike the competitive firm, the monopolist is facing a downward-sloping demand function (that is, marginal revenue is not constant). We know that revenue is equal to price times quantity: $R = PQ$. We also know that

$$MR = \frac{\partial R}{\partial Q}.$$

---

[1] The mirror image of a monopoly is a market with only one buyer, which is called a monopsony. We focus in this chapter on the monopoly structure, although much of the logic is the same for a monopsony market.

[2] Strictly speaking, the marginal cost function for the firm is the marginal cost function for the market.

[3] Entrance of competitors is not impossible. As we will discuss later, potential entry of competitors is an issue for the monopolist.

Therefore,

$$\frac{\partial R}{\partial Q} = P\left(\frac{\partial Q}{\partial Q}\right) + Q\left(\frac{\partial P}{\partial Q}\right)$$

$$= P\left[\left(\frac{\partial Q}{\partial Q}\right) + \left(\frac{Q}{P}\right)\left(\frac{\partial P}{\partial Q}\right)\right]$$

$$= P\left(1 + \frac{1}{E_d}\right), \tag{10.1}$$

where E_d is the own-price elasticity of demand. Equation 10.1 provides some useful information. First, consider the case when the elasticity of demand becomes infinitely large (that is, the demand curve becomes perfectly flat):

$$MR = P\left(1 + \frac{1}{\infty}\right) = P(1 + 0) = P. \tag{10.2}$$

Equation 10.2 says that when the demand curve becomes perfectly flat, $MR = P$. Recall that in the perfectly competitive case, the demand curve faced by the individual producer was perfectly flat, so that $MR = P$. Equation 10.2 formalizes this situation. Now consider the situation when the own-price elasticity is unitary:

$$MR = P\left(1 + \frac{1}{-1}\right) = P(1 - 1) = 0. \tag{10.3}$$

Thus, when the demand elasticity is unitary, total revenue is maximized and marginal revenue is equal to zero. Recall that in Chapter 1, the relationship between total revenue and elasticity revealed that maximum total revenue was attained when the own-price elasticity of demand was unitary. Finally, consider the case when the own-price elasticity of demand is inelastic:

$$MR = P\left(1 + \frac{1}{-0.2}\right) = P(1 - 5) = -4P. \tag{10.4}$$

Clearly, then, as Equation 10.4 illustrates, a monopolist would never produce in the inelastic portion of the demand curve, because that would reduce total revenue and profit.

10.1.1   Optimal Pricing

With the above conditions in mind, Figure 10.1 shows the optimal price and quantity determination in a monopoly. Assuming a linear demand function, the MR function for the monopolist is 1/2 of the demand function. Given the MC function for the firm, the monopolist will equate marginal revenue and marginal cost, resulting in the optimal price–quantity combination of P^* and Q^*. The general conclusion about a monopoly is that it generates a lower total output and a higher price than a competitive market, which is an important critique of the monopoly structure. This issue will be explored in more detail below. However, it is important to note the there are natural restraints on a monopoly.

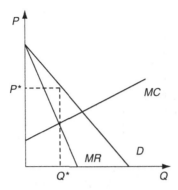

Figure 10.1 Optimal price and quantity in a monopoly.

10.1.2 Restraints on Monopoly

Perhaps the most important restraint on monopoly power is consumer demand.[4] That is, you may be the only firm selling widgets, but if no one wants to purchase widgets, your monopoly power is irrelevant. Assuming, however, there is product demand, the monopolist is still restrained by the demand curve (or consumer behavior). That is, in Figure 10.1, the monopolist is restricted by what consumers are willing to pay. If, for example, the monopolist attempted to charge a price higher than P^*, consumers would only purchase quantities less than Q^*, resulting in lower profits.

Further, pricing decisions have implications relating to market entry. That is, if the monopolist charges too high a price, it will attract competitors to develop substitute products. In perfect competition, these competitive forces drive prices to their lowest possible level given costs and demand, because there is free entry and exit in the market. Restricted entry in the monopoly market affords the monopolist considerable pricing flexibility, thereby allowing the monopolist to charge a price higher than would be observed in a competitive market.

Finally, the monopolist is constrained by production technology (or cost). Restricting output increases price, but restricting output too much will lead to underutilization of plant and equipment, higher cost, and lower profit. Thus, the monopolist is constrained by consumer behavior, potential competitors, and cost. So, while monopolies have significant pricing power, they do not have unlimited pricing power.

10.1.3 Welfare Implications of Monopoly

Previously, it was noted that a monopoly generally generates less output and higher prices than competitive markets. This result has important welfare implications. Consider the situation in Figure 10.2. The optimal monopoly solution of (P^*, Q^*) is shown in the figure. Using MC as the industry supply function and equating MC and D as in a competitive market equilibrium, we see that price would decline and output would

---

[4]We are abstracting here from government intervention to break up a monopoly. Rather, we are focusing on the natural restraints to monopoly.

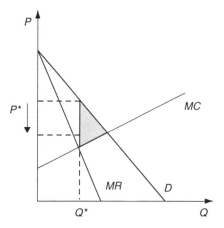

Figure 10.2   The welfare implications of a monopoly.

increase.[5] The result, then, of the restricted output by the monopolist is shown by the gray shaded area, which is called the **deadweight loss** triangle. The deadweight loss shows that, in a *competitive market structure*, producers would have been willing to produce more than Q^* at a price less than P^*, and consumers would have been willing to consume more than Q^* at a price less than P^*. This result makes it quite obvious why the U.S. Justice Department would be concerned with monopoly power exercised by firms. Clearly, egregious[6] use of monopoly power reduces consumer welfare. Anti-trust legislation prevents widespread abuse by monopolies.[7] Nevertheless, the principles of a monopoly are useful in understanding a more prevalent marketing issue in the food and fiber supply chain—price discrimination.

Key Questions

1. How is a monopoly structure different from a competitive structure?
2. What are the conditions for profit maximization in a monopoly?
3. In what part of the demand curve is the monopolist likely (or not likely) to operate?
4. What are the price, quantity, and welfare implications of a monopoly?

10.2   Price Discrimination

In general, there are three forms of price discrimination (Pigou, 1952; Varian, 1992):

Definition 10.1:   first-degree price discrimination   *This is a case in which the seller charges a different price for each unit of the good in such a way that the price charged*

---

[5] We are assuming that the monopolist *MC* represents the summation of individual supply functions in a competitive market, which is not necessarily the case. However, this assumption is sufficient to show the general welfare implications.

[6] I use the term "egregious" because, in practical terms, not all monopolies fully exploit monopoly power. They do not because they (1) do not want to attract potential competitors, and (2) do not want to attract the attention of the U.S. Justice Department.

[7] There are, however, practical difficulties in enforcing anti-trust laws. See Varian (1992) for more discussion.

for each unit is equal to the maximum willingness to pay for that unit (a.k.a., **perfect price discrimination**).

Definition 10.2: second-degree price discrimination *This is a situation in which prices depend on the amount purchased, but the same price schedule is faced by all consumers (a.k.a., **nonlinear pricing**).*

Definition 10.3: third-degree price discrimination *This is a case in which different consumers are charged different prices, but each buyer pays the same amount for each unit of the good.*

First-degree price discrimination is akin to treating each individual consumer differently and is illegal. From the monopolist's perspective, first-degree price discrimination provides the highest profit, because each individual's maximum willingness to pay is being extracted.[8] Thus, while it may be ideal for the monopolist, this form of price discrimination is not likely to be observed in reality.

Second-degree price discrimination is more commonplace in the economy. Nonlinear pricing is used quite frequently and given the positive "spin" of a title such as "volume discounts" or "preferred customer rebates." Whatever title is employed, the practice is to charge different prices for different quantities.

Example 10.1 *Assume that you are purchasing books from Amazon.com. A common advertisement may be that if you purchase $50 or more worth of books, shipping is free.*

In the above example, there is two-tier pricing. For purchases less than $50, you pay the shipping charges. For purchases over $50, you do not pay the shipping charges. Because shipping charges are a part of the total cost to you, by purchasing more than $50 worth of books, you lower your *per unit* cost of books. This, of course, is intended to entice you to purchase more books.

Volume discounting is pervasive in agriculture as well. Seed, chemical, and fertilizer companies regularly use nonlinear pricing schedules. This activity is not illegal. In fact, it is a sanctioned pricing practice used by regulated monopolies such as public utilities. It is seen as equitable because the discrimination occurs on the level of purchases, not on individual consumers. These issues have been investigated empirically by Vercammen and Fulton (1996) for agricultural cooperatives.

Perhaps the most common form of price discrimination is third-degree discrimination. Here, the monopolist is attempting to discriminate between different groups of individuals on the basis of their elasticity of demand. For example, many restaurants provide senior citizen's discounts or bars and pubs have "Ladies Nights." The discrimination is predicated on the different groups having a different response to price.

Tomek and Robinson (1990) provide two necessary conditions for third-degree price discrimination to be effective:

1. The markets must be effectively segmented.
2. The participants in the different markets have different elasticities of demand.

---

[8] We will return to this issue in Chapter 13 and analyze the situation when the monopolist cannot identify the type/behavior of the consumer explicitly.

The segmentation can be natural (e.g., one nation or region segmented from other nations or regions), behavioral (e.g., those desiring organic foods versus those who do not), or physical (e.g., age, or males versus females).

In practice, it is difficult to segment markets effectively. For example, if a firm were to charge one price for medicine in the U.S. and another in Canada, there would be little to prevent some from purchasing the medicine in the low-price market and selling it in the higher-price market (the arbitrage discussed in Chapter 6). Despite the difficulty of segmenting by national boundaries, some countries do attempt to practice price discrimination (Carew, 2000; Schmitz and Gray, 2000; Brown, 2001). Other forms of segmentation, such as age or gender, are more easily conducted, and price discrimination is a popular marketing tool (Larson, 1997; Kiser, 1998). We will assume for a moment that segmentation is effective.

The second condition that must be met is the the price responsiveness in the different markets must be sufficiently different so that the segmentation generates different prices. In plain English, the elasticities of demand must be different.

Example 10.2   *Consider the dry-cleaning market. You will observe two markets for dry-cleaning shirts—one for women's shirts and one for men's shirts. Although there is no difference in cost of cleaning a men's and a women's shirt made of the same fabric, you will notice there is a price difference. Why?*

In the above example, there are two groups that are easily segmented.[9] The two groups also have different elasticities of demand. Men, for example, are known slobs and are likely sensitive to price when it comes to having a clean, pressed shirt. Women, by contrast, are more likely less sensitive to price. The dry-cleaners, therefore, must carefully consider price if they are to retain their male customers.

We can formalize this problem for the dry-cleaner and solve for the optimal prices and quantities. Assuming that the other conditions for price discrimination are met, the dry-cleaner is facing two different inverse demand functions for males (P_1) and females (P_2):

$$P_1 = a - bQ_1,$$ (10.5)
$$P_2 = c - dQ_2.$$ (10.6)

On the basis of these demand functions, we can formulate the profit equation for the dry-cleaner:

$$\pi = P_1Q_1 + P_2Q_2 - TC(Q_1, Q_2),$$ (10.7)

where TC is the total cost function for dry-cleaning shirts. Substituting Equations 10.5 and 10.6 into 10.7 yields:

$$\pi = \left(aQ_1 - bQ_1^2\right) + \left(cQ_2 - dQ_2^2\right) - TC\left(Q_1, Q_2\right).$$

[9] It is important to note that it is the product on which the discrimination occurs, not the gender of the person bringing the clothes into the store. This segmentation occurs because of the "tag" effect. That is, the dry-cleaner will determine whether it is men's or women's garment based on the tag in the shirt.

The first-order conditions for profit maximization are as follows:

$$\frac{\partial \pi}{\partial Q_1} = a - 2bQ_1 - MC_1 = 0,$$

$$\frac{\partial \pi}{\partial Q_2} = c - 2dQ_2 - MC_2 = 0,$$

where MC_1 and MC_2 are the marginal costs for men's and women's shirts, respectively. For now, we will assume $MC_1 = MC_2 = MC$, but different marginal costs could be used. Solving for profit-maximizing quantities yields

$$Q_1^* = \frac{a - MC}{2b}, \tag{10.8}$$

$$Q_2^* = \frac{c - MC}{2d}. \tag{10.9}$$

Substituting Equations 10.8 and 10.9 into Equations 10.5 and 10.6, respectively, yields the profit-maximizing prices for the monopolist:

$$P_1^* = a - \frac{a - MC}{2},$$

$$P_2^* = c - \frac{c - MC}{2}.$$

Note that if the inverse demand functions for men and women were the same (a, b, c, and d in Equations 10.5 and 10.6), the resulting optimal prices and quantities would be the same. Thus, the demand functions (or price responsiveness) must be different for price discrimination to be effective. We can represent this situation graphically as in Figure 10.3. Men, as noted, are more price responsive, so they are viewed as the "elastic"

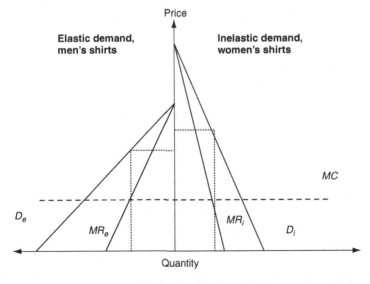

Figure 10.3 Optimal price and quantity for dry-cleaning, third-degree price discrimination.

demand.[10] Women, on the other hand, are less price responsive and are labeled "inelastic" demand. Assuming the marginal cost is constant and the same for both products, we can derive the optimal decisions by the dry-cleaner. The most important feature to note here is that the price is lower in the elastic market as compared to the inelastic market. Thus, one would expect that the dry-cleaner would charge a higher price for women's shirts than for men's shirts, a fact all too real in the marketplace.

This model has many practical applications in food and fiber markets. For example, why are "low-fat" foods priced higher than normal foods? Why are organic vegetables priced higher than other vegetables? Potential differences in elasticities of demand tell part of the story. However, one should be careful not to overextend the logic of this model. There may be cost differences, for example, that generate differences in price. Cost differences can be built into this model as well. Nevertheless, different markets with different elasticities of demand are a powerful tool through which we can filter many of the marketing decisions made by firms.

Key Questions

1. What are the degrees of price discrimination and how are they different?
2. What are the conditions that must exist for third-degree price discrimination?
3. What are the pricing implications of third-degree price discrimination? Who gets the higher and lower prices?

10.3   Summary

We have examined the monopoly market structure, which is the polar opposite of the competitive market structure in the first part of this book. The analysis shows that monopolies generate higher prices and lower output than competitive markets, generating a welfare disruption called a deadweight loss. However, while monopolies have considerable pricing power, their pricing power is not absolute. Pure, unregulated monopolies are rare, but understanding of the monopoly structure aids in understanding a more important issue in economics—price discrimination.

We have analyzed price discrimination, with special attention to third-degree price discrimination. It is apparent that there are rational, legal motivations for discriminating in price. However, the conditions for effective price discrimination are quite stringent and certainly are not applicable in all situations. Nevertheless, the concept of price discrimination helps us understand why some firms behave the way they do in the market.

Exercises

Problem 10.1   *Larger farmers who purchase large amounts of fertilizer often receive price discounts for their purchases. What form of price discrimination is this and what are the characteristics of the price discrimination?*

---

[10]Note that this market does not have to exhibit "elastic" demand. It is only necessary that this market exhibit more elastic (or less inelastic) demand than the other market.

Problem 10.2   *Consumers who prefer organic vegetables are generally less price responsive than those with no strong preference for organic vegetables. Assuming that the marginal cost of producing organic and normal vegetables are the same, graphically and verbally describe the pricing strategy for the retailer.*

Problem 10.3   *Assume that a monopolist is facing an inverse demand function in one market of $P_1 = 150 - 6Q_1$, and an inverse demand function in a second market of $P_2 = 130 - 2Q_2$. Also assume that for technical reasons, the marginal cost of producing for the first market is $MC_1 = 20$, and the marginal cost of producing in the second market is $MC_2 = 40$. Based on this information, solve for the optimal quantities and prices in each market that maximizes the profit to the monopolist.*

References

Brown, J. "Price Discrimination and Pricing to Market Behavior of Canadian Canola Exports." *American Journal of Agricultural Economics*, 83(2001): 1,343–1,349.

Carew, R. "Pricing to Market: Evidence from Selected Canadian and U.S. Agri-Food Exports." *Journal of Agricultural and Resource Economics*, 25(2000): 578–595.

Kiser, E. "Heterogenity in Price Sensitivity and Retail Price Discrimination." *American Journal of Agricultural Economics*, 80(1998): 1,150–1,155.

Larson, R. "Using Price Discrimination Theory to Plan Promotions." *Agribusiness: An International Journal*, 13(1997): 401–408.

Pigou, A. *The Economics of Welfare*, fourth edition, Macmillan, London, 1952.

Schmitz, T. and R. Gray. "State Trading Enterprises and Revenue Gains from Market Power: The Case of Barley Marketing and the Canadian Wheat Board." *Journal of Agricultural and Resource Economics*, 25(2000): 596–616.

Tomek, W. and K. Robinson. *Agricultural Product Prices*, third edition. Cornell University Press, Ithaca, NY, 1990.

Varian, H. *Microeconomic Analysis*, third edition. W.W. Norton and Company, New York, 1992.

Vercammen, G. and M. Fulton. "Non-Linear Pricing Schemes for Cooperatives: The Equity/Efficiency Tradeoff." *Canadian Journal of Economics*, Special Issue Part 1, 29(1996): S303–S307.

Chapter 11

Strategic Interaction

~

A common criticism of neoclassical economics (the models presented in the previous chapters) is that it does not explain the interaction between economic agents—be they individuals, companies, or countries—in any meaningful way. Neoclassical economics is based on the notion that Adam Smith's "Invisible Hand" allocates resources (land, labor, and capital) to their highest and best use, but does not explain how individuals interact within this framework to allocate those resources or carry out transactions. The mathematician von Neuman and the economist Morgenstern (von Neuman and Morgenstern, 1944) developed a framework, called game theory, to explain cooperative and noncooperative strategic interaction.

This theory is based on the supposition that rational economic agents devise strategies in interactions to maximize their economic returns. John Nash generalized this theory with his solution to the bargaining problem.[1] This chapter introduces the basic concepts in game theory. You should note that game theory is a broad and rich field in economics, and this chapter only provides as introduction into the most basic models. This chapter is necessarily short, but sets up the basic models used in the following chapter.

11.1 The Prisoner's Dilemma

One of the most basic forms of a game is the **static game of complete information** (Gibbons, 1992). In this game, players make simultaneous moves (or make simultaneous decisions) and, thus, there are no dynamic considerations. Complete information means that each player's **payoff function** (or the payoff that results for each player from the combination of actions by all players) is common knowledge to all players in the game.

---

[1]Nash's life was popularized by the book *A Beautiful Mind* and the Academy Award winning movie by the same title. Although Nash won the Noble Prize in Economics for his work on game theory, he was a mathematician with only one formal course in economics!

The objective of each player is to follow a strategy that maximizes his or her benefit given the best strategy for his or her opponent—a concept called the **Nash equilibrium**. This game is most easily illustrated in the context of the **Prisoner's Dilemma**.

Assume that an armed robbery has been committed. The police have arrested two suspects, but lack sufficient evidence to convict either suspect unless one of them confesses.[2] The police place the suspects in separate interrogation rooms, so as not to allow any communication between them. Each interrogating officer then explains the possible courses of action each suspect can take and the consequences of those actions. If neither suspect confesses, both will be convicted of a misdemeanor charge of weapons possession and sentenced to one month in jail. If both confess, they will plea bargain their sentences to six months in jail. However, if one confesses and the other does not, the confessor will be released without charges filed and the other will be convicted of armed robbery and will serve nine months in jail.

We can represent the payoff matrix for both suspects by the following:[3]

		Prisoner 2	
		Keep quiet	Rat out
Prisoner 1	Keep quiet	$-1,-1$	$-9,0$
	Rat out	$0,-9$	$-6,-6$

Each prisoner has two potential strategies: keep quiet or rat out. By convention, the payoffs in each cell of the matrix are denoted (Prisoner 1, Prisoner 2). For example, if Prisoner 1 keeps quiet but Prisoner 2 rats out, the payoff to Prisoner 1 is -9 (or nine months in jail) and the payoff to Prisoner 2 is 0 (he or she is free to go). In this construction, it is obvious that both suspects would be better off if both kept quiet. However, there is no communication between suspects, so neither suspect is guaranteed that the other will keep quiet.

How do we solve this dilemma? Examine the best strategies for Prisoner 1. The Nash equilibrium concept dictates that Prisoner 1 must choose a strategy that maximizes his or her payoff given the best strategy of the opponent. If Prisoner 2 keeps quiet, the best outcome he or she would receive is one month in jail and the worst is nine months in jail. By constrast, if Prisoner 2 rats out on Prisoner 1, the best outcome for Prisoner 2 is to be set free, while the worst outcome is six months in jail. Given that the worst outcome for Prisoner 2 for ratting out is better for Prisoner 2 than keeping quiet, Prisoner 2 will always choose to rat out. By this logic, then, Prisoner 1's best decision is to rat out also. Both suspects will rat out and receive six months in jail, which is obviously a worse outcome than if they were able to cooperate and both keep quiet!

The important outcome here is that cooperation would have yielded a better outcome for both players, but because communication is not possible, they both receive a lesser payoff. Although simple in construction, the Prisoner's Dilemma game has many applications in the real world. Consider the arms race between the United States and the former Soviet Union. It obviously would have been better for both sides not to have

---

[2] For those fans of the television series *Law and Order*, this setup should be familiar.

[3] This is one way to view the game. We can also use the *normal-form* representation of the game. A generalized presentation of the normal for representation is shown in the appendix to this chapter. Alternatively, we may present the *extensive-form* representation of the game. We will utilize the extensive-form representation later in the chapter, when we examine sequential bargaining games.

nuclear weapons. However, the payoff to one country for not having nuclear weapons while the other did was such that it created the perverse result of an arms race. These concepts are central to economic interactions as well, as we shall see in the following sections.

Key Questions

1. What is a payoff function?
2. How do we select the optimal strategy?
3. What is a Nash equilibrium?

11.2   Games with Mixed Strategies

Some games will have multiple Nash equilibria—so-called **mixed strategies**. A classic example of a game with mixed strategies is *The Battle of the Sexes*. Assume that a husband and wife are trying to decide on a destination for vacation.[4] The husband prefers the cool crisp mornings and quiet serenity of the mountains. The wife prefers the warm sea breezes of the beach. Both would prefer to be together on vacation. The payoff matrix for this game is as follows:

		Wife	
		Mountains	Beach
Husband	Mountains	2,1	0,0
	Beach	0,0	2,1

Clearly, both (Mountains, Mountains) and (Beach, Beach) represent Nash equilibria. How, then, do we decide which strategy is the best? The short answer is that there is no real way of telling which is the best answer. The Nash equilbrium concept does not provide guidance in these situations. In many games with mixed strategies, a rule of thumb about the solution will present itself (for example, in ties, the husband will defer to the wishes of his wife), but in many cases, these conventions will not present themselves. We are then forced to make judgments about the outcome, because no clear strategy emerges.[5]

11.3   Sequential Bargaining

Many economic relationships do not lend themselves to the simultaneous move construct of the above games. In many cases, one party gets to observe the move made by the other party before making a decision about his or her chosen strategy. This implies a sequence

---

[4] The couple do not have children, so Disney World is not a destination of choice!

[5] Readers interested in expanding their understanding on mixed strategy games are referred to Gintis (2000). In his book, Gintis provides a rich number of examples and solutions to problems with mixed strategies, many of which are based in biology. This is a burgeoning field in game theory and is rich with possible applications in economics.

of events that transpire: player 1 chooses an action a_1 from a feasible set A_1. Player 2 observes a_1, and then chooses an optimal strategy a_2 from a feasible set A_2. The payoffs to each are $u_1(a_1, a_2)$ and $u_2(a_1, a_2)$.

Sequential bargaining games are solved through a process of backward induction.[6] That is, when Player 2 gets to move second in the game, he or she will face a maximization problem subject to the move, a_1, made by player 1:

$$\max_{a_2 \in A_2} u_2(a_1, a_2).$$

We assume that, for each $a_1 \in A_1$, Player 2's optimization problem has a unique solution that is denoted by $R_2(a_1)$. This is equivalent to saying that for every possible strategy that Player 1 can play, Player 2 has a unique strategy or best response.[7] Player 1 is an intelligent individual, so he or she can solve Player 2's maximization problem as well as Player 2 can. That means that Player 1 should anticipate Player 2's response to any move Player 1 makes. Thus, Player 1's maximization problem at stage 1 of the game is

$$\max_{a_1 \in A_1} u_1(a_1, R_2(a_1)).$$

If we also assume that Player 1's response is unique, called a_1^* the *backward induction solution* to the game. This solution does not involve *noncredible threats*. That is, Player 1 anticipates that Player 2 will respond optimally to any action a_1 that Player 1 chooses and Player 1 gives no credence to any threat that Player 2 makes that he or she will play any other strategy besides the optimal.[8] We can visualize this interaction through the following extensive-form representation of a three-stage game in Figure 11.1. This game can be represented verbally as follows:

1. Player 1 chooses L or R, where L ends the game with payoffs of 1 to Player 1 and 0 to Player 2.
2. Player 2 observes Player 1's choice. If Player 1 chooses R, Player 2 chooses L' or R', where L' ends the game with payoffs of 1 to both players.
3. Player 1 observes Player 2's choice (and remembers his or her own choice in stage 1). If the earlier choices were R and R', Player 1 chooses L" or R", both of which end the game. The choice L" ends with payoffs of 3 to Player 1 and 0 to Player 2, and R" ends with payoffs of 0 to Player 1 and 2 to Player 2.

---

[6] For this section, we are again assuming complete information. That is, the payoffs to each player are common knowledge and the moves made by each player are observable. However, unlike the previous models, this model is dynamic. That is, there is a sequence of events. For an application of the dynamic model with incomplete information, see Hudson and Lusk (2004).

[7] This is an important assumption, because it guarantees that no matter the strategy followed by Player 1, we can identify one optimal strategy for Player 2 in response. If this assumption did not hold, we would have no way of telling what Player 2's response would be to Player 1.

[8] From this, you should note that a noncredible threat is a threat to play a nonoptimal strategy. Rational players are assumed to play rational responses, so that a threat to play a nonrational response is noncredible.

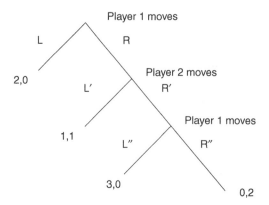

Figure 11.1   The extensive-form representation of a sequential game.

The backward induction solution is established by beginning in stage 3 of the game, which is Player 1's second move. Here, Player 1 faces a payoff of 3 from L″ and 0 from R″, so L″ is obviously optimal. Thus, at the second stage, Player 2 anticipates that if the game reaches the third stage, Player 1 will choose L″, yielding a zero payoff for him or her. The choice at the second stage for Player 2, then, is between a payoff of 1 for L′ and 0 for R′ (because of the optimal choice by Player 1 if the game goes to stage 3), so L′ is optimal. Thus, at the first stage, Player 1 anticipates that Player 2 will play L′ at the second stage, yielding a payoff of 1 for Player 1, which is obviously less than the 3 Player 1 will receive if he or she plays L in stage 1. Therefore, the backward induction solution to the game is for Player 1 to play L in stage 1, ending the game with payoffs of 3 for Player 1 and 0 for Player 2.

11.4   Summary

Game theory is a burgeoning field in economics and adds a new dimension for understanding how individuals interact in markets. We have only scratched the surface here in order to introduce you into this field. We will utilize the tools presented in this chapter later in this book to examine more concrete examples of strategic interaction. However, you are encouraged to seek additional readings in game theory. There are literally hundreds of books on game theory, which provide explicit detail and examples.

References

Gibbons, R. *Game Theory for Applied Economists*. Princeton University Press, Princeton, NJ, 1992.

Gintis, H. *Game Theory Evolving: A Problem Centered Introduction to Modeling Strategic Interaction*. Princeton University Press, Princeton, NJ, 2000.

Hudson, D. and J. Lusk. "Activists and Corporate Behavior in Food Industries." *Journal of Agricultural and Resource Economics*, 29(2004): 79–93.

von Neumann, J. and O. Morgenstern. *Theory of Games and Economic Behavior*. Princeton University Press, Princeton, NJ, 1944.

Appendix 11A: Normal-Form Representation

The following is a discussion of the normal-form representation of a game. It is intended to formalize the concepts discussed within the chapter and it utilizes more advanced mathematical terminology. You are encouraged to examine this presentation, but it is necessarily intended for more advanced students.

The normal-form representation of a game, in general, specifies (1) the players in the game, (2) the strategies available to each player, and (3) the payoff received by each player for each combination of strategies that could be chosen by the other players. To generalize, we often refer to n-player games, where players are numbered arbitrarily (no specific ordering) from 1 to n, and any individual player is number i. We denote S_i as the set of potential strategies available to player i, which is called player i's *strategy space*. We also call s_i any member of that strategy space. We note that $s_i \in S_i$, or that s_i is a member of the strategy space S_i. We let $(s_1, \ldots, s_n)$ denote a combination of strategies, one for each player. We let $u_i(s_1, \ldots, s_n)$ denote player i's payoff function, which is the payoff to player i if the strategy combination $(s_1, \ldots, s_n)$ is chosen. Given these, Gibbons (1992) gives the following definition:

Definition 11.1   *The* **normal-form representation** *of a n-player game specifies the players' strategy spaces $S_1, \ldots S_n$ and their payoff functions $u_1, \ldots u_n$. We denote this game by $G = [S_1, \ldots S_n; u_1, \ldots u_n]$.*

Using the example from the text of the Prisoner's Dilemma, we get the following normal-form representation of the game:

$$G = [S_1(\textit{keep quiet}, \textit{rat out}), S_2(\textit{keep quiet}, \textit{rat out});$$
$$u_1(-1, -9, 0, -6), u_2(-1, 0, -9, -6)].$$

From this, we can construct the payoff matrix found in the text. As you can see, the normal-form representation can become quite complex with complicated problems. This complexity is the reason why people often prefer to utilize the *extensive-form representation* of the game. It is easier for many to visualize the interaction in the tree diagrams, but these can also be quite complex to construct.

Chapter 12

Imperfect Competition

~

Imperfect competition is a broad term used to describe market structures that are neither perfectly competitive nor monopolies. Structures can range from fairly competitive structures such as **monopolistic competition** (Chamberlin, 1933) to structures with only two buyers or sellers, called **duopolies** or **duopsonies**, respectively. The fact that there is more than one seller distinguishes **oligopolies**[1] from monopolies.[2] And the fact that firms see themselves as rivals with some impact on market price distinguishes oligopoly from perfect competition (Scherer and Ross, 1990; Tomek and Robinson, 1990).

The nebulous nature of imperfect competition has made economic analysis difficult, as will be discussed below. But, given the fact that agricultural markets are predominantly imperfectly competitive to some degree, gaining a basic understanding of imperfectly competitive models is essential to a complete understanding of the world in which we live. Often, agricultural producers are facing a limited number of buyers for their products. In this case, producers are facing an oligopsony. These same processing firms may also act as oligopolists in the wholesale market, but also may be facing oligopsonist retailers. Thus, imperfect competition pervades agricultural supply chains. In this chapter, we will focus on the basic structure of imperfectly competitive market models to gain some insight about the impacts of these structures on market outcomes. The chapter will also address some basic empirical tools for analyzing and understanding imperfectly competitive markets.

---

[1] From this point forward, we will follow the convention of Scherer and Ross (1990) in using "oligopoly" as a generic term for imperfect competition. However, you should note that there are different shades of imperfect competition, of which some authors label oligopoly as a specific type. Oligopoly is defined here as two or more sellers, but with few enough sellers so that firms see themselves as rivals with some impact on price.

[2] Here, again, as with monopolies, an oligopoly refers to sellers and oligopsony refers to buyers. The cases are symmetrical, but the focus is on oligopoly for simplicity.

12.1   Pricing and Behavior

We will begin our investigation by examining the most direct case of imperfect competition—duopoly. Consider the following example.

Example 12.1   *You are a farmer in central Kansas. There are two retailers in your local area from whom you can purchase herbicides. By definition, you are facing a duopoly in herbicides.*[3]

Given that there are only two sellers in the market, the question is how this structure affects the pricing of herbicides. The answer, as it turns out, depends on how one believes the firms will behave. Augustin Cournot developed a model of behavior in 1838, assuming that firms choose their profit-maximizing quantity of output believing that the quantity marketed by rivals is fixed. So, in our input example above, Cournot would argue that firm A would choose to sell its quantity of herbicide given a fixed quantity being marketed by firm B. Under these assumptions, Cournot demonstrated that there existed a stable equilibrium where no firm had an incentive to change its quantity given the quantities of other firms. Assume that the market price for herbicides in the local market is a linear function of total output:

$$P(Q) = a - bQ,$$

where $Q = q_A + q_B$ is the total quantity of herbicide offered by the two firms, and q_A and q_B are the offerings by firms A and B, respectively. Firm A's profit is the difference between its revenue and total cost:

$$\pi_A = P(Q)q_A - cq_A,$$

where c is the constant unit cost of selling the herbicide. If we substitute the price equation into the profit equation, we get

$$\pi_A = (a - bQ)q_A - cq_A.$$

Because Q is involved in the profit function for firm A, it is apparent that the output decision of firm B affects firm A's profit (recall the definition of Q above). Thus, firm A cannot make its profit-maximizing decision without making an assumption about what firm B is going to do. To do this, Cournot assumed that firm A differentiates its profit with respect to q_A and sets the resulting equation equal to zero (also known as the first-order

---

[3]It is interesting to note that the Internet has changed the dynamics of this problem. Currently, farmers can "surf the net" and find the cheapest prices for inputs and have those delivered directly to the farm. Nevertheless, this example suffices to frame the problem in your mind.

condition for profit maximization):[4]

$$\frac{d\pi_A}{dq_A} = P(Q) + \left(\frac{dP}{dQ}\right)q_A - c = 0$$

$$= a - 2bq_A - bq_B - c = 0.$$

If we solve the above for q_A, we get

$$q_A = \frac{(a-c)}{2b} - \frac{1}{2}q_B.$$

This equation is known as firm A's **reaction function**, which shows how firm A will react to changes in firm B's offering of herbicide in the market. Clearly, then, how much herbicide firm A chooses to sell is related to how much herbicide firm B sells, as well as the market demand situation (that is, elasticity of demand for herbicides through the coefficient b). In general, in a market with n firms and identical marginal costs, each firm has a limited degree of monopoly power, which is defined as price being elevated above marginal costs. The "profit" margin is defined as the percentage by which the market price will fall with increases in the number of firms or the elasticity of demand:

$$\frac{(P-MC)}{P} = \frac{1}{nE},$$

where E is the elasticity of demand and MC is the marginal cost.[5] Here, we see that this percentage declines as n (number of firms) increases and/or demand becomes more elastic. Thus, if a new input firm were to open in our area, we would expect profit margins to decrease through decreases in price. As n grows larger and larger, perfectly competitive behavior is approximated.[6] The Cournot model also demonstrates the connection between industry profit margins and industry concentration. If we define $\overline{MC}$ as the weighted average industry marginal cost[7] and HI is the Herfindahl–Hirschman concentration index,[8] we find that

$$\frac{(P-\overline{MC})}{P} = \frac{HI}{E}.$$

---

[4] Recall that what is going on here is that differentiating profit yields the **slope** of the profit function. We are setting this equal to zero, which yields the maximum point on the profit function (assuming second-order conditions are met, which we assume holds). Thus, this process yields the amount of q_A that maximizes profit.

[5] Here, we are assuming that marginal cost is the same across all firms. When marginal costs are different, the Cournot model is constructed much the same, but market shares are different. As you might expect, more efficient firms have higher market shares due to lower marginal costs (Schrerer and Ross, 1990).

[6] It is important to note that the number of firms that can operate in an industry is affected by scale economies (Novshek, 1980). There may be a situation in which scale economies imply that only three or fewer firms can operate in an industry with nonnegative profits. But just because the number of firms is small does not mean that competitive behavior cannot result. Elasticity of demand also plays an important role.

[7] If industry marginal costs are assumed constant, this is simply the marginal cost for the industry. Calculating the weighted average generalizes our model to cases where marginal costs are different across firms.

[8] We will discuss the construction of the Herfindahl–Hirschman index later in the chapter.

Thus, as the industry becomes more concentrated (*HI* increases), we expect the profit margin for the industry to increase. This relationship helps explain the preoccupation of analysts and politicians with concentration in agricultural markets (Collins, 2001).

The Cournot model has intuitive appeal because it exhibits characteristics we usually associate with oligopolies—higher prices than the competition and interdependence of firms. However, Cournot's analysis was based on some rather unrealistic assumptions. First, Cournot assumed that quantity is the decision variable, not price. But even casual observation suggests that firms set price to clear quantities.[9] However, if we assume some degree of product differentiation, we can preserve the heart of the Cournot model. So, if we assume that the two herbicide dealers sell slightly different herbicide products, we can maintain the core of our analysis.

A second weakness of the standard Cournot model is the assumption that firm A takes the output of firm B as given. That is, we are essentially assuming that firm B will not react to changes made by firm A. Does it seem rational that one firm will not react to another? To address this issue, economists have developed the **conjectural variations** Cournot model (Cowling and Waterson, 1976; Holloway, 1991).

In our model above, the effect of a change in firm A's output, dq_A, by firm A on industry output Q was one for one because firm B's output was assumed unchanged:

$$\frac{dQ}{dq_A} = \frac{dq_A}{dq_A} = 1.$$

But, what if firm A had some reason to believe that firm B would alter the quantity of herbicide it sells in response to firm A's changes? In this case, $dq_B/dq_A \neq 0$, or the change in firm B's quantity with respect to a change in firm A's quantity is not equal to zero. Thus, in our herbicide market, dq_B/dq_A is defined as firm A's conjectural variation about firm B's response. The full effect now on total industry output of a one-unit adjustment in output by firm A will be 1 (the direct effect) plus the conjectural variation (the rival's reaction).

The full conjectural variations model is presented in Appendix 12A, but the resulting equilibrium condition is

$$\frac{(P - MC_A)}{P} = \frac{s_A}{E}\left[1 + \frac{dq_B}{dq_A}\right],$$

where s_A is the market share for firm A. If the conjectural variation is negative, firm A expects firm B to at least partially offset its quantity changes. In the extreme case of $dq_B/dq_A = -1$, firm B completely offsets the output changes of firm A. Here, the right-hand side of the equation is zero, which implies a zero profit margin for firm A (and this would also be the case for firm B). Thus, in the extreme case of complete offsetting, a perfectly competitive result arises. In cases where the conjectural variation is greater than zero, firm A expects firm B to at least partially match its quantity changes. In the extreme case here, $dq_B/dq_A = 1$, or there is a one-to-one correspondence between firm A changes and firm B changes. This result mimics perfect collusion, which gives the same result as if both firms were combined and acted as monopolists.

---

[9] The use of quantities as the decision variable has been defended by Kreps and Scheinkman (1983) by arguing that firms first choose plant capacity and then engage in price rivalry.

The conjectural variations model has a number of advantages over its more restrictive cousin introduced previously. First, it allows for a range of possible outcomes, as discussed above. This feature is appealing because we do observe a range of behavior in different industries. Second, the conjectural variations model makes explicit the concern that firms will have about the reactions by other firms to its own decisions. But a weakness of this model is the typical assumption that output is at least initially divided equally among the firms (see Holloway, 1991), which, by its nature, implies that it only takes a few firms to generate competitive behavior. Nevertheless, there is some evidence that at least some agricultural industries behave consistently with the conjectural variations explanation of oligopoly behavior (Holloway, 1991; Hudson, 1998).

Key Questions

1. What are the key characteristics of an imperfectly competitive market relative to perfect competition and monoploy?
2. What is an oligopsony?
3. What is a reaction function and what does it indicate?
4. What is a conjectural variation and how is it different than a reaction function?
5. Using conjectural variations, what conditions must exist to approximate competitive behavior, and in monopoly behavior?

12.2   Duopsony/Oligopsony

A particularly acute phenomenon in the agricultural sector is the situation in which there are many sellers (agricultural producers), but only a few buyers (agricultural processors). This structure is commonly referred to as duopsony (two buyers) or oligopsony (a few buyers). As stated above, an oligopsony is theoretically equivalent to an oligopoly, but in reverse. In an oligopoly, we would expect that prices paid by consumers would be higher than in perfect competition. So, in an oligopsony, we expect the prices received by producers to be lower than in perfect competition.

Hudson and Anderson (2006) analyzed this problem using experimental economics.[10] First, they used an experimental market with an equal number of buyers and sellers to simulate a perfectly competitive market. Subjects were provided with supply and demand functions with an equilibrium price of $0.60. Subjects were allowed to buy and sell a product in this simulated market for a fixed time period. Figure 12.1 shows the resulting transactions prices by round. As can be seen, the transactions prices centered around the predicted equilibrium price of $0.60.

Next, a different set of respondents participated in a market with the same supply and demand functions. But this time, there were only two buyers (a duopsony). The resulting transactions are shown in Figure 12.2. Here, you can see that the prices were generally well below (and significantly different) than the $0.60 competitive equilibrium price. Thus, the work by Hudson and Anderson (2006) clearly demonstrates that the

---

[10] A more complete discussion of experimental methods is found in Chapter 16. We omit many of the details here, but readers are encouraged to investigate this approach in Chapter 16.

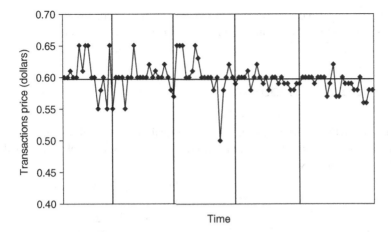

Figure 12.1 Transaction prices in a double-oral auction experiment with equal numbers of buyers and sellers. Note that vertical lines delineate trading rounds. The horizontal line represents the predicted equilibrium price based on given supply and demand functions.

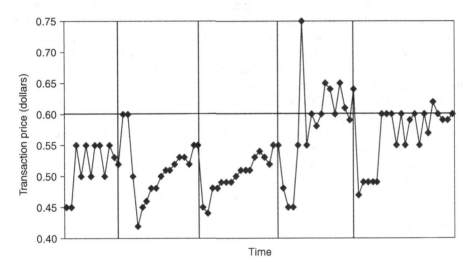

Figure 12.2 Transaction prices in a double-oral auction experiment with two buyers (duopsony). Note that vertical lines delineate trading rounds. The horizontal line represents the predicted competitive equilibrium price based on given supply and demand functions.

oligopsonistic structure of agricultural markets can have important price impacts for agricultural producers.

Now recall that in the beginning chapters of this book, the topic of "conspiracies" against agricultural producers was discussed, and was dismissed because agricultural producers were found to be receiving the highest possible price given consumer demand. Here, we find evidence that agricultural producers may, in fact, be receiving prices lower than would be the case in competitive markets. It is important to remember, however, that this result is not a function of conspiracies, but of the market structure that exists. This result does point out the importance of understanding the impact of market structure on prices. At the same time, collusion, coercion, and other noneconomic/nonlegal behavior are always a possibility. So, an understanding of both the legal and economic environment is critical.

12.3   Strategic Behavior

Yet another method of viewing the behavior of oligopolists is through game theory, as discussed in Chapter 11. Returning to our herbicide example above, consider the following payoff matrix:

		Firm B's price strategies	
		$45	$30
Firm A's price strategies	$45	112,112	58,123
	$30	123,58	91,91

This represents a simple Prisoner's Dilemma model, as discussed in the previous chapter. Here, firm A must decide what to do given what it thinks is firm B's best strategy. Firm B's dominant strategy is to lower its price to $30, because the worst outcome under $30 is better than the worst outcome under $45. Knowing this, it is obvious that firm A is better off lowering its price to $30 as well, so the Nash equilibrium solution in this case is for both firms to lower their prices. But, as can be seen, this is an inferior result as compared to the situation in which neither firm lower its price. As is often the case in games of this type, the underlying incentives are such that the firm's best action in anticipation of the other firm's best action leads to a result that is detrimental to both firms.

The above model, however, is what is known as a **single-period** game. That is, the firms are making a decision today that is binding for all subsequent periods. But it does not make sense that adjustments to strategy will not be made. For this situation, we really need to consider the strategies in **repeated games**. For simplicity, let's assume that industry profits are denoted by π_M. Let us further assume that in the first period, if a firm fractionally lowers its price, it captures all of π_M. But, if all firms charge the monopoly price, they divide the profits, π_M/n, in perpetuity. The present value of receiving one dollar each year forever is simply the reciprocal of the interest rate, so the present value of the profit stream is

$$\frac{\pi_M}{nr},$$

where r is the interest rate. A firm could lower its price to capture the entire market today, but it would expect its rivals to do the same in subsequent periods, eventually resulting in a price equal to marginal costs (the competitive solution). In the equation above, as long as $nr < 1$ because the number of firms is small, the interest rate is small, or both, the firm has no incentive to price below the monopoly price. Thus, in a game with repeated relationships, we move out of the suboptimal Nash equilibrium in the Prisoner's Dilemma to a Nash equilibrium where profits are maximized at the monopoly level.

There are certainly a number of variants to these two games, including games with incomplete information and sequential games, but the insight remains generally the same. Namely, the decision by firm A depends in large part on what firm B is expected to do in response. Certainly, we see evidence from repeated games of various types that the Nash equilibrium solution results in prices that are higher than those in competitive markets, and many times approach or equal prices found in a monopoly structure. From an economic perspective, this result implies that agricultural markets certainly do not achieve the level of efficiency and income distribution found in competitive markets. From a managerial perspective, this discussion highlights the importance of understanding strategy to effectively operate a business within the agricultural supply chain.

Key Questions

1. What is a Prisoner's Dilemma?
2. What differentiates a single-period game and a repeated game in terms of the oligopolist's incentives to act?

12.4 Empirical Analysis

Empirical analysis of imperfectly competitive markets can be quite complex. In this section, we will discuss some basic techniques for gaining perspective on the structure of markets and introduce some ideas of econometric techniques for market structure analysis.

12.4.1 Market Concentration

One of the most fundamental techniques for analyzing the structure of the market is to examine **market concentration**. There are a number of methods of estimating market concentration, but the most basic is called the **market concentration ratio**, which is simply a measure of the percentage of total market sales that is held by the top firms. The most common measure is called the **four-firm concentration ratio**, which is the percentage of total sales held by the top four firms in the market. Table 12.1 shows the four-firm concentration ratios for major agricultural supply chain sectors.

As can be seen, agricultural seeds (especially cotton), corn exporting, and food retailing all appear to be highly concentrated, while food processing remains relatively unconcentrated. The difficulty with relying solely on the concentration ratio is that there is no clear-cut means of discerning the impact of this concentration on market performance (that is, departure from competitive conditions). There are many cases in which highly concentrated industries may still exhibit competitive behavior, and conditions in which moderately concentrated industries behave as monopolists. Nevertheless, there appears to be some degree of correlation between concentration and imperfectly competitive behavior.

A slightly modified version of the simple concentration ratio is called the **Herfindahl-Hirschman index**, or *HI*, which is defined as follows:

$$HI = \sum_{i=1}^{N} S_i^2,$$

Table 12.1   Four-firm concentration ratios in agriculture, 1998

Sector	Four-firm concentration ratio
Agricultural seed	
Corn	67%
Soybeans	49%
Cotton	87%
Exporting firms	
Corn	70%
Wheat	47%
Food processing	20%
Food merchandising	40%
Food retailing	72%

Note: Food retailing is for retail food stores in the largest 100 cities.

Source: Collins (2001).

where N is the number of firms and S_i^2 is the squared market share of firm i. When in an industry is a monopoly, the index attains its maximum value of 1.[11] The construction of the index accounts for two key variables—firm numbers and inequality in market share. Consider the following cases. First, we assume there are two firms that equally divide sales (equal market shares):

$$HI = \sum_{i=1}^{N} S_i^2 = 0.5^2 + 0.5^2 = 0.5.$$

Next, consider the case in which there are two firms, one with a 75% market share and one with 25% market share:

$$HI = \sum_{i=1}^{N} S_i^2 = 0.75^2 + 0.25^2 = 0.625.$$

Clearly, in both cases, the top two firms account for 100% of the output. But in the first case, market shares are divided, leading to a lower *HI*, suggesting less concentration. In the second case, however, the *HI* is higher, suggesting a greater degree of concentration within one firm. Now consider the case in which there are three firms, with market share equally divided among them:

$$HI = \sum_{i=1}^{N} S_i^2 = 0.33^2 + 0.33^2 + 0.33^2 = 0.33.$$

So, the *HI* decreases as the number of firms increases or the inequality in market share across firms decreases. There is still no clear-cut way to determine market performance,

---

[11]That is, the market share for the monopolist is 1. Thus, $1^2 = 1$, so the *HI* is equal to 1.

but the *HI* at least accounts for the heterogeneity in firm size within the market, to get a clearer picture of market concentration.

12.4.2   New Empirical Industrial Organization

A newer vein of analysis in market structure is something called **New Empirical Industrial Organization** (NEIO). NEIO methods have the benefit of combining game-theoretic ideas of market behavior with the empirical methods of market concentration analysis and econometrics, to develop a richer, more complete understanding of imperfectly competitive markets. These techniques are sometimes quite complex, and beyond the scope of this text. Nevertheless, it is worth mentioning that NEIO has been used to address such issues as profit persistence (Lau, 1982; Hall, 1988) as well as market power exertion (Applebaumn, 1982; Schroeter, 1988; Sumner, 1991; Raper et al., 2000). Those of you who are interested in pursuing deeper studies of market structure using NEIO techniques are encouraged, to start with Schmalensee and Willig (1989) as a primer.

Key Questions

1. What is market concentration?
2. What is a four-firm concentration ratio?
3. What are the weaknesses of simple concentration ratios?
4. How is the Herfindahl–Hirschman index different than a simple concentration ratio?

12.5   Summary

This chapter has laid out some basic foundations for understanding imperfectly competitive markets. Because agriculture is imperfectly competitive in most instances, an understanding of the implications of imperfect competition is important to understanding why our markets work the way they do and to beginning to develop a sense for how to operate within the these markets. This chapter, however, is simply an introduction to the concepts of imperfect competition. One can literally take several courses on the subject and still not have covered all relevant topics. Nevertheless, if you understand the basics presented here, other models simply build upon the basic structures that have been discussed. As agricultural markets continue to evolve, a greater understanding of imperfectly competitive markets will become increasingly important.

Exercises

Problem 12.1   *Assume there are two firms selling a new seed variety (firms A and B). Firm A is attempting to determine how many tons of seed to offer for sale. It believes that firm B will sell 10 tons. The industry inverse demand function is given by $P = 220 - 4Q$. The per ton cost of selling seed is 20. What is the equilibrium quantity firm A should offer for sale according to the Cournot model?*

Problem 12.2   *In the problem above, if the elasticity of demand (in absolute value) is 1.67, what is the predicted profit margin for the industry?*

Problem 12.3   *Assume there are five firms in an industry with market shares of 0.40, 0.20, 0.15, 0.15, and 0.10, respectively. Based on these data, what is the Herfindahl-Hirschman index for this industry? Suppose now that the first and third firms merge. What is the new Herfindahl–Hirschman index for the industry?*

Problem 12.4   *Assume that firm A in an industry currently holds a 0.40 market share (40% market share). Also assume that the own-price elasticity of demand (in absolute value) for the industry is 1.20. If firm A conjectures that its competitors will increase their output by half for every one unit of output it increases (that is, $dq_B/dq_A = 0.5$), what is the predicted profit margin for firm A? What if firm A conjectures that its competitors will decrease their output by 50% for every one unit it increases its output? From these results, can you surmise the impact that competitor response is having on firm A's profit margin? Explain your answer.*

References

Applebaum, E. "Estimation of the Degree of Oligopoly Power." *Journal of Econometrics*, 19(1982): 287–299.

Chamberlin, E. *The Theory of Monopolistic Competition*. Harvard University Press, Cambridge, MA, 1933.

Collins, K. "Statement to the U.S. Senate Committee on Appropriations Subcommittee on Agriculture, Rural Development and Related Agencies, May 17, 2001." Available online at http://www.usda.gov/oce/speeches/051701co.html, accessed 2/23/2005.

Cowling, K. and M. Waterson. "Price–Cost Margins and Market Structure." *Economica*, 43(1976): 267–274.

Hall, R. "The Relation between Price and Marginal Cost in U.S. Industry." *Journal of Political Economy*, 96(1988): 921–947.

Holloway, G. "The Farm-Retail Price Spread in an Imperfectly Competitive Food Industry." *American Journal of Agricultural Economics*, 73(1991): 979–989.

Hudson, D. "Intra-Processor Price-Spread Behavior: Is the U.S. Catfish Industry Competitive?" *Journal of Food Distribution Research*, 29(1998): 59–65.

Hudson, D. and J. Anderson. "The Impacts of Market Structure on Agricultural Markets." Paper presented to the Food and Agricultural Marketing Policy Conference, Washington, DC, March 2006.

Kreps, D. and J. Scheinkman. "Quantity Precommitment and Bertrand Competition Yield Cournot Outcomes." *Bell Journal of Economics*, 14(1983): 326–337.

Lau, L. "On Identifying the Degree of Competitiveness from Industry Price and Output Data." *Economics Letters*, 10(1982): 93–99.

Novshek, W. "Cournot Equilibrium with Free Entry." *Review of Economic Studies*, 47(1980): 473–486.

Raper, K., A. Love, and R. Shumway. "Determining Market Power Exertion between Buyers and Sellers." *Journal of Applied Econometrics*, 15(2000): 225–252.

Scherer, F. and D. Ross. *Industrial Market Structure and Economic Performance*, third edition. Houghton Mifflin Company, Boston, MA, 1990.

Schmalensee, R. and R. Willig (editors). *Handbook of Industrial Organization.* North-Holland, Amsterdam, 1989.

Schroeter, J. "Estimating the Degree of Market Power in the Beef Packing Industry." *Review of Economics and Statistics*, 70(1988): 158–162.

Sumner, D. "Measurement of Monopoly Behavior: An Application to the Cigarette Industry." *Journal of Political Economy*, 89(1991): 1,010-1,019.

Tomek, W. and K. Robinson. *Agricultural Product Prices*, third edition. Cornell University Press, Ithaca, NY, 1990.

Appendix 12A: The conjectural Variations Model

In this appendix, we relax the original Cournot assumption that when a firm makes a quantity decision, it takes the quantity offered by the other firm as fixed. Continuing with our herbicide market example, if we assume that firm A's profit function is

$$\pi_A = P(Q)q_A - cq_A,$$

we can now incorporate firm A's conjecture about firm B's reaction into the first-order condition for profit maximization. This can be seen as

$$\frac{d\pi_A}{dq_A} = P(Q) + \left(\frac{dP}{dQ}\right)\left[1 + \left(\frac{dq_B}{dq_A}\right)\right]q_A - c = 0$$

$$= a - \left[2b + \left(\frac{dq_A}{dq_B}\right)\right]q_A - bq_B - c = 0.$$

Solving for q_A yields firm A's reaction function:

$$q_A = \frac{(a - c - bq_A)}{\left[2b + \left(\frac{dq_B}{dq_A}\right)\right]}.$$

As can be seen, the reaction function using conjectural variations is significantly more complex than under the standard Cournot assumptions. However, this reaction function explicitly accounts for the anticipated reaction of firm B to changes made by firm A.

Chapter 13

Vertical Coordination and Contracting in Agriculture

~

We have been treating market price determination as a transaction (or transactions) that occur within a market with little regard to how those transactions are conducted. Implicitly, we are assuming that all transactions occur within a spot market, where individual buyers and sellers interact to arrive at a mutually agreed upon price. These relationships are "one-shot." That is, once the transaction is completed, there is no continued relationship between the parties. This "faceless" view of transactions is useful in understanding general market, as well as individual optimization, behavior, but is not particularly useful in understanding the more complex relationships between parties in the market. In this chapter, we shall peel away the layers around transactions. This chapter only provides an introduction to the rich and varied literature on market organization, but provides some perspective on the different viewpoints about market behavior.

13.1 Defining Transactions

There is a wide variety in type and implications of transactions. Consider the description in Figure 13.1. The exchange process can be viewed as a continuum. At one extreme, there is the well-known spot market, where a product is produced by one party and purchased by another party. The producer owns the factors of production and makes all production decisions. At the other end of the continuum is complete vertical integration. In vertical integration, one party owns the factors of production, produces the product for itself, and then consumes it (or further processes it).

Example 13.1 *Assume that you have a market for wheat flour. At one end of the market, you have the wheat miller who produces wheat flour. At the other end of the market, you*

Figure 13.1 The continuum of exchange.

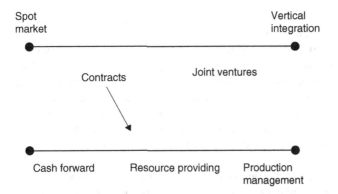

Figure 13.2 An extension of the continuum of exchange' showing contract types.

have the bread maker. In a spot market system, the wheat millers would offer their product for sale in the market to anyone who wished to buy. The bread makers would search the market for the flour with the best price and/or quality and purchase from that miller. Note that the bread maker is not obligated to buy from any particular miller in either this transaction or any future transaction. Likewise, the miller is not obligated to sell to any particular bread maker in either this or any future transaction. Once the transaction is complete, the relationship is essentially terminated.

Example 13.2 *At the other extreme, we could also have vertical integration. In this case, the bread maker may buy a wheat miller's operation, then produce his own wheat flour. Note that the transaction still takes place. That is, someone is producing wheat flour and delivering it to a bread maker. In vertical integration, it is simply the single firm that is carrying out that transaction internally. The market is circumvented by vertical ownership. If all firms in the market were vertically integrated, then there would be no "price" for wheat flour in the sense of a market price that is observable. Rather, the "price" for wheat flour would be an internal calculation for the individual firms.*

At this point, you are probably thinking about the different arrangements that exist that do not fit either the spot market or the vertical integration description. As with other real-world phenomenon, there are variants to the extremes. Contracting in agriculture provides a ready example with which you may be somewhat familiar. Figure 13.2 shows an extension of the continuum of exchange.

The continuum of contract types is viewed similarly as the overall continuum of exchange. Cash forward contracts lie closest to the spot market exchange mechanism, with resource-providing contracts and production management contracts moving up the continuum toward vertical integration. Note that all of the contract types may be viewed as lying below joint ventures on the overall continuum. However, production management contracts take on characteristics of vertical integration, and thus, in some cases, may closely resemble vertical integration. Kohls and Uhl (1998) provide useful definitions of different contract types represented in Figure 13.2:

- **Cash forward contract**. A contract between the producer and buyer of a product that typically specifies the quality, quantity, delivery time, delivery place, and/or price of the product. A cash forward contract does not typically specify production practices or provide inputs or management advice.

- **Resource-providing contract**. A contract that often specifies certain production resources to be used and the place of their purchase. The contractor/integrator usually provides the producer with financing, ranging from operational to fixed investment financing, and a degree of managerial help and supervision. Product prices are usually based on the open market, and income guarantees to the producer are minimal. In such contracts, the contractors/integrators may influence the technology and size of the operations of the producer in order to increase and stabilize the market for their own products.

- **Production management contract**. A contract that often includes the marketing and production stipulations of the above two types of contract. In addition, it provides for the transferring of part or all of the market price and income risks from the producer to the contractor/integrator. This is usually done by paying the producer a prearranged return per unit of product or by guaranteeing against market-oriented financial loss. In these contracts, the contractor/integrator assumes a substantial part of the managerial responsibility of the producers. These contracts come the closest to obtaining the managerial and financial control and risk that occurs when the integration is effected through complete ownership.

These are only general definitions. There are variations on each type of contract. The key element to note is that the involvement of the buyer in the decision-making at the production level becomes progressively more prominent as one moves across the continuum. These contracts make of the overall form of integration called **contract integration**. This is compared to **ownership integration**, which is where all the decisions and assets in a supply chain are owned by one firm.

Key Questions

1. What differentiates spot markets and vertical integration?
2. What differentiates the different types of contract?
3. What differentiates contract integration from ownership integration?

13.2   Governance Structure

The previous discussion can be referred to loosely as the **governance stucture** of the firm or transaction (Williamson, 1979). That is, whether the transaction takes place in a spot market or a vertically integrated environment is referred to as the governance structure within the market or firm. An important question, then, is "What determines the governance structure?"

13.2.1   The Importance of Governance Structure

Governance structure is important because it sets the "rules of the game" for participants in the market. Williamson (2000) discusses the difference between the concept of governance structure and the normal neoclassical optimization that has been discussed in previous chapters (Figure 13.3). The highest order of optimization lies at the level

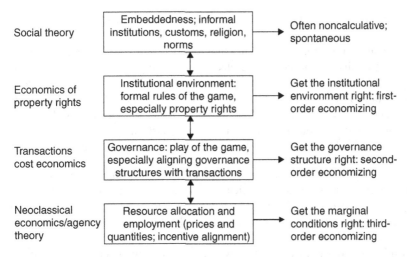

Figure 13.3 The economics of institutions and governance.
Source: Williamson (2000).

of social norms and customs. This superstructure is a consequence of the historical development of a society. It provides a framework for the development of political and economic systems. Further down the line, we find the establishment of governance structures for transactions. Governance structures include legal conventions, organization of firms, and so on, and provide a structure through which individuals make decisions. Finally, we arrive at the level of individual allocation decisions. Most of your academic training in economics is focused at this level. It describes the optimization (either utility or profit) behavior of individuals given a particular governance structure.

This distinction appears somewhat foreign at first. However, the traditional economic theory with which you are likely most familiar is simply a description of economic behavior within the context of a spot market governance structure. You have likely been exposed to additional concepts such as franchises, cooperatives, and so on, but you have not discussed these in terms of their governance structure. Understanding what drives the development of a particular structure is important for understanding overall economic behavior.

It is also important to point out another distinction between neoclassical theory and transactions cost economics. In neoclassical theory, we assume that economic agents are rational. That is, they optimize according to their situation—consumers maximize utility and producers maximize profit. While seemingly benign, this assumption implicitly assumes that individuals are capable of working through very complex problems.[1] By contrast, transactions cost economics adopts a more modest assumption of **bounded rationality**.

Bounded rationality holds that individuals do not have the mental capacity to solve these complex problems "in their heads." That is, individuals adopt "rules of thumb" that approximate optimal behavior, but are not fully optimal. This is a minor distinction in assumptions, but it implies that individuals are not fully rational in the neoclassical sense.

---

[1]This is not to say that everyone works through and solves the first-order conditions for utility maximization. It simply says that they act as if they solve these equations.

13.2.2   The Determination of Governance Structure

Neoclassical economic theory assumes that transactions occur in a frictionless environment. That is, there is no cost associated with carrying out a transaction of any type in the market. This, of course, is not a particularly realistic assumption. **Transactions cost economics** (TCE) relaxes this assumption and assumes that the transactions cost will affect the manner in which transactions are conducted. Specifically, TCE holds that transactions are carried out in a manner that minimizes the transactions cost. Transactions costs can be thought of as being of three general types (Milgrom and Roberts, 1992):

- **Information costs.** Costs associated with gathering information about market conditions, costs, prices, and so on, which also includes the opportunity cost of time spent by the producer or buyer gathering, analyzing, and understanding the information.
- **Negotiation costs.** Costs associated with collecting products for shipment, finding buyers, and actual legal expenses of negotiation.
- **Monitoring and enforcement costs.** Costs of examining performance, quality control, and legal expenses associated with enforcing contracts or market arrangements.

Information costs are composed of many common activities with which you are probably familiar. For example, agricultural producers commonly acquire price information through information services, newspapers, or local buyers. The monetary cost of this information is a transactions cost. However, producers also spend time collecting, analyzing and understanding the information, which is an opportunity cost. Thus, both monetary and opportunity costs are considered as transactions costs in each of the categories above.

Another important concept within TCE is asset specificity. According to Williamson (1979) and Klein, Crawford, and Alchain (1978), asset specificity is defined as follows:

- **Asset specificity.** The magnitude of economic costs associated with redeploying an asset to its best alternative use and by its best alternative user.

Two key concepts are associated with asset specificity: **quasi-rents** and the **"hold-up" problem**. A quasi-rent is the difference between the best alternative use of capital before it is invested in the asset and the return it must earn to prevent alternative use of the capital after it is invested (Hennessey and Lawrence, 1999). The "hold-up" problem arises when the buyer (seller) attempts to appropriate the rents from the seller (buyer) by forcing disadvantageous contractual terms. The buyer (seller) has this leverage because the seller (buyer) has invested in a specific asset.

Example 13.3   *Assume that a farmer has invested in facilities to produce poultry. Obviously, there is little alternative use for the poultry houses and it would be costly to dismantle the poultry houses (redeploy the asset). According to TCE, the poultry producer will seek out a contract with the poultry buyer in order to insure demand for his product to cover investment costs.[2] Now, the poultry buyer may recognize this investment as*

---

[2]In this simple example, we are not considering the impact of contract length. Obviously, the producer would prefer a longer contract to a shorter contract, depending on the length of amortization of investment in the poultry houses. We are extrapolating from the problem of contract length in this example, but this issue will be addressed below.

specific and use that as leverage to force unfavorable terms upon the producer. Thus, the asset specificity may lead to a "hold-up" problem to the disadvantage of the producer.

It is important to note that the effects of asset specificity can also work in the other direction. That is, producers can use the investment in specific assets by processors to force unfavorable terms as well.

Example 13.4 *Assume that a group of producers act together to market a product, say catfish, through a marketing pool. The processor has obviously made investments in specific assets related to catfish processing. If the output of the producers makes up a large enough portion of the processing of the firm, the producers may use this leverage to force higher prices from the processor. The producers have this leverage because the investment in catfish processing facilities would be expensive to redeploy.*

The Role of Governance Costs

Now that we have some concept of transactions costs and asset specificity, we can explore the determination of governance structure. Williamson (1996) provides a simple model that is useful in this regard. Assume that there are two possible profit functions faced by a producer:

$$\pi^i = R(X) - C\,(X, k; \alpha) - \gamma k - G_i$$

and

$$\pi^m = R(X) - C\,(X, k; \alpha) - \gamma k - G_m,$$

where π^i is the profit associated with contract type i, π^m is the profit associated with spot market sales, $R(X)$ is the revenue associated with selling a given output X, $C\,(X, k; \alpha)$ is a twice differentiable, concave cost function, k is the degree of asset specificity with a per unit cost γ, G_i and G_m are the governance costs associated with contract type i and spot sales, respectively, and α is a shift parameter. It is assumed that $C_X < 0$, $C_k > 0$, and $C_{Xk} < 0$. A higher value of α has greater cost-reducing consequences for asset specificity: $C_{k\alpha} < 0$ and $C_{X\alpha} < 0$.[3]

Assume that governance costs are given by the following:

$$G_i = \beta + V(k)$$

and

$$G_m = W(k),$$

where $\beta > 0$ is the bureaucratic cost parameter and $V_k > 0$ and $W_k > 0$. Further, it is assumed that $W_k > V_k$ for all common k, or the marginal cost of governance with respect to asset specificity is greater for spot markets than for any type of contract. It is clear from this that output is chosen to equalize marginal revenue with marginal cost

---

[3] The subscripts denote the partial derivative. For example, C_X is the first derivative of the cost function with respect to X, and $C_{X\alpha}$ is the second derivative of the cost function, first with respect to X and then with respect to α.

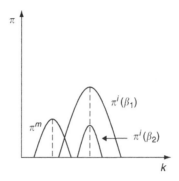

Figure 13.4   The impacts of bureaucratic governance costs on choice of contracting.
Source: Williamson (2000).

(the first-order conditions for profit maximization). However, optimal asset specificity will be chosen (given an output level) to minimize the joint production and governance costs. Examining profits as a function of asset specificity yields a central hypothesis (Figure 13.4). It is assumed that the output is optimal for each level of asset specificity. There is only one profit function for spot sales, but a family of profit relations for contract types depending on the bureaucratic cost parameter, β. The choice of mode of production, then, depends on the profit relation with the highest peak. For example, with a relatively low bureaucratic cost parameter, β_1, integration would be chosen. This is because the additional governance cost coming from the bureaucratic cost is less than the difference in marginal costs between spot sales and the contract (recall that we assumed that $W_k > V_k$, so that in this case, $\beta_1 < W_k - V_k$). However, with a higher bureaucratic cost, β_2, spot sales would be chosen. Clearly, then, it is the *relative* transactions cost between spot sales and contracts that determines the mode of production.

To summarize, transactions costs are composed of three main types of costs: information, negotiation, and monitoring and enforcement costs. More generally, we can summarize transactions costs in two concepts: governance costs and asset specificity. Asset specificity is important because of the associated quasi-rents, and the attempted appropriation of those rents, called the "hold-up" problem, by the other party to the transaction. Governance costs are important through the potential profit relations of contracts versus spot sales. As bureaucratic costs associated with contracts increase, the likelihood of choosing spot sales increases. Thus, transactions costs affect our choice of mode of production (spot markets versus vertical integration and contracting). However, our optimal output and marginal conditions are unaffected by these costs.

Risk and Risk Shifting[4]

There is no universally accepted definition of risk. However, Fleisher (1990) provides a relatively succinct definition:

> When a decision is made under certainty, each possible action has only one possible consequence. This one-to-one correspondence between the action and its

---

[4] It should be noted that this section is not a comprehensive treatment of risk. You are referred to any standard risk or production economics text for a more complete treatment on this subject.

consequences occurs because the decision-maker knows both the event that will occur and its effect on the action selected . . . In contrast, a decision made under uncertainty has at least one action choice with more than one possibe consequence. Many different events may occur between the time the decision is made and the time the consequences are felt. (pp. 13–15)

This definition contains two key elements. First, there is a decision that must be made. That is, the decision-maker is faced with a problem or decision that must be made. Second, for there to be risk, there must be multiple potential outcomes. The decision-maker, then, must make a decision where he or she does not know the final outcome.

Example 13.5   *A producer must make a decision as to whether to plant a crop. Prior to planting, the producer must determine the potential outcome of that decision. The price of the product may go up after planting, thereby increasing the value of the crop. The price of the product may go down after planting, thereby decreasing the value of the crop. Finally, the price may stay the same. The producer does not know the final harvest price of the product. Thus, the producer faces price risk.*[5]

In this example, we are assuming no external forms of risk shifting, such as futures markets. It should be clear from this example that the producer is making a decision under uncertainty. Sandmo (1971) has clearly shown that this risk has an impact on the producers output decision. Specifically, output price risk leads to lower input usage and lower production.

A second element of importance is the producer's attitude toward risk. An individual can be **risk neutral**, which implies that individual is not affected by the risk he or she faces. In contrast, individuals can be **risk averse**, which implies that the individual would prefer less risk to more. In this case, these individuals will seek out methods of reducing their risk. Finally, individuals can be **risk seeking**, which implies that individuals prefer risky situations. Most commonly, individuals, in this case producers, are assumed to be risk averse.

Risk averse producers are assumed to be willing to forgo some level of income, called a **risk premium**, in order to have some assurance about minimum income.

Example 13.6   *A classic example of the risk premium/risk aversion concept is insurance. You purchase automobile insurance to protect against the loss of income (cost of repairs) in case of an automobile accident. The premium that you pay is the risk premium associated with the level of protection you choose to have. A higher-coverage amount means a higher premium (or a lower deductible amount means a higher premium). At the same time, the level of the risk premium is related to the underlying level of risk. If you live in a heavily populated area with a high frequency of accidents, the premium that you pay will be higher for a given level of protection as compared to the same level of coverage in a rural area.*

This example highlights the relationship between the risk premium and the level of risk. Another element is the level of risk aversion. Individuals who are highly risk averse

---

[5]This, of course, abstracts from potential yield risk that occurs because the producer does not know the final yield. In this case, the producer faces yield risk.

are willing to forgo a larger portion of their income to insure against the same level of risk as compared to individuals who are less risk averse. That is, if you highly fear risk, you will be willing to pay a much higher insurance premium as compared to a friend who is less afraid of potential adverse outcome. The level of risk aversion an individual exhibits is potentially a function of many things, but most economists associate risk aversion with the level of wealth and the magnitude of consequences or outcomes.

Example 13.7 *Two individuals are facing an equally risky outcome; say, a bet on a roulette table. The first individual is a millionaire, while the second individual is poor. The millionaire is less likely to be concerned with the inherent riskiness of a $100 bet with maximum potential winnings of $200, while the poor individual is likely to be highly hesitant in making the bet. However, if the same $100 bet had a maximum potential winning of $1 million, even the poor individual might make the bet.*

Risk aversion, then, is a central concept in understanding motivations underlying contracting and vertical integration. If the producer is risk averse, then he or she will be willing to forgo some potential income if someone will be willing to take on that risk. This **risk shifting** is a central underlying concept behind contracts. Buyers of products are assumed to be risk neutral because they have a portfolio of assets, which means that risk does not affect their decisions. The buyers are thus willing to take on risk from the producer in exchange for income. There are several forms of risk shifting, but the most typical is some form of price guarantee.

Example 13.8 *A cotton producer faces price risk. Assume that the producer expects the harvest-time price of cotton to be 60 cents per pound, but is not certain about the harvest-time price. A buyer may offer a cash forward contract of 58 cents per pound. If the producer is sufficiently risk averse, he or she will accept that contract. In this case, the producer has shifted the risk of price changes through the growing season to the buyer. In exchange for shifting this risk, the producer has accepted a 2 cents per pound reduction in the expected price. Now, the price of cotton could increase, in which case the producer will still receive 58 cents per pound. However, if the price of cotton declines, the producer is still protected from price changes.*

Thus, the theory of risk suggests that increases in risk should lead to a greater use of contracting/vertical integration on the part of the producer. It is also important to note that risks faced by downstream processors will also increase the use of vertical integration. These risks may be related to price risk, but they may also be related to **supply risk**. Supply risk is the risk of not being able to find a sufficient supply of appropriate quality product to run production facilities efficiently or meet consumer demand.[6] These processors will seek out contracts or vertically integrate with producers in order to insure that they will have an ample supply of product. These alternative sources of risk affect decisions in a similar manner—*increases in risk lead to a greater desire to shift risk.*

---

[6] A symmetrical relationship exists at the producer level in terms of *demand risk*. If producers grow a unique product, say blueberries, where there is not an active market with many buyers, producers run the risk of not having a buyer for the product. In this case, they will search out contracts to insure a buyer for their product.

Another factor that is related to risk is **diversification**. Diversification is the spreading (or combining) of risk across different sources that are unrelated, in order to reduce the overall amount of risk exposure. Diversification can come from a number of sources:

Example 13.9 *An individual owns stock in two companies. The income of company one is positively related to increases in interest rates, while the income of company two is negatively related to increases in interest rates. Thus, as interest rates increase, the stock price of company one increases, while the stock price of company two decreases, and vice versa.*

Income diversification is also an important component of diversification. That is, if an individual's income comes from several different, unrelated sources, income risk will be reduced. For agricultural producers, a primary method of achieving income diversification is through off-farm income. For example, a producer may derive income from the farm, while the spouse works off the farm. If the spouse's income is not related to agriculture, total household income is diversified and income risk is reduced.

Diversification is important because it reduces risk. As such, increased levels of diversification should reduce the desire to shift risk, and thus decrease the use of contracting/vertical integration, *ceteris paribus*. Thus, both risk and diversification, in addition to transactions costs, are expected to influence the choice of governance structure.

Key Questions

1. What differentiates neoclassical theory from transactions cost economics?
2. What are the types of transactions costs?
3. How is asset specificity important? How does the concept of asset specificity fit with the concept of "not making decisions based on sunk costs"?
4. How does governance cost affect the choice of governance structure?
5. What is risk and how does it affect governance structure?
6. What is diversification and how does it affect governance structure?

13.3 Contracts

Given that the governance structure has been determined, it becomes relevant to understand how it is implemented. In this case, we are interested in how contracts are formulated. We typically assume in neoclassical theory that both parties to a transaction (producers and consumers) have complete, accurate information and that these parties agree on the implications of that information. However, this is not a particularly realistic assumption. You are probably keenly aware of any number of examples. A classic example is selling a used car. Obviously, the seller of the car has more information in this transaction than the buyer. The seller knows if the car has been wrecked, whether the oil has been changed in a regular manner, whether the car has any electrical defects, and so on. The buyer can seek out additional information, but is never likely to know the full history of the car. This is only one type of **asymmetric information**.

In models of asymmetric information, we are working within the **Principal–Agent framework**. There are two "people" in the Principal–Agent model. There is the *leader* (who proposes the contract), who is called the **Principal**, and the *follower* (the party who has to simply accept or reject the contract), who is called the **Agent**. Generally, one of these two is the informed party, whose information is relevant to the common welfare, and the other is the uninformed party. We will assume that the Principal offers a "take-it-or-leave-it" contract and expects a yes-or-no answer. The Agent is not free to counter-offer on the contract.

Given our description of the Principal–Agent model and the concept of asymmetric information, we can now describe two general situations of asymmetric information (Salanie, 1998):

- **Adverse selection** is a situation in which some characteristic of the Agent is not observable by the Principal. This term comes from a phenomenon well known to insurers: If a company only offers a premium tailored to the average risk in the population, this premium will only attract the higher risks and the insurer will therefore lose money. This effect may even induce the insurer to give up insuring some risks. Other terms sometimes used are "self-selection" or "screening."
- **Moral hazard** arises when the Agent takes a decision ("action") that affects his utility and that of the Principal. The Principal only observes the "outcome," which is an imperfect signal of the action taken. Finally, the action the Agent would choose spontaneously is not Pareto-optimal. Thus, because the action is unobservable, the Principal cannot force the Agent to choose an action that is Pareto-optimal.

13.3.1   Adverse Selection

The simplest way to understand adverse selection is through an example. Let the Principal be a butcher and the Agent be a buyer. The Agent may be a keen amateur of good steaks or he may have more modest tastes. Let's assume that there are two "types": the sophisticated Agent (who is ready to pay a large sum of money for a good steak) and the coarse consumer (whose tastes, or means, are less developed and who either cannot afford or cannot recognize a quality steak). Let's assume further that the Principal cannot observe the type of any given Agent, or at least the law (as is often the case) forbids him to use nonanonymous prices that would discriminate between the two types.[7]

The key to the solution of the adverse selection problem is that if the sophisticated Agent is willing to pay more than the coarse Agent for a given increase in the quality of the steaks, then the Principal can segment the market by offering two different steaks:

1. A steak of high quality with a high price.
2. A steak of a lower quality with a lower price.

Ultimately, contract theory concludes that the coarse type buys a lower quality than would be socially optimal.[8] The whole point of adverse selection is to make the Agents reveal their type without incurring too high a social distortion. The critical element is that the Agent has **private information** about his preferences that is of value to the Principal. To get the Agent to reveal that information, the Principal must ultimately create a contract

---

[7] This is essentially an assumption that the Principal cannot practice first-degree price discrimination.

[8] A mathematical solution to this problem is found in Appendix 13A.

that is socially distorting—the idea being that the contract should minimize the social distortion.

Here are some additional examples of adverse selection:

- In life insurance, the insured surely knows more about his or her own health (and therefore the risk of dying soon) than does the insurer, even if he or she has to go through a medical visit. This suggest that the insurer should offer several insurance packages, each tailored for a specific risk class.
- Banks face borrowers whose default risk they can only imperfectly assess. A natural idea is to use interest rates to discriminate between borrowers.
- Employers face potential workers who have an informational advantage in that they know their ability better than the firms. The latter must then screen workers so as to attract the gifted and discard the others.

13.3.2   Moral Hazard

It is difficult to imagine many economic relationships that do not have at least some elements of moral hazard. Again, some examples may make the concept moral hazard easier to understand:

- Moral hazard is common within firms. Employers can rarely control all the decisions of their employees. The term *effort* is often used to designate all employee inputs that are not directly observable; the employer can only condition wages on production or other observable variables to induce employees to put in effort.
- In property insurance, the moral hazard aspect stems from the fact that the insurer cannot observe the self-protection efforts of the insured, even though these positively affect his profits.

The important aspect is that the action of the Agent is not directly observable by the Principal. So, if you have crop insurance, you may not be quite as interested in protecting the crop from pests and thus do not spray the additional insecticide. Thus, like adverse selection, moral hazard implies that the Agent has private information about himself. However, in the case of moral hazard, the private information relates to the Agent's action, not preferences.

13.3.3   Contract Length

As mentioned earlier in this chapter, contract length is a variable of obvious interest to the parties in a contract. The relationship between asset specificity and contract length is one that has received considerable theoretical and empirical attention (Joskow, 1987). Returning to the poultry producer example:

Example 13.10   *A poultry producer has invested in poultry houses at considerable cost. Assume that this investment is amortized over a 10-year period. As stated above, the investment in a specific asset likely leads to the producer seeking out contracts, ceteris paribus. At the same time, the poultry producer is also interested in contract* *length. That is, a one-year contract does not significantly protect the producer from rent appropriation or risk over the life of the investment. Thus, the producer is interested in a contract that has a longer term, so that risk is shifted for the greatest amount of time.*

One obvious question is whether the producer would prefer a contract of 10 years over any other contract (with equal terms such as price, quantity, etc.). The answer is not necessarily. As time passes, the producer increases his equity position in the operation (by paying down debt). With a greater equity position, financial risk (that is, the leveraged position) is reduced and the producer may be less inclined to contract. There are many variables that affect this decision, but it is important to note that one may not simply wish to match contract length with amortization schedules.

The example above brings out another important term—**contract risk**. Contract risk is defined as the probability of having contract terms change during the life of an investment. Again, returning to the example above:

Example 13.11 *Assume that the maximum contract length that a poultry buyer will offer is five years. Also assume that this buyer has offered a lucrative contract to attract a producer into making the investment in poultry houses. Over the initial five years, the producer is protected from risk and is making an adequate rate of return on the investment. However, at the end of the five-year contract, the producer still has five years left on his amortization, but no contract. At this point, the buyer may attempt to change the terms of the contract to the detriment of the producer.*

Thus, contract risk is essentially the embodiment of the "hold-up" problem discussed above in conjunction with asset specificity. Because the producer has invested in a specific asset, in this case poultry houses, the buyer has leverage to force unfavorable terms on the producer. It is important to note that, in practice, these phenomena are significantly more complicated to detect or discern. For example, the buyer may actually provide the financing to the producer at a lower rate of interest than the producer could get at a bank. The buyer may provide inputs, management advice, and so on. These all complicate the problem of detecting whether the buyer has forced "unfair" terms on the producer. In addition, many buyers have nondisclosure clauses in contracts prohibiting producers from discussing the terms of their contracts. There is currently a movement in many state legislatures to implement more transparency and openness in contracts, to prevent buyers from having an informational advantage over producers.

13.3.4 Complete versus Incomplete Contracts

We have been considering the most basic of economic relationships: a contract was signed, the parties took actions in relation to their preferences and the terms of the contract, and then they separated. It is also useful to distinguish between complete and incomplete contracts. In the former, all possible contingencies have been foreseen and entered into the contract. For example, what happens when you get hailed out during the growing season? A complete contract would include a provision for nondelivery. This is a simple example and one that is often included in contracts. However, what if Martians come down and gamma-ray your fields, making the crops inedible? I bet that one is not in your contract. We make the assumption that all possible contingencies have been planned for in the contract.[9]

Second, contracts are not typically static. That is, contracts are typically a result of relationships that exist over some period of time. This brings up the issue of **commitment and renegotiation**. While the theory of commitment is beyond the scope of this text, it is useful to have some idea of the levels of commitment (Salanie, 1998):

- **Spot commitment** is when the contract only holds for the current period (the exact definition of period depends on the context).
- **Full commitment** is when the contract that is signed covers the whole duration of the relationship and it cannot be breached or renegotiated.[10]
- **Long-term commitment with renegotiation** is when the contract covers the whole duration of the relationship, but it can be renegotiated multilaterally. It can only be reconsidered if both parties agree.
- **Limited commitment** is when the contract does not last as long as the relationship and can be renegotiated. This is most similar to our example of poultry houses.

A simple analogy is that of marriage. Some would argue (philosophically, that is) that signing a prenuptual agreement shows that the people getting married are either "spot" or "limited" commited to the marriage. The prenuptual agreement provides an easy "escape" from the marriage. However, "full" commitment would come from not being concerned about the post-marriage dissolution of assets.

The theory on incomplete contracts is much less developed. In this case, we are assuming that the parties do not specify provisions for all possible occurences over the life of the contract. There are two possible reasons for these omissions. First, the parties simply cannot foresee all possible outcomes. This is not unlike the analogy of the Martians from above. We simply are not capable of foreseeing everything (remember the reference to bounded rationality from above). Alternatively, we must recognize the simple fact that negotiating contracts is an expensive business, which requires significant time on the part of managers and significant money for lawyers, researchers, and so on. It should be simple to see that at some point, the cost of taking into account an improbable contingency outweighs the benefits of writing a specific clause into the contract. In this case, the contract will be signed without the contingency.

Key Questions

1. What is adverse selection?
2. What is moral hazard?
3. What influences contract length?
4. What are the types of commitment?
5. What is the difference between complete and incomplete contracts?

---

[9] Obviously, Martians are not going to gamma-ray your crops, but then this would not be a "possible" contingency.

[10] As Salanie (1998) notes, this conjures up the image of Cortez buring the boats when he reached the New World. To motivate his crew, Cortez is said to have burned his boats as a symbol (and reality) that there would be no return. Thus, he fully commited himself and his crew to conquering and exploring the New World.

References

Fleisher, B. *Agricultural Risk Management*. Lynne Rienner Publishers, Boulder, CO, 1990.

Hennessey, D. and J. Lawrence. "Contractual Relations, Control and Quality in the Hog Sector." *Review of Agricultural Economics*, 21(1999): 52–67.

Joskow, P. "Contract Duration and Relationship-Specific Investments: Empirical Evidence from Coal Markets." *American Economic Review*, 77(1987): 168–185.

Klein, B., R. Crawford, and A. Alchain. "Vertical Integration, Appropriable Rents, and the Competitive Contracting Process." *Journal of Law and Economics*, 21(1978): 297–326.

Kohls, R. and J. Uhl. *Marketing of Agricultural Products*, eighth edition. Prentice Hall, Upper Saddle River, NJ, 1998.

Milgrom, P. and J. Roberts. *Economics, Organization, and Management*. Prentice Hall, Upper Saddle River, NJ, 1992.

Salanie, B. *The Economics of Contracts: A Primer*. The MIT Press, Cambridge, MA, 1998.

Sandmo, A. "On the Theory of the Competitive Firm under Price Uncertainty." *American Economic Review*, 61(1971): 65–73.

Williamson, O. "Transactions Cost Economics: The Governance of Contractual Relations." *Journal of Law and Economics*, 22(1979): 233–261.

Williamson, O. *The Mechanisms of Governance*. Oxford University Press, New York, 1996.

Williamson, O. "The New Institutional Economics: Taking Stock, Looking Ahead." *Journal of Economic Literature*, 38(2000): 595–613.

Appendix 13A: Price Discrimination in Steak Attributes

In this appendix, we will provide a mathematical solution to the problem of price discrimination on different steak qualities, using a simple discrete model of price discrimination. This section is intended for the more advanced reader with some knowledge of mechanism design (Salanie, 1998).

Let the Agent be a beef consumer who will consume at most one steak during the period of study. We will assume that his utility is given by

$$U = \theta q - t,$$

where q is the quality he buys and θ is a positive parameter that indicates his taste for quality of steak (say choice versus select beef). If he decides not to buy a steak this period, his utility is just zero. Based on this assumption, we can surmise that

$$\frac{\partial[u(q,\theta') - u(q,\theta)]}{\partial q} > 0, \ \forall \theta' > \theta.$$

That is, for any given quality of steak, the more sophisticated consumer, θ', will be willing to pay more than the coarse consumer, θ, for any given increase in quality. This is analogous to having a different elasticity of demand, and it gives us the ability to segment the market. There are two possible values for θ: $\theta_1 < \theta_2$. The proportion of the population that is of type 1 is π, and by consequence, the proportion of the population that is of type 2 is $1 - \pi$. For this example, the coarse consumer is type 1 and the sophisticated consumer is type 2.

The Principal is a local monopoly on the steak market. He can produce any quality of steak: $q \in (0, \infty)$. The production of a steak of quality q costs him $C(q)$. Assume that C is twice differentiable and strictly convex, that $C'(0) = 0$, and that $C'(\infty) = \infty$. The utility of the Principal is simply $t - C(q)$, or the difference between the revenue, t, and the costs, $C(q)$.

The first-best solution is of course first-degree price discrimination. That is, the seller offers two qualities at two different prices and the sophisticated consumers purchase the higher quality for a higher price (q_2^*, t_2^*), while the coarse consumers would purchase the lower quality at a lower price (q_1^*, t_1^*). In this case, the seller knows the types of consumers (sophisticated or coarse), and can therefore identify and discriminate between the two. However, we know that first-degree price discrimination is not legal. We also know that the seller does not know the type of consumer who walks through the door.

Now, let's assume that the information is asymmetric and that the producer only knows the proportion of the population that are coarse consumers, π. If the seller proposed the first-best contracts (q_1^*, t_1^*) and (q_2^*, t_2^*), the sophisticated consumer would not choose (q_2^*, t_2^*), but choose (q_1^*, t_1^*), because

$$\theta_2 q_1^* - t_1^* = (\theta_2 - \theta_1)q_1^* > 0 = \theta_2 q_2^* - t_2^*.$$

That is, the utility that the sophisticated consumer derives from consuming the lower-quality steak at the lower-quality price is greater than the utility derived from consuming the higher-quality steak at the higher-quality price. The two types are no longer segmented, but both will choose (q_1^*, t_1^*).

The question, then, is how the seller can segment the market so that he maximizes his profit. This is obtained by solving the following maximization problem:

$$\max_{t_1, q_1, t_2, q_2} \{\pi[t_1 - C(q_1)] + (1 - \pi)[t_2 - C(q_2)]\}$$

subject to

$$\theta_1 q_1 - t_1 \geq \theta_1 q_2 - t_2, \tag{IC$_1$}$$

$$\theta_2 q_2 - t_2 \geq \theta_2 q_1 - t_1, \tag{IC$_2$}$$

$$\theta_1 q_1 - t_1 \geq 0, \tag{IR$_1$}$$

$$\theta_2 q_2 - t_2 \geq 0. \tag{IR$_2$}$$

- The two (IC) constraints are *incentive compatibility* constraints; they state that each consumer prefers the contract that was designed for him.
- The two (IR) constraints are the *individual rationality* constraints; they guarantee that each type of consumer accepts his designed contract.

In the optimum situation, the following will be true:

1. (IR$_1$) is active, so that $t_1 = \theta_1 q_1$.
2. (IC$_2$) is active, so that $t_2 - t_1 = \theta_2(q_2 - q_1)$.
3. The higher quality is greater than or equal to the lower quality: $q_2 \geq q_1$.
4. We can neglect (IC$_1$) and (IR$_2$).
5. Sophisticated consumers buy the efficient quality: $q_2 = q_2^*$.

Proof. We will use IC$_2$ to prove property 1. $\theta_2 q_2 - t_2 \geq \theta_2 q_1 - t_1 \geq \theta_1 q_1 - t_1$, since $q_1 \geq 0$ and $\theta_2 > \theta_1$.

If (IR$_1$) was inactive, so would be (IR$_2$), and we could increase t_1 and t_2 by the same amount. This would increase the Principal's profit without any effect on incentive compatibility. Thus, (IR$_1$) must be active. ∎

Proof. Property 2 is proven by assuming that (IC_2) is inactive. This yields $\theta_2 q_2 - t_2 > \theta_2 q_1 - t_1 \geq \theta_1 q_1 - t_1 = 0$.

We can augment t_2 in this case without breaking incentive compatibility or the individual rationality constraint (IR_2). This obviously increases the Principal's profit, and therefore we cannot be at an optimal solution. ∎

Proof. Property 3 is proven by adding (IC_1) and (IC_2) together. The transfers (prices) t_i cancel out, leaving:

$$\theta_2(q_2 - q_1) \geq \theta_1(q_2 - q_1)$$

and

$$q_2 - q_1 \geq 0,$$

since $\theta_2 > \theta_1$. ∎

Proof. For Property 4, (IC_1) can be neglected since (IC_2) is active, so using Property 3:

$$t_2 - t_1 = \theta_2(q_2 - q_1) \geq \theta_1(q_2 - q_1).$$

The proof of Property 1 shows that (IR_2) can be neglected as well. ∎

Proof. For Property 5, we will prove that $C'(q_2) = \theta_2$. If $C'(q_2) < \theta_2$, for example, let ε be a small positive number, and consider the new contract (q_1, t_1), $(q_2' = q_2 + \varepsilon, t_2' = t_2 + \varepsilon\theta_2)$. From this, we can see that $\theta_2 q_2' - t_2' = \theta_2 q_2 - t_2$ and $\theta_1 q_2' - t_2' = \theta_1 q_2 - t_2 - \varepsilon(\theta_2 - \theta_1)$, so that the new contract satisfies all four constraints. Further, $t_2' - C(q_2') \simeq t_2 - C(q_2) + \varepsilon(\theta_2 - C'(q_2))$ and the new contract yields higher profits than the original contract, which is nonsensical. We can prove in the same way that $C'(q_2) > \theta_2$ is impossible as well. Thus, in the optimum, the sophisticated consumer will consume the efficient quality. ∎

To explore the implications of this model, we take Property 5 as given and express the values of t_1 and t_2 as functions of q_1, using

$$t_1 = \theta_1 q_1$$
$$t_2 - t_1 = \theta_2(q_2 - q_1),$$

which yields

$$q_2 = q_2^*,$$
$$t_1 = \theta_1 q_1,$$
$$t_2 = \theta_1 q_1 + \theta_2(q_2^* - q_1).$$

We then substitute these values in the expression of the Principal's profit and solve:

$$\max_{q_1} (\pi \, (\theta_1 q_1 - C(q_1)) - (1 - \pi)(\theta_2 - \theta_1)q_1).$$

This is called the *virtual surplus*. The difference between social surplus and virtual surplus comes from the fact that when the Principal increases q_1, he makes the type 1 steak (select) more attractive to the sophisticated consumer. To prevent the sophisticated consumer from choosing the steak intended for the type 1 consumer, he must therefore reduce t_2 and decrease his own profits.

We finally get

$$C'(q_1) = \theta_1 - \frac{1 - \pi}{\pi}(\theta_2 - \theta_1) < \theta_1,$$

so that $q_1 < q_1^*$. That is, the quality that is sold to the coarse consumer is subefficient.

So what, then, can we conclude from this analysis about choice versus select steak price discrimination? There are several general properties that hold from this model:

1. The sophisticated consumer gets an efficient allocation of quality. That is, the sophisticated consumer gets the exact quality he or she demands.
2. The sophisticated consumer gets a positive surplus, or *informational rent*. This is because the sophisticated consumer can always pretend to be a coarse consumer. Thus, the Principal must lower the price of the choice steak in order to get the sophisticated consumer to "reveal" himself.
3. The coarse consumer gets a subefficient allocation of quality. That is, in a world of continuous quality, he or she would receive a quality that is not what he or she demanded.
4. The coarse consumer gets zero surplus: $t_1 = \theta_1 q_1$. Thus, the monopolist seller has fully extracted all of the surplus from the coarse consumer.

Part III
Advanced Techniques with Surveys and Experimental Economics

Chapter 14

The Basics of Survey Design

~

Increasingly, economists are being called upon to answer questions for which there are no readily available secondary data. Issues such as new product acceptance (Nalley et al., 2004), anticipated responses to potential policy programs (Hite et al., 2002), and farmer responses to new technology (Hudson and Jones, 2001; Hudson and Hite, 2003) are all examples. For these sorts of problems, researchers often turn to surveys. In this chapter, we will address the basic issues of survey design and implementation, which will serve as a foundation for the following chapters on specific techniques of economic analysis using the data derived through surveys and sampling. While we will touch on many issues here, this chapter only serves as an introduction to the subject. There is a vast literature in statistics, sociology, psychology, and economics that deals with survey design that should be examined for those serious about pursuing survey-based research.

14.1   Sample Selection

The sample to be surveyed is the first issue to be decided (after identification of the problem to be addressed). The following sections address two key sample selection issues: sample composition and sample size.

14.1.1   Random and Nonrandom Samples

Generally speaking, researchers prefer to use **random samples**, which are subsets drawn at random from the larger group, or **population** (Dillman, 2000).[1] If properly drawn, random samples have the advantage of being representative of the population on key

---

[1] Here, we are focusing on single surveys. There is a whole other realm of surveys using panels. Panel data is beyond the scope of this text, but extremely useful in many contexts.

sociodemographic characteristics (and, presumably, attitudes), so that a researcher can make inferences about the whole population with a predictable degree of error, called **sampling error**.

Example 14.1   *According to a recent Gallup Poll, 56% of Americans between the ages of 18 and 35 favor partial privatization of Social Security. The poll has a margin of error of ±3%.*

In this hypothetical poll example, the "margin of error" statement refers to the sampling error. Because we are drawing a sample of the population, the 56% support for privatization is just an estimate. The margin of error allows for potential variation between the estimate and the true proportion of the population that supports the program. In this case, we would expect (with probability of $1 - \alpha$) the true proportion of the population to lie somewhere between 53% and 59% (or ± 3% from the point estimate). The degree of sampling error depends on a number of factors, including sample size, to be discussed in the next section.

Definition of the population from which to sample depends on the problem to be addressed. In the above example, the population was defined as "Americans between the ages of 18 and 35." If you want to gather information about likely voting behavior, the population of interest is registered voters.[2] If, however, you would like to know about potential demand for a new food product designed for diabetics, the population of interest is people with diabetes. It is crucial, however, not to define the population too narrowly. A narrow definition of a population necessarily limits how broadly you can draw conclusions. For example, defining your population as only those with diabetes means you can say nothing about other individuals without diabetes, but with health concerns about sugar intake nonetheless. Thus, careful consideration must be given to the population to be sampled, and it should only be defined as is narrowly as is necessary to answer the question of interest.

Once a population has been identified, sampling procedures must be identified. That is, if you wish to pull a random sample, you must find a way to identify members of the population and contact them. A popular method using the phone is **random-digit dialing**, where a surveyor uses a computer program to randomly dial numbers to contact potential respondents (Dillman, 2000; Hudson et al., 2004). Random-digit dialing is advantageous because it avoids problems or biases arising from unlisted numbers. However, what about people who do not have phones?[3] Because some people cannot be contacted, some members of a population do not have an equal probability of being chosen in a sample. To the extent that these people have different characteristics than the rest of the population, a potential bias, called **coverage error**, may arise. Coverage error is difficult to identify or rectify. The only real guard against coverage error is to strive to utilize the widest possible listing of the population.

---

[2] In some cases, researchers may use a definition such as "likely voters." There is tremendous research that goes into these terms and considerable debate about the implications of using alternative definitions of a population.

[3] This may sound silly to you, but a considerable number of people do not have telephone access in their home because of personal choice, lack of phone access in rural areas, or lack of monetary resources to maintain phone access. While the numbers not having phones on a percentage basis of the U.S. population are probably small, this subgroup can still be important, especially for many public policy questions.

Another method of generating a random sample using mail surveys is to secure a random sample mailing list. While one could do this manually, there are many marketing companies that specialize in maintaining updated mailing lists, from which a random sample can be purchased. Although most of these companies are reputable and do attempt to maintain updated lists, people move, leaving no forwarding addresses. Thus, mailing lists suffer the same potential problems with coverage error as phone lists. Nevertheless, mailing lists can be an effective means of generating random samples.

In some cases, random samples are either not desired or are not necessary. For example, perhaps you would like to know the attitudes of people with environmental concerns about a particular environmental problem. As a result, you may contact members of the Sierra Club.[4] Sampling a particular subgroup or organization is fine as long as one does not attempt to extrapolate findings from the group to other populations. Many times, researchers are faced with an inability to secure a random sample of a population due to a lack of organized information about that population, so that using subgroups such as civic, political, or other organizations is the only means of securing a list of individuals. This limitation does not nullify the results of the research, but it does limit how one makes inferences about other populations.

At the same time, random samples may not be necessary, especially when testing behavioral hypotheses. For example, we may wish to test the rationality of individuals in decision-making. We operate with a null hypothesis that individuals are rational and search for evidence to reject that hypothesis. If we find sufficient evidence to reject that hypothesis for any group (whether random or not), it constitutes evidence that our hypothesis should be rejected. For example, List (2002) investigated purchasing decisions of sports card traders at a sports card convention. He found evidence that people behaved "irrationally" through a phenomenon called preference reversal.[5] Certainly, we could not claim attendees to a sports card convention constitute a random sample of the population.[6] But, in this case, it does not matter, because we have found evidence that *some* group behaves inconsistently with our assumption, which is sufficient evidence to question the validity of the assumption we made. Despite this exception, researchers prefer to use random samples because this alleviates concerns about spurious results related to sample selection and allows one to focus more clearly on the hypotheses being tested or the question being examined.

14.1.2   Sample Size

The size of the sample to be drawn is an important question that must be decided prior to implementation. Two criteria drive the sample size decision—statistical validity and cost. Statistical validity relates to the minimum number of observations (or respondents) needed to insure that the sample adequately represents the population and achieves the

---

[4] Just because you contact members of the Sierra Club does not prohibit you from taking a random sample from the membership list of the club. But, even if one does collect a random sample of the club membership, the important element is that the results are only generalizable to the club, not to the population at large.

[5] Recall from Chapter 1 that the axioms of choice require transitivity in preferences. List's research shows that, in some cases, people reverse preferences when they should not, known as preference reversal.

[6] Although they may be closer to the norm than attendees of a Star Trek convention!

desired margin of error. The general formula for determining the necessary number of completed responses given a desired margin of error is as follows:

$$n_s = \frac{N(p)(1-p)}{(N-1)(B/C)^2 + (p)(1-p)},$$

where n_s is the required number of completed surveys, N is the size of the population being studied, p is the proportion of the population expected to choose one of the two response categories, B is the desired sampling error, and C is the Z statistic associated with the confidence level (e.g., $Z = 1.96$ is the Z statistic for a 95% confidence level). For example, assume that you wish to survey farmers in a particular state about their acceptance of a new technology (a yes/no question). The National Agricultural Statistics Service reports that the population size of farmers in this state is 40,000. You anticipate that there is an equal split between those who will and will not accept the new technology, and you wish to estimate the acceptance level with a 5% margin of error. Thus, the required number of completed survey responses is given by

$$n_s = \frac{40,000(0.5)(0.5)}{39,999(0.05/1.96)^2 + (0.5)(0.5)} = 381.$$

If, however, one wanted to decrease the margin of error to 3%, the number of completed responses would have to increase to 1,040. The 50/50 split represents the most conservative estimate of the number of required responses. Consider the same case as above, but instead of an equal split, you anticipate an 80/20 split on the question of acceptance. The equation would be recalculated as follows:

$$n_s = \frac{40,000(0.8)(0.2)}{39,999(0.05/1.96)^2 + (0.8)(0.2)} = 244.$$

Thus, any anticipated split other than the 50/50 split results in a required number of responses that is lower than the 50/50 split. This is what is meant by the 50/50 split being the most conservative, because it results in the highest number of required responses.

Increasing the number of required responses may increase one's confidence in the derived results, but that increased confidence comes at a cost. Survey research can be quite costly. My personal estimation is that it costs between $20 and $25 for each completed mail survey. This cost includes mailing and printing costs as well as costs associated with personnel to collect, tabulate, and analyze results.[7] At $20 per completed survey, the 50/50 split design for our hypothetical question would cost around $8,000. If the anticipated split was 80/20, the cost would be around $5,300. Thus, being conservative in this case and using the 50/50 split increases the cost by 51%. Phone surveys can also be expensive. Most marketing or survey research companies will charge around $2 per minute for the survey. Assuming that it takes just five minutes to do our hypothetical survey (and this is a short survey), the cost would be $3,800, which does not include

---

[7] This cost, however, does not include personnel time to develop the survey or the primary researcher's time; only clerical staff time for mailing and data entry.

the cost of hang-ups, disconnected numbers, fax machines, and so on.[8] Thus, in either mail or phone surveys, mistakes can be costly, and so sample selection is very important. Finally, personal interviews can be conducted (and are often required for very complex questions), but the cost here is $100 per interview or more in many cases.[9]

It should be noted that the equations above are based on the assumption that the question being asked is a yes/no type question. This generally complicates the calculation of an appropriate sample size, but does not alter the fundamental concept. In most cases, over 1,100 completed responses is sufficient for most situations, but many complex studies with different versions of questions require larger sample sizes; of course, depending on the size of the population to be studied. In this section, we have been referring to "completed" responses, which is different than the original sample size due to people not responding to the survey. The concept, called the **response rate**, will be discussed later in the chapter.

Key Questions

1. What is a random sample?
2. What is sampling error?
3. What is coverage error?
4. What variables affect sample size?

14.2   Questionnaire Design

The item that will take the most time, and be the most complex and most difficult task to complete in survey research is design of the questionnaire. A **questionnaire** is the instrument used to elicit responses from participants on the issues of interest. For mail-based surveys, the questionnaire is the actual document received by the respondent, filled out, and returned to the researcher. For phone surveys and personal interviews, the questionnaire is usually formulated as a script for the interviewer to follow when asking questions of the respondent. In this section, we will address some key elements of questionnaire design.

14.2.1   Defining the Problem and Questions

The first, and most critical, step to survey design is to clearly define the problem that one wishes to address. This, of course, is not unique to survey research, but is the first step in any reseach endeavor (Ethridge, 2004). One should not even attempt to formulate a questionnaire until this step is complete. Problem definition allows the researcher to identifty the question to be answered, which guides survey development on a number

---

[8] The proliferation of personal fax machines, Automatic Teller Machines (ATMs), business phone connections for credit card machines, and so on, has meant an explosion of phone numbers. This, in turn, means that many of the numbers called through random-digit dialing are not actually personal phone numbers, thus increasing the time spent to locate a viable sample, which increases the cost.

[9] We will discuss the strengths and weaknesses of the different survey approaches later in the chapter.

of fronts. First, a clear definition of the question identifies the key pieces of information that must be gathered in the questionnaire.

Example 14.2   *Suppose you have been asked to develop a model that explains acreage allocation decisions by farmers. You identify the key problem as understanding the impacts of critical economic variables on planting decisions by the target group … farmers.*

Identification of the problem in this manner gives you the information you need to begin to formulate a questionnaire. First, you would begin with an economic model of acreage allocation decisions. Recall from Chapter 2 that a firm's supply function is affected by a number of variables, such as expectations about future prices/profitability of different crops, current technology levels, management, risk, and so on. Based on this economic model, we can begin to develop a set of questions designed to gather information about expectations, current equipment complements, and risk tolerances, as well as other variables of potential importance, such as farm size, the education level of the farmer, and so on.

A second key benefit of clear problem definition is identification of the population to be sampled. Obviously, farmers are the target in the above example. But we could perhaps refine that population to "commercial farmers," or farmers with over 500 acres in production, or farmers of a particular commodity, and so on. As discussed above, definition of the population has important implications for the sample size, generalizability of results, and so on. Thus, clear definition of the problem has important implications for the execution and quality of research results.

Once we have defined the problem, the appropriate economic model, and identified the key variables of interest, we must design the questions. The upshot of question design is that *wording matters*. Consider the following example.

Example 14.3   *Do you support the legalization of abortion, which results in the murder of over 1 million innocent babies a year?*

Obviously, this question is designed to elicit a particular response. If one is truly interested in learning something about a population, questions must be designed so as to avoid cueing responses from individuals. But, it does not take inflamatory wording such as above to skew results. Consider the following, more subtle, example.

Example 14.4   *The current price of ribeye steaks is $6.47 per pound. What would you be willing to pay for a choice ribeye steak?*

There are two inherent problems with this question. First, providing the respondent with the price of steaks in the market leads to a potential problem called **anchoring**, whereby respondents will fix their responses to the price level you have provided them. So, rather than eliciting their unconditional willingness to pay, you have elicited their willingness to pay given the current market price. In some cases, anchoring is not a serious problem and may actually improve the accuracy of results. But in others, anchoring can give biased results unintended by the researcher.

A second problem with this question is the open-ended nature of the response. That is, respondents can write down any number they choose. Generally speaking, it is better to give respondents a choice between price levels or some other choice mechanism to confine their responses to a reasonable set of potential answers.[10] The precise type of question will be determined by the type of analysis that is to be conducted. Nevertheless, it should be apparent from the examples above that how a question is worded has a substantial impact on the quality of answers one is likely to get from the respondent.

14.2.2   Economizing for Multiple Objectives

As we previously discussed, surveys can be quite expensive to administer. Thus, economizing within a survey to achieve multiple objectives or answer multiple questions spreads the fixed cost of survey administration across multiple potential studies. For example, in studies by Hudson et al. (2004, 2005), two primary objectives were accomplished in the same survey design. The primary objective was to ascertain public awareness about and attitudes toward marine hypoxia caused by nonpoint-source pollution runoff into rivers (Hudson et al., 2005). Given this objective, the survey was designed to elicit responses on awareness and attitudes, so that the questions in the questionnaire were aimed at this objective. At the same time, however, the researchers were interested in the issue of **nonresponse bias**[11] across different survey modes—mail and Internet surveys. The survey was designed to elicit responses by both mail and Internet,[12] and nonresponse bias was examined. Thus, the researchers were able to accomplish two critical objectives with the same survey instrument, hence conserving expenses.

In some cases, such as that outlined above, it is possible to mold the questionnaire to accomplish multiple objectives. In the example above, however, it is critical to note that the second objective of nonresponse bias analysis did not conflict with the primary objective of ascertaining attitudes toward marine hypoxia. Because of this, respondents were not aware that their responses were achieving two objectives, but were focused on answering questions on a well-defined, confined topic. But, in cases where objectives do not coincide, it is not advisable to attempt to combine them into a single survey instrument. Attempting to survey on multiple topics in a single instrument only serves to confuse respondents and increase their frustration level.

14.2.3   Questionnaires and Response Rates

In the previous section on sample sizes, we referred to the "required number of responses," which we said was different than the original sample size. This is because

---

[10] These issues will be discussed in more detail in the following chapter. Nevertheless, careful consideration of question wording is essential, but is intertwined with the specific type of analysis that is to be conducted.

[11] Nonresponse bias occurs when some people respond to the survey, while others do not. If the characteristics of those not responding is different than those who do, potential nonresponse bias occurs. For example, if a survey is sent to a random sample of individuals, but only upper-income people respond, the results may be biased in favor of the attitudes of those with higher incomes.

[12] First, a pre-screening telephone survey was conducted to identify the sample and gather basic sociodemographic data from the respondents. Then, respondents were mailed a survey. Some respondents were mailed the questionnaire and asked to return it by mail. Others were simply mailed a letter with an Internet address to access and fill out the survey. The research then focused on nonresponse bias from both the mail and Internet versions.

some people do not respond to surveys, meaning that we must sample more people than we need to get the required number of responses for statistical validity. The proportion of people who respond to a survey is called the **response rate**. Typical response rates to mail surveys are between 20% and 40% (Dillman, 2000; Pennings et al., 2002), but some surveys see very low response rates (e.g., Isengildina and Hudson, 2001), while some have response rates in the 70–80% range (Hudson and Jones, 2001). Using a 30% response rate, our hypothetical question from earlier with a required number responding of 381 would mean we would need to initially sample 1,270 (or 381/0.3) people to achieve our desired margin of error level. Thus, you can see that achieving a higher response rate is desirable, both from a logistical standpoint of identifying viable samples as well as for controlling cost.

There are a number of factors that influence response rates. The first is respondent interest in the question being addressed. For example, many people are interested in general interest questions about politics, such as voting behavior or social security, and are thus more likely to respond when questioned about those subjects.[13] But those questions with more confined audiences or that are overly complex lead to disinterest or frustration, thereby decreasing response rates. The second is questionnaire length. Generally, the longer the questionnaire, the lower is the response rate. Do you really want to be caught on the phone for 20 minutes answering a lengthy survey? Streamlining the questionnaire to minimize length (that is, only asking the questions that are necessary) will improve response rates. Tied with questionnaire length is the level at which you ask the questions. It is important to remember that the average of the population converses and thinks at an eighth- or ninth-grade reading level. Complex questions using technical jargon only serve to frustrate respondents, leading them to hang up the phone or throw the mail survey in the trash. Keep the audience in mind when designing the questionnaire wording.

Third, question ordering has an influence on response rates (Dillman, 2000). Consider the following questions in order.

1. Do you own your home?
2. Have you ever heard of marine hypoxia?
3. Do you regularly fish or engage in water-based recreational activities?
4. How old are you?
5. Have you ever heard of nonpoint-source pollution?

If you were bombarded with this seemingly unrelated set of questions, you would immediately question why you are being asked these questions, become confused, and likely give up and throw the survey in the trash. Organizing the questions to be asked in a logical manner improves the readability of the survey and makes some sense of why the questions are being asked in the first place. Dividing questionnaires into logical sections also improves the respondent's ability to organize his or her thoughts and answer the questions in the most efficient manner, which improves the quality of your results.

Finally, there is always the question "What's in it for me?" That is, you as the researcher must be cognizant of the respondent's opportunity cost of answering your questions. For

---

[13] This fact can actually be a double-edged sword. That is, if the question is about an environmental problem, those with a greater interest in the environment are more likely to answer, which may influence results toward the opinions of those with environmental concerns. This is an example of the nonresponse bias discussed earlier.

some, you are asking them to skip part of a re-run of *CSI*, while for others, they could be earning money, fixing dinner, or any other of a litany of demands on their time. At the least, you want to outline the purpose of the research in a brief cover letter telling them how their responses will benefit scientific understanding of the question being addressed. You want to make some effort to relate the benefits of the research to them on as personal a level as is possible. In some cases, it may be possible to provide some small monetary payment, say $1, which has been shown to increase response rates. In either case, outlining the purpose of the research is critical for the respondent to feel engaged in the research process and increase response rates.

14.2.4   Ethical Considerations

Because we are dealing with human subjects, careful attention must be paid to ethical considerations of our survey. All university- and government-sponsored survey research must be approved by an appropriate **Institutional Review Board** (IRB) for compliance with rules and regulations regarding the protection of human subjects. The IRB is a group of qualified scientists whose job is to examine proposed research **protocols**, or plans, to insure that potential human respondents are protected. There are several key features of research that are needed to satisfy IRB requirements. First, respondent participation must be **voluntary**. That is, nobody can be coerced into participating by any means. Second, participant responses must be **confidential**. Because university and government research is in the public domain, all data and results must be available to the public upon request. Thus, no identifying information for individual respondents can be included with data collected from human subjects. After all, would you want your next-door neighbor to be able to find out your opinions without your permission? Third, human subjects cannot be exposed to any unnecessary risks of either physical or emotional pain or stress, and certainly cannot be exposed to them without their consent. Subjects must be able to withdraw from participation at any time without loss of access to any benefits provided by participation, and must be clearly informed of their rights as participants and told what they will be expected to do as part of their participation.

All of the information must be contained within something called **informed consent**. That is, participants must be informed of all these conditions and must formally consent to participation. Ethically, we as scientists have a responsibility for the welfare of our participants. Pragmatically, respondents who are put at ease about what you are going to do with their responses and who are comfortable with their rights and responsibilities, as well and benefits and costs of participation, are more likely to participate. While IRB requirements appear difficult to implement on paper, they are actually quite easy in practice. Implementing them will both satisfy your ethical requirments and probably increase response rates at the same time.

Key Questions

1. What is a questionnaire?
2. How does wording affect responses?
3. What is nonresponse bias?
4. What is the response rate? What factors affect the response rate?
5. What are some ethical considerations when conducting a survey?

14.3   Survey Administration

Once the problem has been defined, the population and sample identified, and the questionnaire designed, it is time to move on to the implementation stage of the survey. In this section, we will address methods for improving the survey construction prior to final implementation, for actually conducting the survey, and for data collection procedures.

14.3.1   Pre-Testing

Before final completion and implementation of the survey, it is always a good idea to **pre-test** the survey instrument, or have the instrument completed by a small group of individuals. The purpose of pre-testing is twofold. First, it allows the researcher to get feedback on the questionnaire from people who would likely be receiving it in the mail (or phone or interview). These people should be probed as to whether the questions were understandable, the format and ordering were easy to follow, and so on. It will be amazing the little details you will overlook or the assumptions you will make about how people read questions when you have someone examine it in a pre-test.[14]

Second, a pre-test allows the researcher a brief view of how questions are being answered. For example, you may have asked the respondent for the number of acres farmed. One of your pre-test subjects reported 2,000 acres, but you know that the respondent actually has a farm with 2,000 acres, 1,500 acres of which are cropland, with the remaining 500 acres in pasture. If your intention was to collect the number of acres where crops were grown, the pre-test is telling you that you need to modify that question accordingly to elicit the correct information. Naturally, pre-test subjects are going to be individuals with whom the researcher is familiar and can discuss the questionnaire. Ideally, you want your pre-test subjects to be members of the population from which you are sampling, in order to get the most realistic response, but sometimes this is not possible. Nevertheless, it is best to have several individuals pre-test the instrument, so that the most number of potential mistakes can be located. It is better to correct the mistakes now than to realize one was made after the fact!

14.3.2   Mail, Phone, and Personal Interviews

Mail, phone, and personal interviews are the most common methods of administering surveys, although the Internet is becoming increasingly popular. Each of these methods has its own strengths and weaknesses. Table 14.1 shows that mail surveys allow larger samples to be drawn because of the relatively low cost of mailing an additional survey. Mail surveys are self-contained. That is, once they are mailed, they need no further

---

[14] Pre-testing should not be confused with editing. When you have someone edit your questionnaire, you are asking them to look for formatting and spelling mistakes, but they are not likely to be carefully considering the questions themselves. When you ask someone to pre-test the questionnaire, you are asking them to answer the questions as if they were being interviewed or surveyed, and are thus more likely to get a true response to the questions themselves.

Table 14.1   The strengths and weaknesses of mail, phone, and personal interview survey modes

Mail	Phone	Personal interview
Strengths		
• Larger samples • Self-contained/no interaction needed • Length less important (but not completely) • Good for simple or complex questions	• More control over final sample characteristics • Higher response rates • Fewer logistical problems • Some feedback between interviewer and respondent • Best for simple questions	• More control over final sample characteristics • High response rates • Excellent feedback between interviewer and respondent • Best for very complex questions
Weaknesses		
• Lower response rates • No feedback between interviewer and respondent • Record-keeping and data recording costs high	• Expensive • Questionnaire length is limited to limit time on phone • Harder to get individuals to devote time "now"	• Very expensive • Time-consuming • Sometimes harder to get people to answer difficult questions "face-to-face" • Requires participants to devote time "now"

interaction between the interviewer and the respondent. Because they are answered at the leisure of the respondent, length is generally less important, but excessively long surveys will be thrown in the trash, so economizing on length still carries some level of importance. Finally, mail surveys are flexible in that they can be used to address relatively simple questions, or can be used to address more complex questions. At the same time, they tend to have lower response rates and do not allow feedback between interviewer and respondent. There are many times when a respondent has thought, "I wonder what that means?" Because he or she cannot simply ask the interviewer, he or she may become confused and cease answering the questionnaire. Finally, because you are dealing with a massive amount of mail going out and coming in, record-keeping and data collection costs tend to be higher than with other survey modes.

Phone and personal interviews tend to share many positive and negative aspects. Both offer more control over final sample characteristics because they are identifying those characteristics immediately. Both offer higher response rates than mail surveys. And, both, because data are being collected as the interview is being conducted, have lower record-keeping and data recording expenses. However, phone surveys tend to work best for very simple, direct questions, whereas personal interviews can be used for rather complex questions. On the negative side, both are relatively expensive to administer and both require participants to respond at the time they are contacted, whereas mail surveys allow respondents to respond when they have the most time.

14.3.3   Data Collection and Record-Keeping

Once the survey is under way, data collection and record-keeping become important. As stated above, phone and personal interviews have the advantage that data are being collected on the spot and/or immediately being entered into a database. For mail, however, the process is a bit more complicated. The most typical method of administering a mail survey is through something called a **three-wave design** (Dillman, 2000). Here, the survey instrument and a cover letter are sent to the initial sample. After about two weeks, either a reminder card or a new copy of the survey are sent to those individuals who have not responded. Finally, after about two more weeks, a final copy of the survey and a reminder letter are sent to those who have yet to respond (thus, the three waves). Experience shows that most of the responses will be returned within the first two weeks, but the subsequent waves can generate an additional 10–15% response.

You should immediately spot the potential record-keeping nightmare. For large mail surveys, 2,000–3,000 initial mailings may have gone out. As those return, you must track those returning the survey so as not to waste money on additional mailings.[15] At the same time, one should enter the data from the mail surveys as it comes in, rather than letting it "pile up," because this allows the researcher to spot potential problems in the responses in the early stages, before additional mailings are sent. Once the data are recorded, however, all records of who participated and any identifying information about respondents used for tracking purposes should be destroyed to maintain confidentiality.

Key Questions

1. What is pre-testing?
2. What are the strengths and weaknesses of the different survey modes?
3. What is the three-wave design?

14.4   Summary

This chapter has outlined the basics of conducting surveys for economic research. Increasingly, you as professionals will be expected to know how to conduct surveys to answer specific questions for which there is no secondary data. We have seen that there any many issues to consider when conducting a survey, such as margins of error, nonresponse bias, question wording, and ethical considerations for the protection of human subjects. Hopefully, you now have some appreciation of the difficulties of conducting survey research, and you have some perspective on the strengths and weaknesses of survey research.

---

[15] Some people forgo tracking returns and simply send reminders to everyone with a "disregard this if you have already responded" statement. This certainly reduces record-keeping expenses, but increases mailing expenses and may make the researcher look "foolish" in the eyes of some respondents.

References

Dillman, D. *Mail and Internet Surveys: The Tailored Design Method*, second edition. John Wiley, New York, 2000.

Ethridge, D. *Research Methodology in Applied Economics*, second edition. Blackwell, Ames, IA, 2004.

Hite, D., D. Hudson, and W. Intarapapong. "Taxpayer Willingness to Pay for Water Quality: The Case of Precision Application Technology." *Journal of Agricultural and Resource Economics*, 27(2002): 433–449.

Hudson, D. and D. Hite. "Producer Willingness to Pay for Precision Agriculture Technology: Implications for Government and the Technology Industry." *Canadian Journal of Agricultural Economics*, 51(2003): 39–53.

Hudson, D. and T. Jones. "Willingness to Plant Identity Preserved Crops: The Case of Soybeans in Mississippi." *Journal of Agricultural and Applied Economics*, 33(2001): 475–485.

Hudson, D., D. Hite, and T. Haab. "Public Perception of Agricultural Pollution and Gulf of Mexico Hypoxia." *Coastal Management*, 33(2005): 25–36.

Hudson, D., L. Seah, D. Hite, and T. Haab. "Telephone Pre-Surveys, Self Selection, and Non-Response Bias to Mail and Internet Surveys in Economic Research." *Applied Economics Letters*, 11(2004): 237–240.

Isengildina, O. and D. Hudson. "Cotton Producers' Use of Selected Marketing Strategies." *Journal of Cotton Science*, 5(2001): 206–217.

List, J. "Preference Reversals of a Different Kind: The 'More is Less' Phenomenon." *American Economic Review*, 92(2002): 1,636–1,643.

Nalley, L., D. Hudson, R. Rogers, J. Martin, and J. Herring. "In-Store Evaluation of Consumer Willingness to Pay for 'Farm Raised' Pre-Cooked Roast Beef: A Case Study." *Journal of Agribusiness*, 22(2004): 163–173.

Pennings, J., S. Irwin, and D. Good. "Surveying Farmers: A Case Study." *Review of Agricultural Economics*, 24(2002): 266–277.

Chapter 15

Individual Utility Estimation and Conjoint Analysis

~

Recall that in Chapter 1, we discussed market demand estimation and noted that it was difficult to estimate individual utility. We now return to the issue of individual utility estimation. This chapter draws on a growing body of literature in random utility theory and stated choice methods of estimation. The econometrics are necessarily more complex and, thus, this chapter is geared for more advanced students. Those of you wishing to maximize your understanding of this chapter should have some background in experimental design, although this is not absolutely necessary. This chapter only serves as an introduction into the methods and applications of stated choice models. Readers who wish to explore stated choice methods in more depth are directed to Louviere, Hensher, and Swait (2000), who provide an treatment of stated choice methods with a wealth of practical applications.

15.1 Consumer Choices

As stated in Chapter 1, consumers make choices about consumption decisions subject to a budget constraint. In addition, we saw in Chapter 8 that quality attributes also play a role in the consumer demand (and thus, price) for a product. Thus, for any given type of product, consumers will examine the attributes of a product and choose to purchase that product that yields the highest level of utility. We now define a model of random utility (Ben Akiva and Lerman, 1985) as follows:

$$U_{ij} = V_{ij} + \varepsilon_{ij}, \tag{15.1}$$

where U_{ij} is the utility that consumer i derives from consumption of a product with j attributes, V_{ij} is the deterministic portion of the utility function, and ε_{ij} is the stochastic (random) portion of utility. What Equation 15.1 states in practical terms is that a product with given characteristics will provide a V_{ij} level of utility. At the same time, there is some random component to utility that is not captured by the characteristics of the good. The random utility model is consistent with Lancaster's theory of product price and reflects the fact that product characteristics provide utility to the consumer. How, then, does the consumer make a choice? We express the probability that a product with *j* characteristics is chosen as follows:

$$\Pr(j \text{ is chosen}) = \Pr\left\{V_{ij} + \varepsilon_{ij} \geq V_{ik} + \varepsilon_{ik}; j \neq k; \text{ for all } j, k \in C_i\right\},$$

where C_i is the set of possible goods from which to be chosen. That is, the probability that a product with *j* attributes is chosen is equal to the probability that the product with *j* attributes yields a higher utility than the product with *k* attributes.

Example 15.1 *Assume that a consumer is faced with a choice of a ribeye steak that is grade Choice and priced at $5.50 per pound and a steak of equal size that is grade Standard and priced at $4.25 per pound. The probability that the consumer will choose the Choice steak is equal to the probability that the $5.50 per pound Choice steak yields a higher utility than the $4.25 per pound Standard steak.*

This example may seem simple at first. However, consider that the consumer's decision is based on two factors. First, there is the effect of the steak grade on the consumer's utility. There is also the effect of the steak's price on consumer utility. One can easily see, then, that the choice of steak forces the consumer to make a trade-off between price and quality. Each individual consumer likely has a different rate of trade-off between these attributes. Aggregate demand analysis, as presented in Chapter 1, does not allow an analyst to examine these individual trade-offs.

15.2 Conjoint Analysis

A popular method of examining individual utility is through conjoint analysis: see, for example, Green and Srinivisan (1978) for a discussion of the theory, and Adamowicz et al. (1998), Lusk and Hudson (2004), Beggs, Cardell and Hausman (1981), and Hudson and Lusk (2004) for empirical examples. Conjoint analysis has the advantage over traditional methods of market analysis in that it allows the researcher to directly manipulate the attributes under consideration.[1] This ability allows for more direct and accurate estimation of consumer preferences (utility). However, experimental techniques such as conjoint analysis are *stated preference* techniques. That is, they are hypothetical choice decisions and, thus, are subject to potential hypothetical bias. Recent work by Lusk and Schroeder (2004) has attempted to examine the issue of hypothetical bias in conjoint experiments.

---

[1] This ability is consistent with saying that the researcher has complete control over the *ceteris paribus* assumption. That is, in traditional market analysis, the researcher is forced to use data taken from the real world where many variables are changing simultaneously. Regression analysis allows the researcher to artificially impose the *ceteris paribus* assumption by holding other variables constant. In conjoint analysis, the researcher has the ability to only alter one variable at a time in choice sets, thereby isolating the effect of that variable on individual utility.

15.2.1 Choice Sets

A primary area of consideration in choice-based conjoint experiments is the design of the **choice set** the consumer will face. Consider the simple choice set presented in Lusk and Schroeder (2004) (Figure 15.1). This choice set was designed to answer the simple question of the effects of steak type (or brand) and price on consumer choice. Individual consumers (or, more specifically, respondents to a questionnaire or personal interview) examine the set of choices presented to them and choose the product (or none) that they would purchase. By changing the price levels, choice sets are replicated and multiple scenarios are examined by the respondent. After completion, the impacts of price and brand on consumer choices, and thus, utility are estimated.

More complex problems necessitate more complex choice sets. Consider the choice sets faced by respondents in the work of Hudson and Lusk (2004) on producer contract choice (Figure 15.2). In this case, the agricultural producer faced three possible choices—"Contract A," "Contract B," and "Cash sales." There were six attributes of each contract—"Expected income," "Price risk shifted to the buyer," "Level of autonomy," "Required investment in specific assets," "Provision of inputs," and "Length of contract." These attributes were motivated by theoretical considerations. Thus, the more complex problem of contract choice necessitated a more complex choice set.

A second issue in choice set design is the number of levels each attribute can take on. For example, in the Hudson and Lusk (2004) analysis, each attribute had three possible

Scenario 11		Steaks				None of these
	Generic $6.75	Guaranteed Tender $7.88	Natural $9.00	USDA Choice $5.63	Certified Angus beef $7.88	
I would choose ...	⇩ ☐	⇩ ☐	⇩ ☐	⇩ ☐	⇩ ☐	⇩ ☐

Figure 15.1 Choice sets of different steak types and prices.
Source: Lusk and Schroeder.

Scenario 1
Options A and B represent two different descriptions for a contract/marketing arrangement. Please check (✓) the option (A, B, or C) that you would be most likely to choose.

Contract attribute	Contract A	Contract B	Cash sales
Expected income	$165,000	$135,000	$150,000
Price risk shifted to the buyer	Fixed	Semifixed	None
Level of autonomy (relative to Cash sales)	Lower	None	Same
Required investment in specific assets	10%	10%	10%
Provision of inputs	50%	100%	0%
Length of contract/arrangement	1	1	0
I would choose ...	☐	☐	☐

Figure 15.2 Choice sets used in the conjoint experiment of producer contract choice.
Source: Hudson and Lusk.

levels. Expected income, for example, could be \$135,000, \$150,000, or \$165,000. The choice of the number of levels is arbitrary, but if all attributes have the same number of levels, the problem of experimental design is greatly simplifed (Louviere, Hensher, and Swait, 2000). One should recognize that as the number of attribute levels (and, indeed, the number of attributes as well) increases, the complexity of the experimental design also increases. We now turn our attention to the issue of experimental design.

15.2.2   Experimental Design

Experimental design is given much consideration by researchers using conjoint analysis (Louviere, Hensher, and Swait, 2000). Most generally, we are concerned with (1) the size of the experimental design and (2) proper identification of relevant effects. First, and foremost, we are concerned with the size of the experiment because personal interviews and/or mail surveys are expensive to administer. The larger the experimental design, the larger is the necessary sample of respondents, and thus, the larger the expense.

The most straightforward experimental design is called the **full factorial** design, which incorporates every possible combination of the attributes (and different levels) in the choice sets. For simple designs with two or three attributes, the full factorial design may not be large. However, in the Hudson and Lusk (2004) example from above, there are six attributes with three levels each, resulting in a full factorial design of $6^3 = 216$ possible combinations. Can you imagine having to sift through 216 combinations of choice sets and making a decision/choice on each one?

At the same time, we must be cognizant of the "effects" we wish to estimate. First, there are the simple, linear effects called the **main effects**. The main effects are typically the most important (Louviere, Hensher, and Swait, 2004) and enter the regression equation as variables in themselves. However, we may be interested in **two-way interaction** effects as well. The two-way interaction effects represent combinations of pairs of the main effects. Finally, we may be interested in the **higher-order interaction** effects, which are combinations of three or more of the independent variables. The advantage of the full factorial design is that it can efficiently[2] estimate main effects as well as two-way and higher-order interaction effects. However, given that main effects are typically the most important, we are able to confine ourselves to simpler experimental designs.[3]

Fractional factorial designs offer a way out of the large full factorial designs by taking advantage of the ability to pull subsamples from the full factorial design. Such fractional factorial designs are necessarily less powerful in identifying interaction effects, depending on the fractional factorial design chosen. There are methods in common statistical packages such as Statistical Analysis Software (SAS) that can be used to establish a fractional factorial design with maximum design efficiency and can be customized to create designs that, for example, properly identify main and two-way interaction effects, but not higher-order effects (Kuhfield, Tobias, and Garratt, 1994). These techniques significantly

---

[2]"Efficiently" refers to the econometric properties of the estimates. An efficient estimate is one in which the standard error of the parameter estimate is a minimum.

[3]Recent work by Lusk calls into question the empirical importance of experimental design in parameter estimate precision and efficiency. However, his findings suggest that more complex designs are still needed if the outcome of interest is willingness-to-pay estimates that are derived from parameter estimates in conjoint models.

reduce the size of the experimental design. For example, in the Hudson and Lusk (2004) analysis with a full factorial of 216 choice sets, the fractional factorial design for main and two-way interaction effects resulted in 76 choice sets. Examining 76 choice sets is obviously less taxing on the respondent than 216!

We can further reduce the workload of the respondent by **blocking** the choice sets into smaller groups. That is, we can divide the 76 choice sets in the subgroups about about 20, so that any individual respondent is only asked to examine 20 choice sets. The result of blocking, however, is that, in this example, you need about four times as many respondents to get the same number of observations. Nevertheless, most researchers would prefer to ask respondents fewer questions, lest they overtax respondents and get less cooperation from respondent in future work!

15.2.3   Estimation

In this section, we address the basic assumptions and estimation methods used to analyze conjoint models. Empirical applications are often complex, with many subtle, related issues. This section provides an introduction to the concepts, but you are cautioned that there is an extensive body of literature that has developed around estimation procedures and issues, and you should refer to Greene (2000) and Louviere, Hensher, and Swait (2000) for a broader exposure to these issues.

Necessary Assumptions

The conjoint model is expressed in terms of discrete choice. That is, the consumer either chooses good A, B, or C, but no more than one choice is made in each choice set. Therefore, we are modeling the probability of choosing A relative to B, A relative to C, and B relative to C. Thus, we are necessarily operating in an environment of discrete choices, which has its own type of statistical models.

The main axiom for modeling these relationships is Independence from Irrelevant Alternatives (IIA). As Louviere, Hensher, and Swait (2000) point out, the IIA axiom holds that "the ratio of probabilities of choosing one alternative over another (given that both alternatives have nonzero probabilities of choice) is unaffected by the presence or absence of any additional alternatives in the choice set" (p. 44). This axiom is both a strength and weakness of the discrete choice model. It is a strength because it simplifies the computation process necessary to derive parameter estimates, and means that we can either introduce or delete choices from choice sets without having to reestimate the model. It is a weakness because the observed and unobserved portions of utility may be correlated.[4]

In addition to the IIA axiom, Freene (2000) adds the following assumptions:

1. **Positivity**. Given a respondent's socioeconomic characteristics and the alternatives in the choice sets, the probability that a particular alternative is chosen must be greater than zero for all alternative choice sets.

---

[4] This is consistent with saying that the error term is nonnormally distributed and correlated with the independent variables. In standard regression analysis, we would say that the model is misspecified and exhibits omitted variable bias.

2. **Irrelevance of alternative set effects**. Without replications on each individual, it is impossible to identify alternative choice set effects.

Empirical Model

The IIA axiom implies that the random component of utility (the ε_j's) are independently and identically distributed across alternatives. There are a variety of potential distributions that can be used to describe the random component, but by far the most popular is the Extreme Value Type 1 (EV1) distribution.[5] Use of the EV1 distribution yields the following general model of choice:

$$P_i = \frac{1}{\sum_{j=1}^{J} e^{-(V_i - V_j)}}, \tag{15.2}$$

where V_i and V_j are the deterministic portions of the utility derived from alternatives i and j, respectively, and P_i is the probability that alternative i is chosen.

The model is a conditional logit, or multinomial logit (MNL), model of choice. We typically use Maximum Likelihood Estimation procedures to fit the MNL model. Many common software packages are available to estimate MNL models, but perhaps the most convenient is *LIMDEP* (Greene). [6] We operationalize Equation 15.2 across each individual, q, by the following equation to be estimated:

$$P_{iq} = \frac{e^{V_{iq}}}{\sum_{j=1}^{J} e^{V_{jq}}}.$$

We assume that each alternative, j, is described by a vector of attributes, X, which are assumed to be linear and additive. Thus, we can describe the deterministic portion of utility for alternative j, V_{jq}, as follows:

$$V_{jq} = \sum_{k=1}^{K} \beta_{jk} X_{jkq}.$$

If a constant term is included, it is interpreted as the *alternative specific constant*.

Continuous versus Discrete Explanatory Variables

Most practical applications of conjoint analysis will have alternatives with explanatory variables that are both discrete and continuous. For example, the Hudson and Lusk (2004)

---

[5]The EV1 distribution takes the form

$$Pr(\varepsilon_j \leq \varepsilon) = \exp(-e^{-\varepsilon}) = e^{-e^{-\varepsilon}}.$$

[6]This should not be construed as a product endorsement. Many computer programs will estimate these models quite easily.

analysis has continuous variables for expected income, required investment in specific assets, provision of inputs, and contract length. At the same time, it has discrete variables for price risk shifted to the buyer and level of autonomy. The choice of continuous or discrete variables is a function of the attribute that is being analyzed, and there are no rules against either.

Data for continuous variables enter the regression as they do in any other regression analysis. Data for discrete variables are treated as dummy variables, but the researcher has a choice of how to treat them. On the one hand, one can treat them as standard dummy variables.[7] The researcher may also recode them as **effects coded** dummy variables. Effects coded variables are similar to standard dummy variables, except that they take on a value of -1 when the attributes are at their "base" level, making the base equal to the negative sum of the other dummy variables.

For example, Autonomy in the Hudson and Lusk (2004) study contains three levels. Assume that "None" is the base. If Autonomy was equal to "Same," the effects coded dummy variable from Some would equal 0 and Same would equal 1. However, if Autonomy was equal to "None," the effects coded dummy variable for Some would equal -1 and Same would equal -1. The advantage of the effects coded dummy variables is that they allow direct recovery of the marginal utility with respect to the base category.

A Practical Example

Consider the following practical example from Hudson and Lusk (2004) alluded to above. The objective of this analysis was to examine the impact of a variety of attributes of contracts on producer contract choice. The research involved personal interviews of 19 agricultural producers in Texas, who were presented choice sets to be examined. The MNL model was estimating using maximum likelihood estimation in *LIMDEP*. The following table represents the estimated parameters and related diagnostic statistics:

Variable	Estimated coefficient	t-value
ASC1[a]	0.6178	1.765*
ASC2[a]	0.8405	2.333**
Expected income	0.00004	4.945***
D_{Fixed}	0.3164	2.308**
$D_{Semifixed}$	0.4145	2.725***
D_{None}	-0.5925	3.896***
D_{Some}	0.1610	1.135
Asset specificity	-0.0249	3.791***
Provision of inputs	0.0069	2.664***
Contract length	-0.2254	3.516***
χ^2 value	103.4917*	
Number of observations	276	

[a] Alternative specific constants.

---

[7] With choosing an appropriate base category to avoid the dummy variable trap!

The D-variables are effects coded dummy variables for fixed-price contracts, semifixed-price contracts, no (none) autonomy, and some autonomy, respectively.

The resulting model is statistically significant, as indicated by the χ^2 value. The number of observations is a result of replicated choice sets presented to the 19 participants. To interpret, we see that both alternative specific constants are positive and statistically significant. Because cash sales was the base alternative, these results suggest that producers prefer some type of contract to cash sales. The sign on the coefficient for expected income is positive and statistically significant, indicating that income has a positive marginal utility (let's hope so!). We also see that any level of price risk shifted to the buyer provides positive marginal utility to the producer. Conversely, eliminating producer autonomy (as expressed in the D_{None} effects coded variable) significantly reduces producer utility. Additional investment in specific assets[8] reduces producer utility, while provision of inputs by the contractor increases producer utility. Finally, longer contracts have negative marginal utility, suggesting that producers prefer shorter contract length.[9]

15.3 Alternative Choice Models

15.3.1 Contingent Valuation

Contingent valuation (CV) models provide another avenue for analysis of consumer choice.[10] Often called dichotomous choice models, CV models present respondents with a discrete choice of choosing to consume or not consume a product. The respondent is faced with a choice with a set of potential attributes and is asked whether or not he or she would be willing to purchase that product given its characteristics.

Example 15.2 *Assume you wish to examine the willingness to pay for steam pasturization of beef to decrease the likelihood of exposure to* E. coli *bacteria. You could formulate a question to be asked as follows: "Steam pasturization of beef eliminates 99.99% of* E. coli *bacteria. However, steam pasturization increases the cost of ground beef to the consumer. Assume that normal ground beef costs $0.99 per pound in your local grocery store. If the price of steam-pasturized ground beef was $1.60 per pound, would you purchase it?"*

The value of the steam-pasturized ground beef is the variable of interest here. We would select a range of values for this variable, called a **bid vector**. The construction of the bid vector requires careful consideration. Bid vector construction can be quite complicated. Cameron and Quiggin (1994) provide a detailed discussion. Intuitively,

---

[8]These are assets that can only be used in one productive enterprise. An example would be investment in chicken houses.

[9]In addition to parameter estimates, researchers can utilize these estimates to generate measures of willingness to pay, or monetary trade-offs between attributes. These details are not covered here, but are explicitly treated in Louviere, Hensher, and Swait (2000).

[10]CV models are, by no means, limited to consumer analysis. In fact, the most common use of the CV model is in environmental economics applications of evaluating respondent willingness to pay for nonmarket goods such as pollution abatement. See Hite, Hudson, and Intarapapong (2000) for an example.

one is tempted to create a bid vector around the added cost of steam pasturization. For example, if steam pasturization adds $0.20 per pound, on average, to the cost, we are tempted to construct a bid vector around a value of $1.19 per pound. Some researchers frown on this practice because it may bias the responses of true willingness to pay. Say, for example, that the true willingness to pay was $2.20 per pound. If the bid vector was constructed around $1.19, it might cause respondents to lower their expectations of the willingness to pay and provide responses that result in a lower willingness-to-pay estimate. This phenomenon is called **anchoring**.[11]

In a **first-price** CV analysis, the respondent is presented with a single price, as in the example above, and asked a yes-or-no question. The price level is changed across respondents to generate the variability in price to derive the willingness-to-pay function. Because the question is stated in a yes-or-no manner, the resulting model is estimated using either logit or probit models (Greene, 2000). A general form for the model is

$$\Pr(Yes = 1) = f(\mathbf{X}|\mathbf{Z}),$$

where $\mathbf{X}$ is a vector of explanatory variables/attributes of the good and $\mathbf{Z}$ is a vector of sociodemographic and other variables. In the previous example, the attribute of the good is its price.[12] Other variables might be the age, income, ethnicity, education, and so on of the respondent.

The estimated logistic regression model is

$$\Pr(Yes = 1t) = \frac{e^{\beta'\mathbf{X}}}{1 + e^{\beta'\mathbf{X}}},$$

where $\mathbf{X}$ is the vector of explanatory variables.[13] The estimated parameters represent the effects of each variable on the probability of the respondents saying "yes" to the proposed question. However, these parameter estimates do not represent the **marginal effects**. The marginal effects are the impact, at the margin, of a change in one independent variable on the probability of a "yes." This is derived by taking the derivative of the expected value of a "yes" given a change in an independent variable:

$$\frac{\partial E[yes|\mathbf{X}]}{\partial \mathbf{X}} = \frac{e^{\beta'\mathbf{X}}}{(1 + e^{\beta'\mathbf{X}})^2}.$$

---

[11] This phenomenon appears most relevant in a nonmarket valuation setting where there is no preconceived notion of the potential market value of an amenity. In a market setting, respondents already have some notion of the value of a good, and therefore are already anchored to those approximate valuations.

[12] If one were to vary the price of the normal ground beef in order to identify cross-price effects, that variable would be considered an attribute of the good as well.

[13] The probit model is a common alternative to the logit model (Greene, 2000). The primary difference between the two is that the the logit model is based on the logistic cumulative distribution function, while the probit model is based on the standard normal distribution. There is no real theoretical reason to choose one over the other. In most cases, the two models will generate very similar marginal effects (but not necessarily similar parameter estimates).

Note that because the logistic function is multiplicative, the derivative of the expected value with respect to any independent variable includes all other independent variables.[14]

Contingent valuation is a useful device for judging the anticipated acceptance of new products, valuing nonmarket goods such as environmental amenities, and examining sociodemographic effects of preferences for goods. However, CV is not without its criticisms. Some of the main ones are as follows:

1. Contingent valuation is **hypothetical**. Respondents are placed into situations that do not resemble realistic choices and, therefore, are subject to **hypothetical bias**. For example, assume that you were asking respondents if they would be willing to pay a given amount for an environmental amenity such as pollution abatement. Some researchers argue that respondents have no real way to place a value on that amenity and, therefore, results are circumspect. At the same time, in applications where respondents are asked to place a value on an attribute of a known good, such as the steam-pasturized beef example from above, respondents are not actually making a purchase decision (not having to actually pay for that decision). Thus, they may be more likely to answer "yes" than they would if having to actually pay for the good.[15]

2. Results of CV estimates are sensitive to the bid vector. As alluded to above, many researchers are concerned with the issue of **anchoring**. By presenting the respondent with a price in the question, we may induce the respondent into believing that the presented price is appropriate, thereby securing a "yes" response when one would not ordinarily be forthcoming. Thus, careful consideration to bid vector construction must be given in the formative stages of the research. Researchers often attempt to mitigate this problem through the use of pre-testing of focus groups. These focus groups are presented material about the issue under investigation, and the researcher attempts to elicit responses about willingness to pay in an open-ended fashion. The focus group responses are then used to guide the researcher in development of a bid vector that more appropriately captures the range of potential values placed on the good.

3. The CV framework cannot capture intensity of preferences or choices from a set of goods. Standard CV methods present the respondent with a single choice—to choose or not to choose the good at the stated attributes. Because the question is essentially a yes-or-no question, respondents have no way of expressing alternative answers. For example, a consumer may not be willing to purchase the good at the stated price, but would be willing to do so at a lower price.[16] At the same

---

[14] There are two ways to evaluate marginal effects. First, we can evaluate them at the sample means, as we do elasticities. However, we can also calculate the marginal effect for each observation in the data set, and then average those marginal effects. Greene (2000) notes that in many cases, the latter is preferred to the former, but that is a matter of judgment. You should note, however, that popular statistical packages such as *LIMDEP* calculate marginal effects at the sample means.

[15] In the next chapter, we will explore methods of making those purchase decisions nonhypothetical.

[16] Hite, Hudson, and Intarapapong (2002) provide a recent example of an extension of this standard model, which allows this type of choice framework. Based on the censored probit model by Cameron and Quiggin (1994), this paper allows respondents who say "no" to the first price to indicate that they would be willing to pay some positive amount less than the stated price. This refinement improves the efficiency of the estimated willingness-to-pay values.

time, the respondent is faced with a single choice. However, we know that in most real-world applications with actual products, consumers face a choice decision with alternatives.[17]

In sum, then, the CV method represents an alternative method of assessing consumer demand for goods and services. The method is a dichotomous choice model, where respondents reply with a simple "yes" or "no" to a question regarding acceptance of a good with a particular set of attributes. The advantage of the CV method is its simplicity of application and its reduced workload on the respondent relative to the conjoint method. The primary disadvantage of the CV method is its hypothetical nature, sensitivity to bid vectors, and its inability to capture intensity of preferences.

15.3.2   Ordered Models

Another alternative method of addressing potential demand for a product is through rank-ordered models. These models are based on the supposition that the respondent will order preferences of a set of goods with different attributes. For example, let's take the Lusk and Schroeder (2004) example that was originally cast as a conjoint question and rearrange it into an ordered model question:

Example 15.3   *Assume that you are shopping for a steak. When you arrive at the grocery store, you see the following in the meat case: (1) a generic, ungraded steak for $6.75, (2) a guaranteed tender steak for $7.88, (3) a "natural" steak for $9.00, (4) a USDA Choice steak for $5.63, and (5) a Certified Angus Beef steak for $7.88. Please rank these steaks from 1 to 5, with 1 being the most preferred and 5 being the least preferred.*

It is obvious that this question is different than the question posed to the respondents by Lusk and Schroeder (2004) in the conjoint analysis. Instead of choosing one of these, the respondent provides the rank ordering of steaks. Conceptually, if the respondent chose #4 as the preferred steak in the conjoint experiment, he or she should rank the USDA Choice Steak first in the rank ordering. However, with the rank ordering, the consumer is providing the added information about the order of preference for the other steak. Nevertheless, the ordered nature of the data means that the multinomial logit model used to estimated the conjoint model cannot be used to estimate the ordered model.

Zavoina and McElvey (1975) provide ordered probit and logit models that can be used to estimate these relationships. We begin with the following.

$$y^* = \beta'\mathbf{X} + \varepsilon,$$

---

[17] A recent paper by Lusk and Hudson (2004) illustrates how one might include alternatives within a CV choice to estimate the impacts of cross-price effects on willingness to pay for a new good.

where y^* is the unobserved benefits of choice. We do observe:

$$
\begin{aligned}
y &= 0 \quad \text{if} \quad y^* \le 0, \\
y &= 1 \quad \text{if} \quad 0 < y^* \le \mu_1, \\
y &= 2 \quad \text{if} \quad \mu_1 < y^* \le \mu_2, \\
&\vdots \\
y &= J \quad \text{if} \quad \mu_{J-1} \le y^*,
\end{aligned}
$$

where the μ's are unknown parameters to be estimated with β. The primary advantage of the ordered model is that it allows the respondent to express his or her intensity of preferences about a set of goods, thereby allowing the researcher to estimate the impacts that other goods will have on the good under question. There are two primary disadvantages of this approach, however.

1. In complex choice questions where choice sets are replicated across individuals, preference reversals may occur. Using the Lusk and Schroeder (2004) example from above, assume that the respondent says that he or she prefers the USDA Choice steak to the Certified Angus Beef steak. In a later choice set with the same prices for both steaks, the consumer switches preferences to the Certified Angus Beef steak. These are generally just mistakes on the respondent's part because of the number of choices that are being faced, and not a violation of the transitivity assumption in utility maximization. However, how do you know this is the case?
2. In the conjoint experiment, the respondent was only asked to make a choice of one steak in each choice set. In the ordered model, the respondent is asked to rank order the five steaks. This greatly increases the workload of the respondent, which can lead to problems of mistakes alluded to above. In addition, respondents may become bored or frustrated with the questions, leading them to "drop out" at the end, or provide answers with no real correspondance to their true preferences. This problem can be remedied by carefully considering the choices you want the respondent to make and minimizing his or her workload for any given question.

15.4 Summary

In this chapter, we have briefly outlined some popular methods of examining individual utility and demand for products. In a world of increasing branding, processing, and marketing of food and fiber products, these methods will likely become even more popular in the future. We have only scratched the surface on the variety of models that are available and the econometric and experimental issues surrounding these methods. The goal here was to provide you with a flavor of the potential applications and methods to be employed. Nevertheless, practitioners should familiarize themselves with these methods because of their growing importance in agricultural market and price analysis.

References

Adamowicz, W., R. Boxall, M. Williams, and J. Louviere. "Stated Preference Approaches for Measuring Passive Use Values: Choice Experiments and Contingent Valuation." *American Journal of Agricultural Economics*, 80(1998): 64–75.

Beggs, S., S. Cardell, and J. Hausman. "Assessing the Potential Demand for Electric Cars." *Journal of Econometrics*, 16(1981): 1–19.

Ben-Akiva, M. and S. Lerman. *Discrete Choice Analysis: Theory and Application to Travel Demand*. The MIT Press, Cambridge, MA, 1985.

Cameron, T. and J. Quiggin. "Estimation Using Contingent Valuation Data from 'Dichotomous Choice with Follow-Up Questionnaires.'" *Journal of Environmental Economics and Management*, 27(1994): 218–234.

Green, P. and V. Srinivisan. "Conjoint Analysis in Consumer Research: Issues and Outlook." *Journal of Consumer Research*, 5(1978): 103–123.

Greene, W. *Econometric Analysis*, fourth edition. Prentice Hall, Upper Saddle River, NJ, 2000.

Hite, D., D. Hudson, and W. Intarapapong. "Taxpayer Willingness to Pay for Water Quality: The Case of Precision Application Technology." *Journal of Agricultural and Resource Economics*, 27(2002): 433–449.

Hudson, D. and J. Lusk. "Risk and Transactions Cost in Contracting: Results from a Choice-Based Experiment of Producer Preferences for Contract Attributes." *Journal of Agricultural and Food Industrial Organization*, 2(2004): Article 2.

Louviere, J., D. Hensher, and J. Swait. *Stated Choice Methods: Analysis and Application*. Cambridge University Press, Cambridge, UK, 2000.

Lusk, J. and D. Hudson. "Willingness to Pay Estimates and Agribusiness Decision Making." *Review of Agricultural Economics*, 26(2004): 152–169.

Lusk, J. and T. Schroeder. "Demand Revealing Auction and Choice Experiments: Are the Mechanisms Compatible?" *American Journal of Agricultural Economics*, 86(2004): 389–405.

Kuhfield, W., R. Tobias, and M. Garrat. "Efficient Experimental Design with Marketing Research Applications." *Journal of Marketing Research*, 31(1994): 545–557

Zavoina, R. and W. McElvey. "A Statistical Model for the Analysis of Ordinal Level Dependent Variables." *Journal of Mathematical Sociology*, Summer 1975: 103–120.

Chapter 16

Experimental Methods

~

Another method of deriving data about consumer preferences, demand, and prices is through the use of economic experiments. In the previous chapter, we discussed a number of methods that generate hypothetical valuations. While effective in many situations, **hypothetical bias**[1] is still possible (List and Gallet, 2001; Lusk and Schroeder, 2004). In this chapter, we will discuss methods that force respondents to "put their money where their mouth is," or actually face the consequences of their choices. These **nonhypothetical** experiments are a means of controlling for hypothetical bias, thereby generating reliable results.

Unlike laboratory sciences such as chemistry or physics, true experiments are a relatively new phenomenon in economics. The first known modern experiments were conducted in the 1950s, although Bernoulli conducted some primitive experiments in the 1700s. This chapter will outline some key experimental methods, with a focus on experimental auctions. There is a rapidly growing body of literature on economic experiments, and interested readers are encouraged to start with Davis and Holt (1993) or Kagel and Roth (1995) for a broad survey of this field as well as more in-depth analysis of experimental methods.

16.1   Experiments as a Research Device

Throughout this book, we have discussed different models and estimation techniques for price analysis. In almost all cases, however, we are viewing the world as or after it happens and we have no control over the relevant variables. Thus, we are forced to make the *ceteris paribus*, or other things being equal, assumption and attempt to account for the levels of these variables in our regression models (Hudson, 2003). Experiments, however, allow the researcher to set the conditions of the experiment and vary only one

---

[1]Hypothetical bias is defined just like it sounds. It is bias, or systematic error, that arises because values are elicited in a hypothetical nature. That is, subjects do not have to face the consequences of their actions, so they may not respond truthfully.

variable at a time, thus providing the most direct test of the research hypothesis. Thus, **control** is a key advantage of economic experiments (Smith, 1994).

For example, consider the situation in which I give a classroom full of students a slip of paper that has a "resale" value on it. This value represents the price at which I, as the monitor, will purchase a good from them if they happen to own the good. Next, I offer the good for sale to the class and ask them to place bids for the good. Here, I am attempting to ascertain whether the students bid rationally. You should never bid an amount to purchase the good that is more than what you can resell it for, should you? What about bidding less that the resale value?[2] The point here is that the good is generic (a "chit" or widgit) and the only economic variable that is changing is the resale value across students. So, this allows us to test whether the students respond in a manner that is consistent with predictions from our economic models.

The above example is something called an **induced-value** experiment. That is, the subjects in the experiment were provided their "value" by the experimenter. Here, it is expected that the respondent will examine the value provided in the experiment and react accordingly. In contrast, there are also experiments using **homegrown values**, which are values carried into the experiment by the subject and have an influence over respondent choices (Hudson, 2003). For example, Lusk et al. (2002) conducted an experimental auction on genetically modified corn chips. Respondents were provided a bag of corn chips made from genetically modified corn and were then asked to bid for a bag of corn chips that were guaranteed to come from nongenetically modified corn. Respondents were not provided induced values. Rather, the experiment was designed to elicit their **private value** for avoiding consumption of genetically modified corn chips.

Generally speaking, induced-value experiments are designed to test specific assumptions about human behavior, to examine the impacts of alternative economic institutions, or to test the effectiveness of alternative policy instruments (Smith, 1994). By contrast, homegrown value experiments are generally used to test consumer preferences, or reactions to alternative policies, or to establish potential demand for new products/services. In either case, experiments are extremely useful, but not a panacea of problem-solving. Because experiments are highly controlled, they are necessarily less complex than the real world. As such, experiments cannot be used to simulate all of the real-world situations that subjects may experience. Nevertheless, when properly used, experiments add a powerful tool to the researcher's tool chest.

Key Questions

1. What are induced values?
2. What are homegrown values?
3. Can experiments accurately reflect all possible situations? Why or why not?

16.2   Experimental Markets

Experimental markets have been a stalwart method of evaluating the performance and structure of markets. Although not necessarily so, experimental markets are typically

---

[2]In fact, the optimal strategy depends in great part on how the auction is constructed. This issue will be discussed later.

used in induced-value experiments to test specific hypotheses about the performance of alternative market institutions, market performance, or individual decision-making. Two primary types of experimental markets are discussed in this section—double-oral auction markets and posted-offer markets—although there are other types in the literature: see Kagel and Roth (1995) or Davis and Holt (1993). These two markets are presented both because of their widespread application in the literature and because their construction simulates well many agricultural and food markets in the real world.

16.2.1   The Double-Oral Auction

One of the first and most widely applied types of economic experiments is the **double-oral auction**, or double-auction market. The popularity of the double-auction market is its striking similarity in structure to what economists think of as a market. There are buyers and sellers, with sellers offering a "product" for sale and buyers making bids to purchase the product. The "oral" part of the market is that sellers announce offers for sale and buyers announce bids for products. Unlike the typical "stock" market, chaotic approach to the bidding, however, bids and offers are controlled in a calm, systematic manner.

Sellers in the experiment are provided with "costs of production," which reflect the cost to them of each unit sold. Obviously, the sellers wish to maximize profits, so they should only offer to sell their product above their cost of production. At the same time, buyers are provided with "values," which represent their "utility" from purchasing the good. Thus, buyers should not purchase the good for more than their value. To make the experiment nonhypothetical, subjects are typically paid the difference between the price paid and their value—profits for the seller, and surplus for the buyer. Paying on this basis should induce the subjects to behave rationally.

The auction proceeds by either one buyer posting an offer for sale at a particular price or a seller posting a bid at a particular price. Subjects then raise their hands to make subsequent offers or bids. Subsequent offers must be sequentially lower than the previous offer, and subsequent bids must be sequentially higher than the previous bid. This process continues until one buyer agrees to the highest bid or one seller agrees to the lowest offer. Once a trade is made, the process starts over. Trading time is usually limited to, say, 10 minutes. As many transactions as can be established during that time are allowed, but the number of units each seller has to offer is limited. So, some trading sessions may have many transactions, while some may have few. It just depends on the dynamics of the subjects and how quickly they engage in the game.

The double-auction experiment was originally designed to test the structure of the market and to determine whether predictions from competitive price theory (the first half of this book) can be simulated in the laboratory. The findings from the double-auction experiment are quite robust (that is, have been replicated many times with the same result), and the general findings are that competitive price relationships do spontaneously arise within the double-auction environment. This result is important, because it suggests that competitive price theory is correct. When the conditions of perfect competition are imposed in the laboratory, the competitive model predicts actual behavior quite well. In fact, we have learned through this experiment that the standard assumption of "many buyers and sellers" is not necessarily needed to generate competitive results. Rather, competitive results arise with only small numbers of buyers and sellers. Thus, it is the structure of the market institution (or rules of the game) that matters, not necessarily the number of participants.

The double-auction market can also be used to examine the impacts of other market assumptions. For example, some researchers have examined the situation in which the double-auction mechanism is used, but transactions are private. That is, rather than the open outcry format, subjects were allowed to interact with other subjects privately to arrive at transactions, and no market feedback was allowed. This approach simulates a situation is which there is no market information. Findings generally suggest that the lack of market feedback is an advantage to sellers, resulting in higher market prices than in the perfectly competitive situation. Thus, the double-auction market can be quite useful in analyzing many market situations that deviate from the perfectly competitive case, and because of its property of generating competitive market results, it provides a useful, direct comparison with the outcomes found in competitive markets.

16.2.2   Posted-Offer Markets

Another important type of experimental market is called a **posted-offer market**. The posted-offer market is constructed in a manner that is very similar to current retail markets for food and other items (Williams, 1973; Davis and Holt, 1993). Unlike the double-oral auction discussed above, prices are "posted" on a take-it-or-leave-it basis, and no revisions of offers are allowed during the trading period. The market can be constructed to be where the seller posts prices or the buyer posts prices, but we will focus on the case where the seller is posting the offers.

In this experiment, sellers in the market are given costs of production for their product, which is private information to them. They are also provided information on the number of units they have to sell. An example of the information provided to the seller is shown in Table 16.1. The sellers then privately determine the price they are going to charge and that information is provided to the buyers (but not the quantity information). In the figure, the seller must examine the unit costs for each item and determine a price they believe will be attractive to buyers, given that other sellers will be in the market and that will maximize their profits. Obviously, the seller does not want to price products below cost, resulting in negative profits.

Each buyer, on the other hand, has personal "values" for each unit purchased, as shown in Table 16.2. Buyer wish to pay a price that is less than their value, thereby maximizing their earnings. They will select to purchase from sellers whose posted prices are less than their earnings. After the sellers have posted their prices, one buyer is selected at random and allowed to purchase as many units as he or she would like from any seller until that

Table 16.1   An example of the information provided to a seller in a posted-offer experiment

Unit	Price	Unit cost	Profit
1		2.36	
2		2.95	
3		3.25	

Table 16.2 An example of the information provided to a buyer in a posted-offer experiment

Unit	Unit value	Price	Earnings
1	4.05		
2	3.35		
3	2.75		

seller exhausts his or her available supply. Once the first shopper is finished, another is selected at random. This process continues until all buyers have shopped or all available units for sale have been purchased (Davis and Holt, 1993).

Generally, posted-offer markets have been used to examine imperfectly competitive market structures such as oligopolies or oligopsonies. But they may also be useful in understanding consumer behavior related to alternative information about sellers. For example, examination of anonymous sellers versus known sellers may provide insight into how consumers respond to certain information about the sellers, such as race, gender, brand or store, and so on.

Key Questions

1. What is a double-auction market? What is it used to test? What are its properties?
2. What is a posted-offer market? What is it used to test? What are its properties?

16.3 Auctions

Experimental auctions are rapidly growing in their popularity as a research tool (Lusk, 2003). They are appealing to agricultural economists both because of their theoretical properties and because of their flexibility in answering many questions for which there are no existing secondary data. Example of issues that have been addressed through experimental auctions include the value of food safety, consumer willingness to pay for nongenetically modified foods, and consumer values for food attributes and labeling, among many others. This section will address the different types of experimental auctions, issues to consider when using experimental auctions, and provide some examples of auction contruction and implementation from the literature to address specific problems.

16.3.1 Auction Type

There are many types of **auction mechanisms** in the literature. One type probably most familiar to you is the **English auction**, where bidders bid sequentially higher bids until only one bidder remains. The winning bidder pays the highest bid to acquire one unit of the good. The English auction has a number of advantages and disadvantages, as shown in Table 16.3. Because the English auction is typically an open outcry type of market, there are large amounts of **market feedback**. That is, market participants are able to instantly see what the bids are and what other bidders are doing. A participant can observe what the current market price is, and decide whether that is higher or lower

Table 16.3   The practical advantages and disadvantages of different auction mechanisms

English	Uniform *n*th price	BDM	Random *n*th price
Advantages			
• Familiar to most people and easy-to-explain procedures • Open market with large amounts of market feedback	• Relatively easy to explain to participants and easy to implement • Control over numbers of units sold, so ease in experiment preparation	• Can be used with individual subjects in settings such as grocery stores • Values can be elicited relatively quickly	• Keeps all bidders engaged in all rounds • Relatively high degree of market feedback if desired
Disadvantages			
• Difficult to implement with multiple goods • Difficult to control market feedback	• Some evidence that subjects overbid; but evidence is mixed • Subjects with low values become disinterested in multiple bidding rounds	• No active market • No market feedback	• Difficult to explain to participants • Determining market price can be lengthy if sessions are large; less control over numbers of items sold, so more difficult in experiment preparation

Source: Adapted from Lusk (2003).

than his or her personal willingness to pay. Despite these advantages, researchers often wish to auction multiple goods. That is, you may wish to determine what willingness to pay (WTP) is for two goods in a side-by-side comparion. This scenario is difficult to achieve with an English auction. Also, because the market is open outcry, it is also difficult to control market feedback.[3]

Perhaps one of the most popular mechanisms is called the **uniform *n*th price** auction, of which the 2nd price auction is the most widely used (Vickrey, 1961). All *n*th price auctions are **sealed tender**, or sealed bid, auctions. That is, participants submit a sealed

---

[3] Recall that control is one of the desired attributes of experiments. As experimenters, we wish to have only one variable changing at a time. Having market feedback, *per se*, is not always a detriment to the experiment, but we would typically like to have control over the type and amount of feedback that is allowed.

bid for the good. The monitor then ranks the sealed bids from highest to lowest. In the case of the 2nd price auction, the highest bidder wins the auction, but pays the second highest price. This auction is called "uniform" because all winning bidders pay the same price. For example, in a 5th price auction, the four highest bidders would all pay the 5th highest price. As can be seen in Table 16.3, the uniform nth price auction has a number of advantages. As seen above, it is relatively easy to explain the procedures to participants. Second, the number of units sold is determined by the n, so experiment preparation is easy (as compared to the random nth price discussed below). At the same time, there is some evidence that participants "overbid" in the uniform nth price auction (Kagel, Harstad, and Levin, 1987; Lusk, Feldkamp and Schroeder, 2002). And, because participants with low values have little chance of winning, they become disinterested in multiple bidding rounds. Feedback is controlled by the monitor. The monitor can choose to post winning prices in multiple round auctions or not.

The Becker–Degroot–Marschak (BDM) mechanism is not an auction, *per se*. Subjects do not bid against each other in an BDM. Rather, they are bidding against a random number generator. For example, a bidder will place a bid for an item. The random number generator will generate a price (within specified bounds), and if the subject's price is higher than the random price, the subject wins the auction and pays the bid amount. So, while the BDM is not an auction as strictly defined, its structure is nonetheless similar. The advantage of the BDM is that is can be used to elicit WTP from subjects individually, which makes it particularly well suited to field experiments in places such as grocery stores. Values can be elicited quickly, implying that individuals can participate at relatively low cost to them.[4] A common critique of the BDM is that it does not represent an active market. That is, because bidders are not in competition with one another, it does not "feel" like a market, which may lead subjects to behave differently than they would inside a market mechanism. And, because there is no market, there is also no possible market feedback.

Finally, the random nth price auction was proposed by Shogren et al. (2001) to address the "off margin" bidder problem of the uniform nth price auction. As discussed above, the uniform auction suffers from the problem that low-value bidders often become disinterested or disengaged in multiple round auctions. The random nth price auction remedies this by making all bidders (less one) potentially a winner. The auction proceeds as the uniform auction in that all bidders submit a sealed bid for the good. The monitor then ranks the bids from highest to lowest. In the random nth price auction, however, the monitor then pulls a random number between 1 and n, where n is the number of respondents, from a hat (or some other means). The number that is pulled becomes the winning bid number. For example, if there were 10 respondents and the number pulled was 9, the 8 highest bidders would pay the 9th highest price. Conversely, if the random number pulled was 3, the two highest bidders would pay the 3rd highest price. In this manner, subjects do not know from one round to the next who will actually be a winner. Shogren et al. (2001) note that this process results in significant engagement of those bidders who would have been "off margin" in the standard 2nd price uniform auction. At the same time, however, the random nth necessarily increases the complexity of the auction mechanism, making it more difficult for subjects to understand and to implement. Further, the monitor does not know *a priori* how many units of the good will be sold, requiring the monitor to have a sufficient supply of the good to sell $n - 1$ units.

---

[4]That is, the opportunity cost to the participant is low, thereby increasing the likelihood of participation.

16.3.2   Issues to Consider

There are a few issues to consider when designing an experimental auction. The first is the potential for **bidder affiliation**. In the "real world," we use signals and information such as market prices to help us determine our values for goods and services. Market feedback in auctions acts as a mechansim to provide that information to subjects. In many cases, market feedback is necessary for rational decision-making (Cherry et al., 2003), and so market feedback in experimental auctions is a desirable feature. But, by posting prices, we are necessarily influencing the values of at least some of the participants (Milgrom and Weber, 1982). That is, if I am uncertain about my value and I see that others are bidding X, I am likely going to "affiliate" my bid to that X in future rounds. Despite this theoretical possibility, List and Shogren (1999) have found that posted prices have a limited effect on bidder affiliation.[5] Nevertheless, careful attention should be paid to the potential for bidder affiliation, especially in cases where the researcher wants to elicit WTP amounts that are not influenced by the opinions of others.

A second important issue is related to **demand reduction**. That is, suppose you design an experiment that either (1) asks subjects to potentially purchase multiple units of the same good or (2) units of multiple goods. In the first case, imagine that you have already purchased one steak in an experiment, and now you are being asked to place bids on another steak. If you have a downward-sloping demand function, you are likely to bid less for the second steak than for the first. Likewise, if you have already purchased one type of good, are you going to bid less for a second good? Many times, experimenters would like to have multiple rounds of bidding for various reasons, but winners in one round may express demand reduction for subsequent rounds, thus biasing our estimates of WTP. One way around this problem is to have multiple rounds with only one round "binding."[6] The binding round is chosen at random so that all rounds have an equal probability of being chosen. It is important that subjects are made aware of this procedure prior to the experiment, so that they do not express demand reduction during the bidding.

Finally, the issue of potential **wealth effects** should be considered.[7] There are two general types of "wealth" effects—one related to the demand reduction issue above and the second dealing with "windfall" gains (which are sometimes called endowment effects). With regard to demand reduction, when a subject starts with a fixed amount of money, the purchase of one good necessarily reduces the amount of "wealth" that can be expended on other goods. The random binding round procedure outlined above, however, alleviates this problem as well. A second wealth effect problem relates to the issue of windfall gains. Typically, experimenters are paying subjects some nominal fee to participate, and this nominal fee is sufficient to cover any anticipated cost of purchasing the good in question with some left over. The problem is this: What do you do when

---

[5] As an interesting aside, Lusk, Feldkamp, and Schroeder (2002) found that the BDM (no market feedback) and the English auction (complete market feedback) generated statistically equivalent results, suggesting that even when bidder affiliation was not possible, market feedback did not statistically alter the results.

[6] "Binding" means here that for the binding round, the winner(s) of the auction in that round actually pay for the good at the winning price.

[7] This is not to be confused with the idea of wealth effects as it relates to differences in WTP and willingness to accept (WTA). Kahneman, Knetsch, and Thaler (1990) have demonstrated that there exists a difference in WTP and WTA as a result of the wealth effect. That is, I must be paid more to relinquish ownership of a good than I will pay to acquire it. This is a very interesting research issue, but it is not being addressed here.

you find a $20 bill in your pocket that you did not know you had? The answer: You run out and immediately spend it. The same is true for experiments. We are concerned that by providing subjects with this "windfall," they may behave differently than as if they had earned the money.

To alleviate this problem, most experimenters require subjects to fill out lengthy surveys or participate in alternative games, or some other means of making them feel as if they "earned" their participation fee. Research has shown that this procedure tends to eliminate "windfall" effects, and thus generate behavior that is consistent with economic theory (Nalley et al., 2005). Thus, it is advisable when conducting experimental auctions to account for wealth effects.

16.3.3 Example

Lusk et al. (2001) provide an example of an experimental auction for nongenetically modified corn chips. Here, the authors wished to examine consumer WTP to avoid consumption of corn chips made from genetically modified corn. Initially, subjects were given $1 and a 1 oz. bag of genetically modified corn chips and were told that consumption of the chips was mandatory.[8] The subjects were then asked to place a sealed bid (using the Vickrey 2nd price uniform auction mechanism) for the right to exchange their bag of genetically modified corn chips for a bag that was guaranteed to contain no genetically modified corn.

Five rounds of bidding were used, with only one round binding, which was chosen at random. After analyzing the resulting bids, Lusk et al. (2001) found that the average WTP to switch to a nongenetically modified corn chip was $0.07 per ounce. While most subjects bid $0 per ounce, 20% of subjects bid as much as $0.25 per ounce and 2% bid as much as $0.50 per ounce, suggesting that at least some portion of the population has a positive WTP for avoiding genetically modified food consumption.

Now suppose you wish to set up an experiment. The issue you wish to test is whether labeling shrimp as "Product of the USA" increases the WTP over shrimp labeled "Imported." Your null hypothesis is that is does not increase WTP, and your alternative hypothesis is that the labeling significantly increases WTP (note this is a one-tailed hypothesis). Now, how does one construct an experiment? Following the Lusk et al. (2001) model above, we could endow subjects with a 1lb. bag of "imported" shrimp plus some amount of money (say, for example, $5). Next, we want to elicit values for switching from the "imported" shrimp to "USA" shrimp.

To accomplish this, we must decide on an auction mechanism, which is likely related to our choice of sample. If we want to target actual consumers, we may want to conduct this experiment in a store, which suggests the use of a BDM mechanism.[9] Alternatively, if we are satisfied with other samples such as students, using a nth price or English auction

---

[8] By forcing consumption, the authors were making the possibility of eating genetically modified corn real. Otherwise, people who did not want to consume the corn chips could simply bid $0 and not consume the bag they were given.

[9] Although using actual consumers in a laboratory is also possible, it is often more logistically challenging and expensive, as we have to pay them a considerable fee for showing up and we often must schedule the experiment for after hours due to conflicts with work. Thus, it is certainly possible, but more difficult.

in the laboratory is also possible. Once we have decided on an auction mechanism, we must also address the issues of demand reduction, wealth effects, and bidder affiliation. So, for example, assume that we have decided on a 2nd price auction in the laboratory using students as our subjects. We wish to have multiple rounds to allow for learning, and we believe that market feedback is essential. So, we will execute our experiment with, say 10, rounds of bidding and will post the winning price after each round. To account for demand reduction, we will choose one of those 10 rounds at random to be binding. To account for wealth effects, we will make our subjects fill out a survey relating to shrimp and shellfish consumption.[10] Finally, given that we are using a 2nd price auction, we will likely need about 10 subjects. We wish to have enough subjects to make the bidding realistic, but not so many that each individual sees themselves as having no possibility of winning. But with only 10 subjects, we may not capture all of the potential heterogeneity that exists withing the population. Therefore, we likely want to have multiple "treatments," or sets of 10 people bidding. That is, we may want to replicate this experiment a number of times to insure that we are getting the most realistic and consistent answers possible.

Key Questions

1. What is an auction mechanism?
2. What are the different auction mechanisms? What are their advantages and disadvantages?
3. What are market feedback, bidder affiliation, demand reduction, and wealth effects?
4. How do you mitigate the issues in question 3?

16.4   Summary

This chapter has outlined some of the growing experimental methods that are available to researchers for price and utility analysis. Experiments provide an exciting new way to generate primary data where no secondary data exist for traditional analysis. But this chapter has just scratched the surface of this approach, and there are many issues and techniques that are not addressed here. Hopefully, this discussion has whet your appetite to learn more about the subject. Experiments offer a way to rigorously answer real-world questions of practical importance to business and industry, as well as to the economics discipline. However, experiments are not the "silver bullet" of problem-solving. There are many issues that must be considered and, as with any other approach, experiments have their strengths and weaknesses that should be understood before wading off into applied research.

References

Cherry, T., T. Crocker, and J. Shogren. "Rationality Spillovers." *Journal of Environmental Economics and Management*, 45(2003): 63–84.

---

[10] An added bonus of this approach is that we can collect attitudinal and demographic data that can be used to analyze for systematic patterns in bidding behavior in later analysis.

Davis, D. and C. Holt. *Experimental Economics*. Princeton University Press, Princeton, NJ, 1993.

Hudson, D. "Problem Solving and Hypothesis Testing Using Economic Experiments." *Journal of Agricultural and Applied Economics*, 35(2003): 337–347.

Kagel, J. and A. Roth, Editors. *The Handbook of Experimental Economics*. Princeton University Press, Princeton, NJ, 1995.

Kagel, J., R. Harstad, and D. Levin. "Information Impact and Allocation Rules in Auctions with Affiliated Private Values: A Laboratory Study." *Econometrica*, 55(1987): 1,275–1,304.

Kahneman, D., J. Knetsch, and R. Thaler. "Experimental Tests of the Endowment Effect and the Coase Theorem." *Journal of Political Economy*, 98(1990): 1,325–1,348.

List, J. and C. Gallet. "What Experimental Protocol Influence Disparities between Actual and Hypothetical Stated Values." *Environmental and Resource Economics*, 20(2001): 241–254.

List, J. and J. Shogren. "Price Information and Bidding Behavior in Repeated Second-Price Auctions." *American Journal of Agricultural Economics*, 81(1999): 942–949.

Lusk, J. "Using Experimental Auctions for Marketing Applications: A Discussion." *Journal of Agricultural and Applied Economics*, 35(2003): 349–360.

Lusk, J., T. Feldkamp, and T. Schroeder. "Experimental Auction Procedure: Impact of Valuation of Quality Differentiated Goods." Working Paper, Purdue University, Department of Agricultural Economics, 2002.

Lusk, J. and T. Schroeder. "Are Choice Experiments Incentive Compatible? A Test with Quality Differentiated Beef Steaks." *American Journal of Agricultural Economics*, 86(2004): 467–482.

Lusk, J., M. Daniel, C. Lusk, and D. Mark. "Alternative Calibration and Auction Institutions for Predicting Consumer Willingness to Pay for Non-Genetically Modified Corn Chips." *Journal of Agricultural and Resource Economics*, 26(2001): 40–57.

Milgrom, P. and R. Weber. "A Theory of Auctions and Competitive Bidding." *Econometrica*, 50(1982): 1,089–1,122.

Nalley, L., D. Hudson, and G. Parkhurst. "The Initial Endowment Effect Revisited: Further Evidence." *Applied Economics Letters*, 12(2005): 59–63.

Shogren, J., M. Margolis, C. Koo, and J. List. "A Random n^{th}-Price Auction." *Journal of Economic Behavior and Organization*, 46(2001): 409–421.

Smith, V. "Economics in the Laboratory." *Journal of Economic Perspectives*, 8(1994): 113–131.

Vickrey, W. "Counterspeculation, Auctions and Competitive Sealed Tenders." *Journal of Finance*, 16(1961): 8–37.

Williams, F. "The Effect of Market Organization on Competitive Equilibrium: The Multi-Unit Case." *Review of Economic Studies*, 40(1973): 97–113.

Index